END OF T

Reimagining the Street as the
Heart of the City

William Riggs

BRISTOL
UNIVERSITY
PRESS

First published in Great Britain in 2022 by

Bristol University Press
University of Bristol
1–9 Old Park Hill
Bristol
BS2 8BB
UK
t: +44 (0)117 954 5940
e: bup-info@bristol.ac.uk

Details of international sales and distribution partners are available at bristoluniversitypress.co.uk

British Library Cataloguing in Publication Data
A catalogue record for this book is available from the British Library

ISBN 978-1-5292-2514-3 hardcover
ISBN 978-1-5292-2515-0 paperback
ISBN 978-1-5292-2516-7 ePub
ISBN 978-1-5292-2517-4 ePdf

Cover design: River Design
Front cover image: Marco Bottigelli
Bristol University Press use environmentally responsible print partners.
Printed in Great Britain by CMP, Poole

To Fritz, Lee and Menka:
every day you bring life to the potential of
what a street can be

Contents

List of Figures and Tables

Figures

Table

Acknowledgments

Every list of acknowledgments should always begin with an apology for anyone mistakenly omitted. There are so many people who deserve thanks, those who have provided input and ideas for this book, and I know I will forget some of them. At the same time, there are a number of people to whom I am extremely grateful for helping to shape, develop and finalize this manuscript.

Most importantly, I must thank my family. Fritz and Lee, thank you for being beautiful and active boys who inspire me to want to create the best streets possible for you to run, bike, play and live on. Menka, thank you for your patience as I pursued this book and my academic journey. I know it likely came across as vanity much of the time, but I could not have done it without your sacrifice.

My parents, Glenn and Sally Riggs, deserve so much credit for raising me in an environment that challenged me with a passion for hard work and a deep sense of empathy. This book likely began with your patience in letting me strike out on my own, traveling to Africa, England, Belize and many other places at an early age. These were the places where I learned about how my hometown streets were very different, yet very much the same as those elsewhere, and I am grateful that you empowered me with this freedom of exploration.

Ben, Gabe and Haley Riggs shaped a lot of my early experiences with the street and deserve thanks, as did my friend Josh Pedigo, who helped me tunnel under suburban fences as a boy. As the working title of this book was "Kill the Street," my brother Gabe warrants credit for coming up with a new title. Menka said there should be "no killing, no blood" so we spit-balled a bunch of ideas. Ultimately, we started thinking about music we liked, and Gabe started talking about playing off of the U2 song "Where the Streets Have No Name." Pretty quickly we jumped to the idea of "End of the Road." While a song wasn't the first thing that popped into my mind, after the fact I realized we had stuck with a musical tie-in and settled on a name that mapped back to a 1991 song from a Philadelphia R&B group (Boyz II Men).

In terms of other formative assistance, Michael Johnson deserves credit for being there with me while some these ideas began to trickle out over long runs and while he was supporting me during my Achilles recovery. Nathaniel and Evelyn Shober played an important role in dragging me to Tanzania to experience African streets just after college. Also, the Doughty family offered me my first planning job in Lincolnshire, and I'm grateful they gave me my first taste of what the streets in England were like. Thanks to Leo Lozano and Barb Frommel who brought me to the West coast and Alix Bockelman who was probably the first person to set me on a path to becoming a transportation nerd. Other colleagues from my professional work in Berkeley were critical in developing early drafts, including Emily Marthinsen, Beth Piatnitza, Jennifer Mcdougall and Cathy Simon.

Chris Thompson (at Ball State University) was also a huge support, having known me longer than just about anyone involved with this project. Father and President Paul Fitzgerald also deserves credit for his discussions about the idea of "a praxis of streets" and his encouragement for me to integrate how the street can bring about spiritual awakening, in addition to other benefits.

Some of the thinking on street evolution and autonomous vehicles began as part of a rich collaboration between Mark Schlossberg, Elizabeth Shay, Adam Millard-Ball and myself at a conference hosted by Urbanism Next. I'm grateful to this team, as well as the entire Urbanism Next team for supporting this; particularly Nico Larco and Becky Steckler.

My students at Cal Poly and University of San Francisco over the years also deserve a lot of credit. Amanda Grossman-Ross, Sam Gross, Jana Schwartz, Priit Kaskla, Matt Kawashima, Elisa McDade, Therese Perez, Kai Lord Farmer and Louis Yudowitz worked on projects that would eventually become part of this manuscript. Megyn Rugh was the standout among these students and deserves the most credit for helping support most of my own research that is discussed in this book.

There are also many other people who provided some level of intellectual support and partnership that made this book possible. These include Stefan Al, Bruce Appleyard, David Batstone, Geoff Boeing, Michael Boswell, Karen Chapple, Jason Corburn, Sam Davis, Karen Fricke, Eric Guerra, John Gilderbloom, Adrienne Greve, Malo Hutson, Richard Jackson, Judy Innes, Lewis Knight, Matt Mahan, Rebecca Sanders-Carlton, Manish Shirgaokar, Bill Satariano, Suresh Sethi, David Simpson, Alex Schafran, Shivani Shukla, Paul Waddell, Stephen Zavestoski and Stephen Zoepf. My Dutch colleagues Tom Alkim, Bart van Arem and Serge van Dam also deserve thanks for helping to open up opportunities in the Netherlands for me. This list should also include Anita Malnig and Kim Crum, who provided valuable editing support.

I'm especially grateful to Robert Cervero and Betty Deakin for pushing and supporting me so much while I was a student and becoming such great friends and mentors as my academic career has developed. Thank you both from the bottom of my heart. Much of what you have imparted lies within.

Finally, I must thank at Emily Watt, Freya Trand and the entire editorial team at Bristol University Press for helping me refine this idea but also for working with me to make sure it stayed consistent with my own vision. Thank you for that and for helping me get to the "End of the Road."

1

Introduction

We must kill the street! (Le Corbusier, 1930)

In around 1930, renowned architect Le Corbusier is attributed as saying that "we must kill the street." Allegedly, the designer was almost struck by a car on the Champs-Elysées in Paris and took it upon himself to rethink city design and eliminate obsolete streets that were being taken over by cars. Lamenting how vehicles were overrunning the streets that had formerly been dedicated to living, playing and commerce, he decided they were obsolete. He chose to eliminate them. In his radiant city proposal, he suggested restricting human activities—living, working, playing, shopping and so on—to high-rise towers and parks set apart from wide, motor roads for use only by cars.

While this vision of an auto-dependent city might sound like a contradiction to some, Corbusier's obsession with streets is a good starting point. Despite where he ended, in removing all the human activity from the street, he started with an appreciation of what a street can be—the very heart of life in cities. He also chose to separate slower human travel from faster vehicular travel, which to a large degree has been adopted by the modern engineering profession.

In many ways, I have the same obsession with streets, but I don't want to kill them. I don't want to see human life eliminated from streets. In contradiction to the perspective of Corbusier, I hope to see the end of the road. I long for roads to evolve, or even devolve, to be safer, slower and more accommodative of all kinds of travelers and all kinds of activities.

Why is this? In many ways streets, whether they are paved or dirt, or in the US, China or South Africa, are the lifeblood of a city. The way they look, feel and how people behave when interacting with them—whether it be via walking, biking, transit or driving—is important to the very existence of how cities work. Yet, in many places, streets have become more like Corbusier's roads than ever before. They are even more hostile than ever, particularly for people who want to walk or bike. I want to see these roads change. I want to see them evolve to be more well designed for walking,

1

biking and living. I want to reimagine the idea that roads can be designed for more than just travel.

This book starts with that premise: that we can reimagine "roads," which I define as automobile-oriented, as "streets" that are more people-oriented. A well-designed, or "complete," neighborhood street is something that can shape how people live, play near their home and travel to their place of employment. Complete streets that are designed to facilitate walking and biking can increase physical activity levels and reduce obesity risks, as well as improve mental health (Saelens et al., 2003; Badland and Schofield, 2005; Ewing et al., 2006; Mehta, 2007; Glazier et al., 2014). They can be described as "lively" or "livable," with occasional transportation-speak terms like "multi-modal" or a "woonerf," which is the Dutch concept of the street as an extension of the living room.

These terms are important. They relate back to ideas of urban thinkers like Jane Jacobs and Donald Appleyard who argued that streets need to be "livable" for all kinds of travelers; yet most neighborhood streets, particularly in the West, continued to be designed around the automobile. Further, most citizens do not realize that using design features such as bulb outs or sidewalk extensions to make roads less wide (what city planners call "complete streets" design features) slow down driving and make streets safer for everyone. Often, some individuals will even oppose projects that reduce the width of streets and slow driving, not realizing the safety benefits of features that support walking and cycling.

Given this, it is likely that the term "complete streets" is not complete enough. It and other design terms do not embody the true power of the way a street can impact a city. There are many other things that happen on a street—for example creating a public gathering, social or economic space. We saw these kinds of activities take shape during the COVID-19 pandemic, when people stopped driving to the same extent and had a reawakening of how activities such as walking, cycling, playing and dining had a role in the street. Yet, still, most people do not think of streets that way. They consider them as conduits for human travel. They think of them as for transportation not for other activities—this view is limiting. The street can be more. Streets can have movement and activity of all kinds.

In this light, perhaps we should thank Corbusier for the idea that we should "kill the street," or at least the notion that we should put an end to roads. The themes of paths, trails, movement and connectivity involve more than travel. They are cultural and can be traced throughout generations and across nations. And the idea of using the street for something other than transit is woven into many other facets of our human lives. Streets facilitate more than how we travel, but how we live, work and play.

In my life, I have seen the idea that a street can be more than something for travel reflected in many of the locations I have been in—places ranging

Figure 1.1: A slow streets project from the city of San Francisco encouraged creative uses of the street for play, art and music

Source: San Francisco Planning Department https://www.flickr.com/photos/sfplanning/51017374281/

Figure 1.2: The emergence of slow streets during the pandemic provided a softer vision for roads that allow for new experiences of the street

Source: San Francisco Planning Department https://www.flickr.com/photos/sfplanning/50568595991/

from Tanzania, to Belize, to England, to the deep south of the US. In these places, streets are the lifeblood and the heart of the neighborhood in so many ways. They are places of connection, and they can be places of conflict. And I believe that I am not alone in this perception that streets can be more. I think streets tie many people together. It is probably not a stretch to say that every individual has had an experience with a street, and this experience is something that they could talk about with anyone—whether by the side of the road or in the halls of national government.

From the villages of Africa, to the hills of Italy, to the passages of Paris

When I think of these discussions and the global importance of streets, one of the first places my mind goes is my experience working in Sub-Saharan Africa after college. Imagine a narrow road with rich red-brown dirt surrounded by tall fields of corn. You walk down the street kicking up dust and catching brief glimpses of the distant hills and mountains peaking over the top of the corn tassels. You are joined on the street by friends, neighbors and strangers, mostly on foot. The occasional car passes, slowing to squeeze by you on the narrow road. You catch the rich smell of wood smoke in the distance and remember that you'll pass a local who sells barbecued corn just up the road.

For me this was my norm, walking in the street and interacting with my community and fellow travelers just outside of Arusha, Tanzania, and it's really a starting point for how I began thinking about the global experience of the street. I would walk to work each day and see a road that wasn't designed in the same way as the streets of Europe. It wasn't paved and didn't have the most modern kind of engineering. But it had people using it in many ways—walking, cycling, taking the bus, driving. It had people selling corn, avocados and even cellphones. It even had places where young people would congregate and dance.

And what struck me most about the street wasn't the wonderful activities occurring or the fact they happened without specialized infrastructure—it was that this place wasn't dissimilar to the places where I had grown up in Indiana and Kentucky. I had been on many other unpaved dirt roads in the rural US, surrounded by fields of corn. The difference was that I hadn't been on foot. My experience growing up in the US had been framed by the car and not by the human experience.

In contrast, many lessons about people and the human experience are espoused in the hill-towns of Cinque Terre in Italy. I had the opportunity to undertake research there around 2010. In Cinque Terre, a series of walking trails have united coastal trading towns since the days of the Roman Empire. People walk to-and-fro, from town-to-town, not only to fulfill their economic needs but also social needs for interaction with each other and the outside world. The primary forms of transportation are on foot, horse, bike or boat, and the street infrastructure respects this. Dense lodging mixed with businesses sprout from the hillsides, connected by streets no more than eight to ten feet wide in most places, and a spine of train lines connects the towns providing faster access along the coast.

Yet, despite this historic focus on walking, cars have changed many of these travel patterns, just as they have done around the world. Traffic jams and pollution now put pressure on streets and infrastructure not designed to handle such capacity, and, more and more, people are less active. This inactivity is leading to a global weight problem. For example, in 2018, the Organization for Economic Cooperation and Development estimated that 35 percent of Italians were overweight and 10 percent were obese. During the same timeframe, 33 percent of the US population over age 15 were overweight, and 34 percent were obese (OECD, 2018).

While in Italy a few years before these numbers were released, I spoke with people who would make observational assessments of this trend. One that struck me was the owner of a cycling company who said that many of his clients were too out of shape to take a moderate 15-mile bike ride through the region. He blamed it on poor diet and lack of exercise, and based on my observations I might confirm this opinion. I remember sitting and watching a small child play soccer and feeling sad. He had a waist girth of someone three times his height. It was a sobering picture of how even Europe is grappling with the same obesity issue that is present in the US.

Urban development and the advent of the automobile are not the only culprit in this weight epidemic. For example, the stereotypical Italian diet is high in carbohydrates and, while they eat smaller portions than most Americans do, they are exercising less and less. This combination of diet and exercise is exacerbated by continued urbanization that may not respect access to health resources such as parks, green spaces and walking facilities. Although many urban spaces are now being cited for their sustainable and livable environments, many suburban locations, such as the immigrant-heavy outskirts of Paris, still suffer from a lack of resources and progressive planning thought on urban design and the street (Gaspard, 1995). As Rebecca Solnit puts it in her book *Wanderlust*,

> ... In many new places, public space isn't even in the design: what once was public space is design to accommodate the privacy of automobiles; malls replace main streets; streets have no sidewalks; buildings are entered through the garages; city halls have no plazas; and everything has walls bars and dates ... where to be the pedestrian is to be under suspicion ... At the same time, rural land and the

once – inviting peripheries of towns are being swallowed up in car commuter subdivision and otherwise sequestered. (Solnit, 2001, p 11)

This changing cultural and physical landscape is further complicated when 'weighed' against other factors such as: genetic predispositions towards disease, cultural acceptance of habits such as binge drinking or smoking or the seemingly innocuous economic benefits that the auto brings to personal mobility. These benefits are important. Autos have increased autonomy, productivity, tourism and ultimately wealth. Also, in Italy, it is safe to say that they have provided cool art in the many cars I want but can't afford on a professor's salary.

Housing also plays a part in our relationship to the street and has changed significantly from the 19th century to today, and the mention of Parisian post-war suburban growth underscores the issue. In many locations, the great wars and economic booms and busts contributed to expansion beyond the core of cities (Jackson, 1987; Gaspard, 1995). In most cases, single-family bungalows that were once connected as streetcar suburbs became highly auto reliant. And while there have been recent trends to increase bike and pedestrian accommodations, the number of walkable and bikeable locations is still limited and there are issues with affordability. On the surface, one could say that your housing choice is either livable and expensive or drivable and affordable.

This auto-reliance is oppositional to the classic Parisian notion of the flâneur—a French word to describe a person that strolls or wanders (most of the time aimlessly and lazily) and becomes part of society based on what they experience during that jaunt. This concept arose based on the activity of gentry in pre-1800 Paris (called pre-Haussmann Paris), who would wander the night on streets that were designed narrowly and circuitously—sharing the roads with users of all types on wandering and aimless strolls, famously documented in photos by Charles Marville that showed the streets as both irregular and informal. One could look down a street and see odd angles, banners, store signage and even random furniture in their view as the street visibly curved to the right or left in front of them. While to the modern eye they might have looked rather ramshackle, these attributes represented the active nature of the road and only increased people's desires to get out and engage with them.

While these roads were renovated (demolished) as part of modernization (slum-clearance) efforts by Georges-Eugène Haussmann on the orders of Napoleon Bonaparte (Chisholm, 1911), the notion of the flâneur, of being engulfed by the city, has remained. The 18th-century poet Baudelaire described it as:

> The crowd is his domain, as the air is that of the bird or the sea of the fish. His passion and creed is to wed the crowd. For the perfect

flâneur, for the passionate observer, it's an immense pleasure to take up residence in multiplicity, in whatever is seething, moving, evanescent, and infinite: you're not at home but you feel at home everywhere; you see everyone, you're at the center of everything yet you remain hidden from everybody – these are just a few of the minor pleasures of those independent, passionate, impartial minds whom language can only awkwardly define. The observer is a prince who, wearing a disguise, takes pleasure everywhere ... The amateur of life enter into the crowd as into an immense reservoir of electricity. (White, 2001, p 36)

Not just complete: street design and urban vitality

While I recognize that flâneur of Baudelaire's time may have some aristocratic ties, I appreciate this idea of creating streets that are immersive and experiential—that the street can be more than just something for travel. And I believe that this experience can and should be afforded to all social classes in our current society. I like the notion of fully investing in something as a participant-observer, and also of the street transcending the theme of transport and becoming a social space.

This social aspect reminds me of the key refrain in the poem "The House by the Side of the Road" by Sam Walter Foss, "Let me live by the side of the road/ And be a friend to man." Written in 1897, the refrain is borrowed from Homer ("He was a friend to man, and lived in a house by the side of the road.") and, for me, it provides a link between the emissive walking experience described by Baudelaire and the houses where each of us live. My late grandmother Mary Jane used to recite it to me. She was both in the hills of rural Eastern Kentucky where recited poetry continues to be an important part of the local culture—where walking and the small town are still intertwined; perhaps the poor, country version of the flâneur.

The House by the Side of the Road

> *There are hermit souls that live withdrawn*
> *In the place of their self-content;*
> *There are souls like stars, that dwell apart,*
> *In a fellowless firmament;*
> *There are pioneer souls that blaze the paths*
> *Where highways never ran; —*
> *But let me live by the side of the road*
> *And be a friend to man.*
>
> *Let me live in a house by the side of the road*
> *Where the race of men go by —*
> *The men who are good and the men who are bad,*

As good and as bad as I.
I would not sit in the scorner's seat
Nor hurl the cynic's ban; —
Let me live in a house by the side of the road
And be a friend to man.

I see from my house by the side of the road
By the side of the highway of life,
The men who press with the ardor of hope,
The men who are faint with the strife,
But I turn not away from their smiles and tears —
Both parts of an infinite plan; —
Let me live in a house by the side of the road
And be a friend to man.

I know there are brook-gladdened meadows ahead,
And mountains of wearisome height;
That the road passes on through the long afternoon
And stretches away to the night.
And still I rejoice when the travelers rejoice,
And weep with the strangers that moan,
Nor live in my house by the side of the road
Like a man who dwells alone.

Let me live in my house by the side of the road,
Where the race of men go by —
They are good, they are bad, they are weak, they are strong,
Wise, foolish — so am I.
Then why should I sit in the scorner's seat,
Or hurl the cynic's ban? —
Let me live in my house by the side of the road
And be a friend to man. (Foss, 1897)

The visual of the house that embodies the union between housing and transportation provides a good mental picture of the term "livable streets." But, as I alluded earlier, transportation terms like livability, complete streets, walkability or bikeability can be limiting. When we use the term "complete," it could mean many different things (whole, finished, all-inclusive, and so on). Similarly, the verb "walk" is made into a noun for the word "walkability"—a practice which seems somehow sacrilege given the liveliness the term implies.

These terms have been developed for various reasons. For example, academics and practitioners have used terms like walkability and bikeability to compare how good places are for walking and biking. This has led to trademarked industry terms such as "Walk Score" and "Bike Score" (Handy et al., 2002; Frank et al., 2005; Forsyth et al., 2008; Ewing and Cervero, 2010). In particular, 'Walk Score' has entered common lexicon because of the website by the same name that rates one place against another, implying that some areas are a "Walker's Paradise" and others are the opposite. Some studies have suggested that tools like WalkScore provide a direct and replicable manner to benchmark or measure how people will travel via walking or biking (Heath et al., 2006; Brownson et al., 2009; Carr et al., 2010, 2011).

Yet, I would argue that there are limiting aspects to this language and analytical framework. Many terms that relate to transportation, such as "walkability," "livable streets" or "complete streets," only tell a small part of a larger story and are not inclusive of other factors that shape streets and transport. These include things such as social or public space and economics. They are aspects of the street that authors such as Jane Jacobs or Ebenezer Howard might say have to do with beauty, community and sense of place yet are not often accounted for when we plan, design and engineer our streets (Jacobs, 1961). Even Le Corbusier was in touch with this ethos. While he is sometimes derided for his desire to help ease traffic flow by segregating cars from bikes and pedestrians, he also held to a vision of the past where streets were built for people saying, "The road belonged to us then; we sang in it, we argued in it, while the horse-bus flowed softly by ..." (Hurst, 2006).

It is my belief that there are aspects of the "complete street" that we cannot quantify—aspects of the street that defy the technocratic or rationalist approach that is often the default for city planners and engineers. This reduces the full, deeper meaning of terms like walkability and bikeability through a "tyranny" of relying on experts and data (Douglas, 1970; Lieberman, 1970). It divorces streets from the intangible aspects of street design to support quality of life and urban vitality. It essentially degrades the "street" and makes it into a "road."

Urban planning literature tells the story simply—that great streets are highly connected, have many people living in proximity (high residential density) and are designed for a pleasant experience (Cervero and Duncan, 2003; Handy et al., 2005, 2006; Sallis and Glanz, 2006; Ewing and Cervero, 2010, p 201). These areas have lower levels of obesity and increased economic productivity (Saelens et al., 2003; Frank et al., 2004, 2005; Ewing, 2005). They are exemplified by European cities such as Zurich and Copenhagen which have streets designed for active transportation, but they can also be reflected by the streets of Africa that I experienced at a young age. They have lively activity and social interactions, increased property values, less traffic and more healthy environments (Cervero, 2012). In the US, however, there are far fewer examples of these kind of streets.

Whether or not this is due to jargon, terminology, political will or legacy of investing in automotive design, I cannot conclusively say, but I can say that there are few resources that identify this as a problem and provide a more advanced discussion on how to change it—hence, the purpose of this book, to extend beyond the jargon of complete streets and talk about something more dynamic, to put an end to the road. My goal is to provide a greater understanding of the intangibles that make roads more *livable* and *complete*, and to help define and take action to make these streets more *inclusive*, so that they support walking and biking for all.

Through a series of stories (some of which relate to my own experiences), case studies and anecdotes, you will learn about how researchers and thinkers are trying to improve streets holistically, not only with things such as sidewalks, bulb-outs and bike lanes, but with strategies to create equity, economic value and reshape land use for walking and biking. This book will show how qualitative knowledge and intuition can help inform the hyper-rational engineering approach to street design (Riggs, 2014a).

By the end of this book, my hope is that you will have a better understanding of the concept of a "complete street" and how neighborhood streets can be designed to stimulate holistic urban vitality, in both urban and suburban contexts; mega-regions and small towns alike. Streets for walking and biking should not just be an afterthought (Berman, 1983): the most walkable and bikeable neighborhood streets should be accessible for all of us regardless of our age, race or income status (Riggs, 2011; Schafran, 2013; Gilderbloom et al., 2015). You will learn to reimagine the notion of all the things a street can be.

In my 20 years of work designing streets and teaching about roads and how they can be made better, I have been able to observe (on numerous occasions) the limitations of jargons and "planner-speak"—how it can be an impediment to advancing bold ideas that move beyond current paradigms. I have also gained an appreciation about how street design fits into my own story. So, before I launch into a discussion on ending roads and designing neighborhood streets, I feel it is important to explain the origins of how I came to my worldview. It started as a result of one tragic event during my college years and shaped my view of walking, biking and streets for years to come.

An Achilles heel

During the fall of my senior year in college, I was at the peak of academic and athletic performance; or so I thought. I had excellent grades, was interviewing to become a Rhodes Scholar at the University of Oxford and was poised to run a very competitive sub-3-minute and 50-second 1500m time in my final collegiate season as a track and field athlete. I was very active and walking and biking were a big part of my life. I liked to think that I took after Roger Bannister and would run almost everywhere, training between 80 and 120 miles per week.[1]

At the same time, as an urban and architectural history major, I had become transfixed with cities. This was due in large part to Professor Christopher Thompson. Chris, who is now a good friend, was a scholar of Le Tour de France, so did not only understand the history of the street, but also had an excellent grasp of many important locations such as London and Paris that shaped how planners and engineers think about the walkable and bikeable city. I listened to his stories about the advent of the bike and urban migration to the city and they galvanized my interest in walking, biking and the city. I also learned how Corbusier framed a modernist city as auto-oriented and about how much of the reconstruction of cities after WWII adopted this approach.

I distinctly remember the first time Chris showed a photo of an early cyclist in class. It showed a working-class man balanced on a bike with arms spread wide as the wind rushed by him, exclaiming, "Without engine, without wings and … just as fast" ("Sans moteur, sans ailes et… aussi vite"). It captivated me. Chris explained that the wide adoption of the bicycle provided the first opportunity for humans to travel that fast on their own power. He also argued that this was connected not only to women's emancipation but ultimately to the rise of the democratic republic and the French Revolution. I ended up studying the social political and economic development of many Western European cities with Chris. I became his teaching assistant where I was able to share my plans with him—I wanted to cap off my final semester of my undergraduate education by taking a trip to study walking, biking and history in the city of Groningen in the Netherlands.

While that was my intention, that was not what life had planned for me. While I was engaged in these academic and athletic endeavors, I was also having fun with my friends. And one day, while playing basketball (something forbidden for college runners), I had a bit too much fun.

Since I was very quick, my usual strategy on the basketball floor was to try to more-or-less outrun my opponent. This involved driving and stopping with sudden cuts and bursts of speed. On this occasion, I was being closely guarded by my friend Bryan, who was likely channeling Chicago Bulls' great Horace Grant as a defender, given his intimate love for the team. I ran to Bryan's right with the ball to try to score on him. I then took another quick step to try to shake his defense, but suddenly fell to the floor. My mind was shrouded with confusion.

While in my head I saw myself dribbling easily past him and shooting a layup, my body had instead collapsed to the floor as my left leg went out beneath me. It felt as if the floor had given away. Momentarily dazed, I turned to my back and reached for my knee and to get up but could not. Gaining some coherency I winced, now feeling the pain power through the initial shock of my fall. I laid back to the floor almost blacking out. My leg was limp and not able to support me.

Figure 1.3: "No engine, no wings and... just as quickly."

Source: Adapted from Forchey (1890)

What I would find out later was that I had completely ruptured my Achilles tendon. The doctor described it as an explosion in the back of my leg—with tiny sinews of muscle shredded and balled in the top of my calf. As an athlete, this was clearly not the best prognosis. And the doctors did not mince their words in telling my future. Not only did they say I would never run again, but they also said I would be lucky to walk without a limp.

I was crushed; mentally deflated before, during and after my intensive surgeries. The pain was excruciating, which made it hard to focus, and I barely finished out the fall term. There would be no travel to the Netherlands for me. I retreated home to my parents for a month of recovery; preparing for the months of physical therapy that I had been prescribed. My whole identity felt ruptured, along with my tendon. How could I be a student of these places if I could not see them the way I wanted to; walking or biking through them?

Fortunately, my emotion gave way to determination. I was determined to walk again. I was determined to run again. I would experience these places, these streets, that I had wanted to see. And I would also become a better student of how to create streets for people and human experiences—holistic places for people of all abilities. I wanted to explore places where people could walk or bike, but also places for people living with reduced mobility like I had. I threw myself into physical therapy and cross training, and also into my studies—reading more about how cities had developed.

I became transfixed by Peter Hall's *Cities of Tomorrow* and Ebenezer Howard's *Garden Cities of Tomorrow*. I read Jane Jacobs' work to shape the West Village into one of the most coveted walkable areas in the United States. I also researched graduate schools, most in public affairs, until my father suggested I look at an urban planning program in my hometown of Louisville, Kentucky. Just what was this planning thing? I certainly had no idea, but as I looked closer, I discovered that it might be an area where I could combine my many interests. The degree might allow me to focus on creating more livable environments for people to walk or bike in.

In addition to this, I trained by running everywhere I went and chose the longest and most obscure routes to experience difference kind roads. Upon graduating with a master's degree in urban planning, I moved to San Francisco where I got a job as an economist and planner for the US Coast Guard. I gave up my car and told myself that I would never wear anything but running shoes again, even in the work environment (something that I have fortunately given up since). And within two years of my injury I was running competitively again, with a new appreciation for the role of streets in cities.[2]

While the reader may be skeptical about why I told this story and what it has to do with the design and evolution of streets, I would argue it has everything to do with them. A great street is not just about the asphalt, the number of lanes, the division between the bikes and pedestrians or even the accommodation it makes for cars, it is about the exact thing that I came to appreciate as the result of my injury—creating a place of enjoyment for people of all ages and abilities. The individual recipe for success may be different, but the goal of making a place where someone can go for a walk, a bike ride, play or engage with the street is still the same. And my own evolution in thinking after rupturing my tendon is a small reflection of how streets can evolve. They can be the same and yet different, and function in ways far beyond just a purpose for transport in places across the globe.

The organization of this book

Considering this background, this book is organized around themes that evolve the idea of the road and extend the concept of complete streets to be more inclusive. Over the coming years, as our cities face pressure to reduce emissions and grow less reliant on cars, the dialogue on what a street is and how it can evolve (or devolve) will need to be rethought and expanded.

This dialogue must focus not only on the travel, but on the many other aspects of the city that can stimulate urban vitality, such as the economic, social and cultural aspects of cities. I believe that this focus can even extend to the green landscape, where the street can "disappear" into sidewalks, gardens and play spaces.

While this idea of a disappearing street moves beyond the current idea of the "complete street" or "livable street," it can likely best be illustrated by experience and observation—for example taking a walk to experience the way the streets interface with yards and buildings, or as Baudelaire would claim, taking "up residence in multiplicity" of the crowd (White, 2001). This idea of observation and experience is an important keystone of this book, and why I take advantage of many case studies and personal experiences throughout it. This experience lens provides room for instinct and intuition to guide design. The concept embraces the idea that we intrinsically know what a livable or lively street is and prefer them. As one might say: while many of us can't say what comprises good design, we can recognize bad design. Given this idea that good design can be experienced, this book is designed around a handful of *experiences of the street*.

After an introduction of the history of the street in Western cities in Chapter 2, we will dive into a number of thematic *experiences of the street* that extend the discussion of complete streets and develop the concept that roads can disappear and streets can emerge. These experiences first explore *the street as transportation space* (Chapter 3), which also provides a primer of transportation planning and engineering concepts. In Chapter 4, we will then move to exploring *the street as an economic space*, followed by an look at *the street as social space* (Chapter 5), *the street as a cultural space* (Chapter 6) and the street as natural space (Chapter 7). Chapter 8 and Chapter 9 focus on the challenge of urban infrastructure and housing in how we create vibrant and livable streets, and the importance of integrating human behavior into thinking about how we design streets. Chapter 10 offers a window into the future of street design and considers new kinds of vehicles and new kinds of streets. Finally, Chapter 11 summarizes these *experiences of the street* and discusses how we can engage action now.

The aim of this book is to move beyond terminology and help to start reimagining the street—something that is particularly important now technology, such as shared and autonomous vehicles, have us rethinking who "owns" the street. My aim is to help others to start to think of the street as something much more than something for transportation—helping build streets that are economic, social, cultural and natural places that help heal many of the social and political barriers that separate our society. There are very few places that people can meet on common ground to socialize, talk interact and empathize with one another, and I believe streets can be one those rare places.

It took me close to 20 years of work and a traumatic injury to come to this conclusion. My aim is not only to convey the nuances of how streets are designed but also how citizens, planners, engineers and policymakers can work together to shape streets that are more vibrant and safer for human interactions and that help bring our cities together in a new way.

As discussed, while Corbusier said that we can "kill the street" in a way that encouraged auto-mobility, we can adopt this idea of deconstruction as we tear down pre-conceived notions of what a street can be—as we end the road. The act of killing can be also used as a concept that implies a rebirth and evolution. I believe that our roadways can evolve and be reimagined. We can move them beyond the concept of them simply being "complete." We can shape more human-oriented spaces, where people of all types and abilities can live, work, play and connect. And, I believe, as our roads begin to disappear, our streets can emerge, and our cities can thrive.

So let's get on with it.

2

A Recent History of the Street

She had always been fond of history, and here was history in the stones of the street and the atoms of the sunshine. (Henry James, 1917, p 301)

If we are to better understand how the street can be shaped for livability and human interaction, it is helpful to start with a basic understanding of how streets have evolved over the past few centuries. In that sense, the first thing that may come to mind when considering this history might be the cart paths that facilitated trade in medieval Europe and the Middle East or perhaps the dusty road outside a saloon from a glamorized American Western movie. While there may be lessons to learn from these visions of the street, the origins of the modern street stem largely from the urbanization and industrialization following the industrial revolution and post-war reconstruction periods (Boyer, 1986). Given that, this discussion begins at the Industrial Revolution in the early 19th century and the creation of the modern engineered street.

This beginning does not discount the many different forms that a road can take, and I fully realize that the experience of an organized, paved, modern road is not necessarily one that all can say they have. When I was a boy growing up in a rural and poor community near Louisville, Kentucky, seeing an unpaved dirt or gravel road was not uncommon, and this kind of "un-engineered" street is still common in many places around the globe. I have strong memories of walking down dirt roads surrounded on both sides by beautiful fields of corn standing four to six feet high and extending far into the horizon until they met the hills of the Ohio River Valley.

As discussed earlier, after college, I had the opportunity to teach in a village on the outskirts of Arusha, Tanzania, and had a similar experience to what I had already had in Kentucky. Each day my friend Nathaniel and I walked from the house that we had rented to the school where we were working on a dirt street that was flanked by fields of corn. Nathaniel and I liked to joke that some of the potholes we saw cars and buses drive through could swallow a small elephant, but aside from the beautiful Mount Meru in the background the scene in Africa was almost identical to what we had experienced in the US.

And while these unstructured street forms may seem odd or divergent, the principles that they espouse—of simplicity and devolution of formality—are more common than you would think. Many communities are beginning to draw on these kinds of less structured or less infrastructure-intensive design ideas for their roads.

Take, for example, the dialogue happening in some US cities on using gravel for roads instead of pavement (Igarta, 2017b), and the fact that Portland, Oregon, has over 40 miles of unpaved roads in city limits. Portland is using those unpaved areas to reimagine the public right-of-way. They are allocating space to planting and gardens, and modes of travel other than driving. This trend excites me, but it is also an advanced concept. To contextualize and begin applying these ideas, it is important to understand the history of the paved, structured and engineered streets that exist in most of the cities and neighborhoods in the West; and the story starts with the origins of the industrial city.

The street and the industrial city

In the early 1800s as the Industrial Revolution took hold around the globe, most cities in the US and Europe were built for walking and cycling. They were compactly constructed so walking was the primary mode of transportation, but most were also crowded and dirty. City officials placed little control over building placement, size or safety. Garbage and sewage went unmonitored. Water and air quality were poor. Transportation systems were uncontrolled, with travelers overcome by "clacking horse hooves, wooden wagon wheels, street railways, and unmuffled industrial machinery" (Leavitt, 1996).

This was the disease-ridden environment that Jacob Riis uncovered in his 1890 expose on New York slums, *How the Other Half Lives* (Riis, 1890). He found unhealthy slums with crowded conditions that were conducive to diseases like typhoid, yellow fever and cholera. He also related this crowding to criminal behavior (Corburn, 2007). This belief was common at the time, that a person's physical environment determined their behavior. He and other early public health advocates such as Charles Booth wanted to find solutions to mend the "slum problem" because they felt it not only physically unhealthy but caused moral corruption.

As a result, many cities were "sanitized." Housing and street standards were created to deal with health standards and to design rules that might remedy health problems, or "environmental miasmas," and create "sanitary cities". Laws were made to provide appropriate infrastructure systems, resulting in

Figure 2.1: A depiction of New York streets in the late 1800s

Source: Public Domain, https://www.publicdomainpictures.net/en/view-image.php?image=76637&picture=broadway-new-york-old-print

cleaner water, sewers and appropriate disposal of refuse. Riis and Booth's idea was to give proper housing and access to open space to individuals, not only for physical health, but so that they could be reformed. As these rules evolved, building and zoning codes emerged. In New York, for example, these provided for better ventilation and ambient light exposure and limited the proximity of noisy or noxious industrial land uses (for example tanneries or meat packing facilities) around residences.

These urban sanitation changes improved the public health and safety of cities. Along with individuals such as Riis and Booth, other reformers of the time worked to make cities healthier, as well as more equitable, as they continued to identify many of the early problems with the modern city—including lingering human slavery and segregation. Designers, naturalists, politicians and activists such as Daniel Burnham, Lucretia Mott, John Muir, Theodore Roosevelt and Elizabeth Cady Stanton also worked to improve housing and labor standards, abolish slavery, build parks and preserve natural spaces.

Following this work, a gradual shift occurred in the way streets were designed and used, allowing them to support walking and cycling more safely. By rebuilding cities for health, civic leaders enabled the possibility of more active and human-centric travel for all urban residents. This was unique—prior to the Industrial Revolution, in most locations, the notion of using the street for leisure walking or human travel was primarily something for the wealthy gentry. It was written about by those such as Charles Baudelaire, who saw walking as the pastime of the refined gentleman who would engage in social walking and the casual flâneur (White, 2001). While travel via steam train, carriage and buggy were available, they were too primarily used by the wealthy and for longer trips. But, through urban reform in the way cities were designed, citizens of all kinds were able to access more green space for walking and cycling This provided for a more healthy urban environment.

A good example of this design was the idea of the garden city. Ebenezer Howard designed "garden cities" that were conceived to promote peace and egalitarianism. His designs featured a series of ring roads that were connected by radial streets tying together "the factories, warehouses, dairies, markets, coal yards, timber yards" on the outer rings of the town. He placed walkable gardens and elegant public spaces at the center of his ideal city (Howard, 1902). These ringed cities, gardens and public spaces were connected by rail with other similarly designed cities.

Famed landscape architect Frederick Olmstead, Jr. also believed in this idea of walkable cities with well-distributed public facilities and parks "if the health and vigor of the people are to be maintained" (Olmsted Jr, 1911). Yet, despite the attempts to tie physical form (and thereby morality) to health in city design, planners and architects such as Olmsted and others did not understand the way diseases spread. Put simply, they did not understand germs. Take for example this quote by the naturalist John Muir (1894),

> Fear not, therefore, to try the mountain passes. They will kill care, save you from deadly apathy, set you free, and call forth every faculty into vigorous, enthusiastic action. (p 79)

While that phrase sounds majestic, it also illustrates that Muir thought that exposure to nature was directly connected to health. Just like many thinkers in the 1800s, he believed that environment determined biology. This kind of thinking was an oversimplification and a misunderstanding of science. Individuals such as Howard, Olmsted and Muir thought that things such as decomposition, stagnant water, unventilated air and lack of light caused contagious disease. They thought that man was corrupt but that through a better environment and being in nature this corruption could be cured (Corburn, 2007).

While we now know better, this kind of thinking resulted in some dramatic urban benefits. It led to the creation of large greenbelts and parks throughout London and the establishment of national parks such as Yosemite in the United States. The focus on the natural world led to changes in street design and the integration of natural space with housing design.

For example, most roads during this period were designed to be extremely narrow with plenty of green space around them. Homes were built as

Figure 2.2: Late 19th-century street design

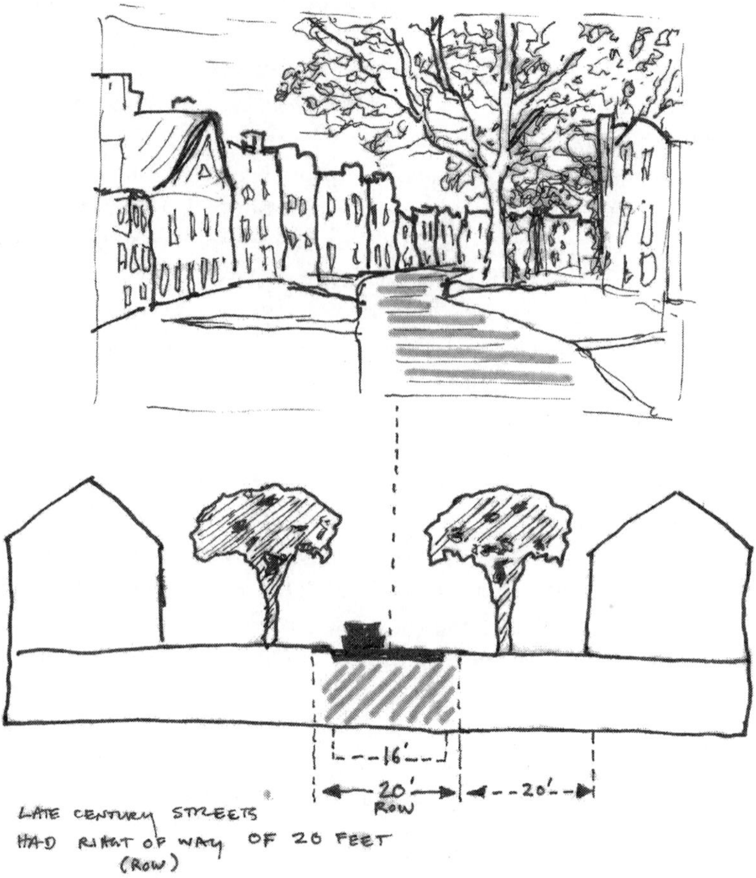

LATE CENTURY STREETS
HAD RIGHT OF WAY OF 20 FEET
(ROW)

Source: Adapted from Southworth and Ben-Joseph (2005)

connected townhouses, dense but with plenty of areas for planting, exercise and play in front of them. In locations such as Hampstead, England, roads were designed approximately 25 to 30 feet wide, and the full right-of-way (or space controlled by the municipality) was around 40 feet. These yielded enough area for a carriage but also ample space for walking, cycling and active recreation (Southworth and Ben-Joseph, 1995). As depicted in Figure 2.2, only 16 feet of the space in between homes was dedicated to roadway. But this did not last long.

20th-century development and housing

A change came as cities expanded at the start of the 20th century. Reformers began to modify city structure through engineering (Peterson, 1979). Despite the "green" approach of their predecessors, most reformers focused on creating a more structured city. This involved complex sewerage projects to dispose of refuse and the "diseases" that cities struggled with previously (Melosi, 2000). Both New York and Boston installed over 100 miles of sewer lines between 1849 and 1873. The reforms also involved miles of newly installed roadway infrastructure. For context, at the end of the 19th century, New York had spent $24 million on subways, bridges, paving and water supplies (Boyer, 1986). In 2022, that closes in on a billion dollars of investment.

During this period, in the early 1900s, transportation in the center of cities was still done primarily by walking or horse and buggy, but this was gradually changing. Formal policy was being put in place to systematically design cities to reduce disease causation and, based on this, they were becoming more structured. In the US, the American Public Health Association's Committee on the Hygiene of Housing issued risk-reducing guidance for neighborhood planning and design (APHA, 1948). These policies formalized the engineering of the streetscape and began to form the principles that would standardize suburban growth as the century progressed. This was a change from the past city planning eras which focused on cities in the "garden", values of nature and ties with walking and transit. City design began focusing on a key invention that was emerging—the motorized vehicle.

Around 1929, American architect Clarence Perry provided design schemes for the ideal "neighborhood unit" that included an array of single-family homes over 160 acres of land and accommodating 5,000 to 6,000 individuals, with streets navigable not only by horse and buggy but also by automobile (Perry, 1929; Silver, 1985, p 19). Perry, assuming that the neighborhood provided organization and homogeneity to human beings, wrote that "automatically it (the neighborhood) draws together a group of people of similar living standards and similar economic ability to realize them." He also believed that,

> the segregation of a city population along racial, economic, social and vocational lines is a normal process and one which is constantly at work ... (and that) the use of a neighborhood formula in suburban building and slum rebuilding schemes (would) promote this grouping process. (Perry, 1929, p 99)

This division of urban spaces and accommodation of the car in city design was emergent and unique at the time. The plan had increased attention on the automobile. It not only created streets that provided wide separation between housing but it outlined a template for auto-oriented, suburban development and sowed the seeds for the racial segregation and social isolation that emerged following World War II. Perry's plan allowed for more efficient travel via automobile for more well-to-do individuals. These people were primarily those who were White and who were able to occupy housing further from the city center (Massey and Denton, 1993; Massey, 2008).

In Perry's layout, the space between buildings expanded to a width of as much as 60 to 80 feet. While the design and layout of these building and street areas was curvilinear, with distributed pedestrian paths and distributed parks and playgrounds, this space outside of the housing unit was restricted to recreation, not circulation (Larice and Macdonald, 2013). Circulation was "to be limited and sufficient only to meet the absolute requirements of utility in the physical operation of a housing project." (Larice and Macdonald, 2013, p 205)

Most of these plans related to the societal pivot to embrace the automobile. There was pressure to accommodate cars and an emphasis on different kinds of roads or road hierarchy. In particular, with the mass production

Figure 2.3: Perry's vision for the neighborhood unit, providing schools, shopping and services within quarter of a mile of residences

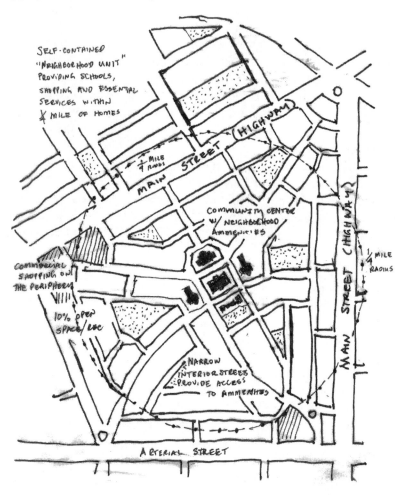

of the Model T Ford that began in 1907, engineers began to classify roads by type. They started to create road hierarchies, with collector and arterial streets allowing for faster and heavier traffic. Neighborhood roads began to be enlarged with more paved areas for traffic around homes. They looked increasingly auto-oriented and less green.

This suburban development trend and its impacts on roadway design rapidly accelerated after World War II. Housing construction boosted the economy as it transitioned from military to consumer-goods production (Hall, 1996). New communities became filled with middle-class troops returning from the war. Expansion occurred outside of the central cities, in places like Levittown—towns largely dependent on private automobiles. Larger homes and more streets designed around cars continued to be the trend.

Linked to these changes in transportation and commute patterns, the functionality of cities changed. Downtowns became less focused on walking and environmental exposure for health and more on providing privacy. Many suburban locations became principally bedroom communities. Ever more developments had large-lot homes with neighbors spread out from each other. While original suburbs were found to have greater neighborhood involvement than their urban counterparts, over time they filled with middle-to-upper class, homogenous, White populations, which created difficulty in social connectedness (Putnam, 2001). Occupants seeking privacy and safety found that they were more isolated and disconnected both physically and emotionally with the loss of the social capital of traditional non-auto-focused communities.

To recap, most of these suburban developments around the globe were designed for automobiles, with little connectivity; thus the ease of moving via walking or cycling to destinations such as schools, stores and workplaces was limited (Sallis et al., 2004). Roadways progressively grew to 40, 50 or 60 feet in width, and the people living in these areas, located away from jobs and transit, became largely dependent on private automobiles. Residents were less likely to walk or bike and became progressively mentally and physically unhealthy (Cervero and Kockelman, 1997; Frank et al., 2004).

Issues of physical and social health related to sprawl

This section turns to urban sprawl. The idea of sprawl, however, may not be clear to all readers of this book. I know that it was not clear to me when I was young. I grew up in a very poor, yet suburban and car-dependent area, and that just seemed to be the norm. Getting into a car to get to housing or jobs that were spread out from one another was commonplace. It was just a part of a city, even if that city was large and ever expanding. We relied on our old Datsun with rusted-out floorboards to get almost everywhere. This included the many places we went that would not have been not ideal for cycling and walking. We lived in a house on the outskirts of the town, on roughly 30 acres, but I remember going to neighborhoods where my friends lived that would have been defined as "sprawling."

In these places, it was hard to connect from house to house, and many walking routes between neighboring homes were cut off. You had to travel almost double the distance on meandering and circuitous roads to visit with friends than if you would have been able to simply walk across a backyard or cut through another lot. I can still remember trying to co-opt this system with an elementary school friend by digging tunnels under the fences in his backyard to access the neighboring property.

This lack of connectivity (where I was forced to dig under a fence in middle-America) was anecdotal evidence of what a researcher might find in examining many places in the US at the time. The researcher would have found suburban locations that limited movement and induced social disconnection. They would have seen that the individuals living in these locations were more likely to have chronic mental or physical health conditions (Sturm and Cohen, 2004). They quite literately might have needed to go over a fence to socialize with a neighbor—or under one in my case.

To put it simply, the suburban locations that many people around the globe grew up in are not healthy. Data has shown that, in general, suburbanization has led to new trends of chronic diseases, despite advances in medicine that have limited how contagious diseases spread (Galea et al., 2005) While you may not die of typhoid, malaria or yellow fever in the US or Europe any longer, you are likely to experience obesity, heart disease, diabetes, depression, osteoporosis or cancer. And much of this is just based on where you live.

A 2006 study by researchers at the Harvard School of Public Health reported that obesity is responsible for 2.6 million annual deaths worldwide (Ezzati et al., 2006). More recent 2020 data from the US Center for Disease Control and Prevent reveals that 40 percent of the American public are considered obese (CDC, 2021). Being overweight increases the risks of high blood pressure, high cholesterol, heart disease, stroke, cancer, gall bladder and respiratory disease, joint and bone disease and many other afflictions such as diabetes (Pi-Sunyer, 1993). Furthermore, work by researchers such as Raj Chetty from Harvard now illustrates what a ripple effect this type of growth has had on American society (Chetty and Hendren, 2018; Chetty et al., 2020). Research shows us that suburban pressures compounded issues with inner-city urban poverty and blight. As affluent people fled the central city, this compounded health and social inequalities for minorities and the poor.

In the 1960s, planners and engineers thought the answer to the problems of suburban (and primarily White) flight the center of cities was "urban renewal"—or attempts to cure and resuscitate the urban slums that had been underfunded for years (Corburn, 2007). To "renew" these areas, planners built massive super-block housing that gave little thought to streets and tore apart many minority and immigrant communities. Many people in these communities remained reliant on cars to access jobs. Most minorities were stuck in these areas of concentrated poverty. They were not able to afford to purchase nicer housing in the suburbs because of predatory lending and insurance practices—a mortgage industry that was pitted against minorities (Cutler et al., 1999).

While undertaking my research on street design, I continually encountered examples of zoning and city design laws that were devised to segregate minorities (Rothstein, 2017). This is commonly called redlining and some studies suggest a housing markup of approximately 7 percent for Black people compared to White people (Kain and Quigley, 1972). For most ethnic minorities, it has also been extremely tough for them to find housing with good transportation access. For example, in Boston, ethnic minorities faced an 8 percent higher chance of being denied a home mortgage in a livable, walkable area than a White individual (Munnell et al., 1996).

To me, this illustrates that the community envisioned by Perry had become a foundation for housing segregation. While the original intent of a classic neighborhood may have been designed to contain relevant services and amenities that you could walk or bike to, in the end these structures have only facilitated suburbanization and segregation. And, unfortunately, these trends have only continued.

As we will discuss in more detail in subsequent chapters, the bulk of urban housing has continued to move out of the downtown core of cities, where the street had traditionally been the most conducive to walking and cycling. As a data point, while the average household size has decreased over recent years, the average house size has increased from 1,500 square feet in 1970 to over 2,300 in 2020 according to the US Census. Most cities around the globe now have developments that form "edgeless cities"—many of which lack diversity in land use and provide inadequate access to jobs and transit (Lang, 2003). This equates to time spent in cars. Both recreational and incidental, utilitarian trips, such as walking to school, to friends' houses, the library, the store or the park are all seen as "active lifestyle" behaviors and have decreased (Forsyth et al., 2007). And, of course, we are only increasing our use of automobiles as innovations like ridesharing make it even easier to access a ride in a car—and it's even driven for you.

The 21st-century response: a contrasting view of urbanism

Given these developments, it may be easy to feel discouraged by the problems our cities have (and we haven't even talked about the implications of emissions from driving) but there are other perspectives. For example, contrasting the negative visions of sprawl, some work has shown that lower-density areas are not all bad for those who do want to walk or cycle and offer more opportunities for leisure walking (Forsyth et al., 2007, 2008). Essentially, people engage in active forms of transportation for different reasons. Those who live in a city or location that is denser will likely walk for their daily transportation needs, but those who live in more suburban areas may walk more for leisure. Research also suggests that streets designed to encourage walking and biking behaviors can decrease crime and increase broader demand for what planners define as "multi-modal" facilities (those that are designed to facilitate multiple "modes" of transportation, inclusive of bicycles and pedestrians in addition to cars) (Leslie et al., 2005; Foster and Giles-Corti, 2008; Handy et al., 2008; Troy and Grove, 2008). This can lead to greater numbers of collisions simply due to the increased number of walkers and cyclists on the road.

At the same time, a growing body of work illustrates that walkable and bikeable neighborhoods have economic value by encouraging business transactions (Litman, 2003) and bolstering real estate property values (Cortright, 2009; Diao and Ferreira, 2010). Research shows the more a city has a grid-like street pattern the higher the home values (Matthews and Turnbull, 2007). Other work finds that walkability and bikeability can be associated with an increase in property value of up to nine percent (Pivo and Fisher, 2011; Pivo, 2013). For example, during the Great Recession from 2008–2012, many neighborhoods struggled with economic decline, yet more dense, walkable and bikeable areas in urban environments had fewer foreclosures and less price decline (Glaeser, 2011; Saito, 2011; Dong, 2015).

In response to these findings, 20th-century planners are continuing to find new city design elements that improve health and community (Keating and Krumholz, 2000). Planners such as Lynch (1960), Alexander (Alexander et al., 1977) and Jacobs and Appleyard (1987) have all suggested that cities should focus on livable streets, density, integration of activities, retention of distinct public spaces and use of architectural variation. These urban planning ideas emphasize that housing, streets and the built environment can define physical and social relationships, encouraging walking and healthy lifestyles (Rutheiser, 2008). This concept that the design of a house or street can be related to behavior has a vague resemblance to some of the same principles espoused in the 18th century, which are often criticized because of the social equity challenges embedded in designing cities (Zavestoski and Agyeman, 2014). Yet the ideas do offer a platform for rethinking the street altogether.

Summary

If roads are to be rethought, we must harness both the historic legacy of neighborhood design as well as the embedded socio-economic tension in changing them into streets. It is clear that creating equitable street regeneration has been a challenge for planners since the 1890s (Cutler et al., 1999). This inequality continues as we have had decades of thinking about roads in one way—as conduits for cars. Truly, the results of suburban trends have been neighborhoods that extend far beyond original central cities, and this presents issues with resource and health equity. This inequality is bad for us—physically, mentally, socially and, I believe, spiritually. The design of our streets—their geometry, their width, the speed that one can travel—plays a role in how we live. And we can choose to plan for and design streets that guarantee equity of opportunity to walk or bike to all (Rawls, 1988).

Just how do we do this? We might start with thinking about planning, design and engineering interventions. In the next chapter, we will focus on exactly that before we transition to a discussion about the economic, social, cultural and natural power of the street. All of this can help facilitate humanistic travel.

So, let's keep moving and discuss the details of designing streets for people of all types.

3

The Street for Transport

... as you see, the cars look out for the cyclists, the cyclists look out for the pedestrians, and everyone looks out for each other. You can't expect traffic signs and street markings to encourage that sort of behavior. You have to build it into the design of the road. (Hans Monderman in McNichol, 2004)

Now that we have spent some time looking at the history of how "streets" developed into our modern iteration of "the road," we can entertain a dialogue about how roadway (and related infrastructure) are currently designed by planners. As Hans Monderman says, this does not need to be an overwhelmingly technical conversation. The discussion can and should include aspects of the street that facilitate the type of activity we want to see, whether it be driving, walking, biking, taking transit or riding a scooter. The dialogue need not just be about engineering details.

For me, this departure from engineering is an act of catharsis, since the topic can sometimes be wieldy and complex, so much so that for the first five to six years that I worked as a professional I downplayed my expertise in transport planning and engineering. I was embarrassed (and perhaps slightly intimidated) by all the terminology and code, lingo and acronyms that city planners and transportation-folk threw around. I liked to joke that I should have written a dictionary entitled "transportation-speak." I was not exactly dumb—I had both a master's and PhD in the field—but it seemed that the terms were created to keep people in the dark. So, all I wanted to do was disengage from the pretense and go back to my spreadsheets.

Why spreadsheets? In 2002, I was hired as an engineering technician and asset manager by the Coast Guard, primarily because of my economic expertise and ability to develop complex life cycle and benefit cost analysis models. While I had expertise in streetscape engineering and design, particularly for walking and biking, I chose to underemphasize it since I was not confident in the technical language. However, confident or not,

I came to understand that this high-minded language did a disservice to the community of transportation professionals, alienating key audiences. I wanted to simplify and dispel the mystery of transportation engineering—which is why this chapter is intended to provide a primer in street planning and design to improve the environment for walking and cycling.

A prime example of this alienation came in 2009, just after I had taken over the management of the transportation program at the University of California, Berkeley. There had been ongoing dialogue about a federally funded bus-rapid-transit project that would provide faster transit services to the eastern portion of the San Francisco Bay Area, running from Berkeley to San Leandro. Planners, engineers and policy makers conducted planning and analysis on all the elements of the project, including things such as improved arrivals times, priority signal timing and raised platforms for boarding. While each of these studies was technically sound, in almost every public meeting, the same planners and engineers failed to clearly explain the functionality and benefit of this technology and its implications on the street.

As a result, the public became skeptical and fragmented, and in 2009 the city of Berkeley decided they would opt out of the project. Berkeley's key players had become convinced that it was of little benefit to them, with many of those players fearing the impact on bicycles, pedestrians and traffic even without evidence for that concern. Clearly something was wrong in that, primarily due to an inability to communicate effectively, a community would turn down tens of millions of dollars in investment without any clear rationale. At the time, I was frustrated and despondent that a decision I viewed as fiscally irresponsible could be made; yet, in retrospect, I believe that a lack of broader understanding of street design was partly to blame. We were speaking different languages.

Simplifying the language of street design

While the idea that differences in terminology and communication impacts the design of streets may be hard to believe, such cognitive dissonance is not abnormal. Many highly technical fields such as computer science and even medical science suffer from the same challenges. You might have experienced this when your doctor has described an illness or medical treatment to you. The language might be overly technical or a specialized language that is hard to understand. This is not abnormal in the transport sector, and the transportation profession sometimes experiences the same problems. It can be very hard to see the future reality of roadway design due to the technical jargon in the transport industry: hence, a need to simplify language for better communication.

Take for example the two side-by-side neighborhood street visions in Figure 3.1. Which one do you think is the more conducive to a better

Figure 3.1: Example of a typical neighborhood street: one designed for cars and the other designed for people

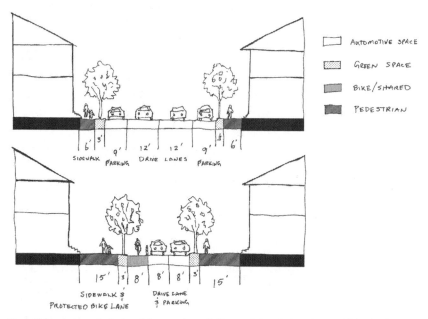

Note: When a street is designed for travelers of all types it is called multi-modal level-of-service (MMLOS)

environment for walking and biking? If you guessed the one toward the bottom, then you are correct. It is narrower (with less than the standard car travel lane width of 12 feet) with wide 10-foot sidewalks and 6-foot buffered lanes for cycling, as opposed to having limited space for biking and walking, and wide unidirectional lanes. The wider street with more generous 12-foot driving lanes is more conducive to driving. While this concept may be simple to communicate graphically, a transportation engineer might refer to the street and say something akin to it having a high "level of service" (LOS) due to the low trip generation of adjacent land uses so that it can support multi-modal goals such as a road diet and reduced crossing distances.

This needlessly complicated language clouds and mystifies a simple point: streets that are narrower have slower-moving traffic. It also serves to stifle innovation since the language is perceived incorrectly. Academics such as Nussbaum (2011) and Sen (2004) refer to this shroud that technical language imposes as "tyrannical," and while I do not believe that most planners and engineers want to manipulate the public, I do believe that by *not* providing simple language many experts and advocates limit our ability to question the appropriateness of such solutions.

For example, do bikes and pedestrians need to be separate from traffic in slower-moving environments? Some of my own research suggests that, just by creating this separation between bicycles, pedestrians and cars in the neighborhood environment, we may create faster and less gracious streets for biking and walking. Perhaps we may want to create both gracious and shared streets for bicycles and pedestrians.

In this light (and keeping with the theme of ending traditional roadway design throughout this book), this street might be a step in the right direction, but it may not go far enough at prioritizing the safety and comfort of active modes of transport, let alone bringing in the co-benefits of economic, social and cultural spaces that are presented later in this book. I have long dialogues with my colleagues about the type of travel experience on most modern engineered streets which are much different than streets in places such as historic Parisian neighborhoods, the Netherlands or even Delhi, India. As dramatized in Woody Allen's movie *Midnight in Paris*, the lead character (played by Owen Wilson) walks all night through streets of Paris, sharing them with cars. The same can be said about certain places in India where shared streets between pedestrians, animals (usually cows) and autos are common.

We will discuss these examples in greater depth later in this book, but it is important to mention this trend of shared streets here, as it provides a part of the rationale for this book. Even those streets that are currently engineered for bicycles and pedestrians do not provide a great environment for those activities; they provide no shared space that moves beyond the traditional engineering, and the focus is on separation for those modes. The idea that streets should be alive and vibrant, even chaotic, is something that many have called for, including people as diverse as Jane Jacobs and Le Corbusier. Both wanted to see transformation of the places we live, whether it be on the streets of the West Village in New York City or in the large grassy meadows of Corbusier's radiant city.

The theory behind why people walk, bike, take transit or drive

These thinkers, and many others, have had the goal of changing the way people travel, giving the option to walk or bike more often, so it is important to spend some time thinking about why people travel the way they do—whether it be by taking a bike, walking, taking transit or driving. A large amount of research has correlated neighborhood walking with higher density communities, street intersections, an increased mix of land uses and green and open space access (Frank et al., 2004). Studies have found that neighborhoods classified as more walkable (using walkability benchmarking tools) have higher levels of incidental walking and less likelihood of obesity (Frank et al., 2007).

For example, Sallis and Glanz (2006) link reduced obesity to aspects of the built environment—things such as living far away from schools or on a busy street. Taking a different perspective, the work of Handy and colleagues looks at walking behavior and how the built environment impacts obesity (Handy et al., 2005). Their work emphasizes the urban design elements of the built environment as important to walking behavior, including safety, quality of the sidewalk and the experience of activity there (Southworth, 2005). Encouraging walking involves thinking about travel for work as well as leisure purposes (Forsyth et al., 2007) and there is a growing theory that walkable neighborhoods have an intrinsic economic value by encouraging economic transactions and social exchanges, and bolstering property values (Cortright, 2009).

By further dissecting the elements that enhance or deter walking, factors such as landform, climate and weather come to light. Research has shown that such factors are more likely to control walking and biking transport behavior than urban design factors (Cervero and Duncan, 2003). Other studies also emphasize this, showing that neighborhoods with a hillier topography have less walking and lower physical activity (Leslie et al., 2005). Further complementary work has discussed how climate and hills deter walking, especially among vulnerable populations like the elderly (Li et al., 2005). Topography is even more important as people age because of cognition and balance issues (Tranter et al., 1991). For example, a study by Lövdén found that older adults have more trouble with directions and what we call "wayfinding" because of these kind of geographical issues, perhaps because of their age (Lövdén et al., 2008).

It is important to mention older adults since there is a recognition that vulnerable populations (which include those with disabilities and children) may be most in need of the intervention of walkable, bikeable or "active-living" communities (Prohaska et al., 2009). Research has shown that certain features of the physical or built environment (such as bulb-outs and the presence of sidewalks, which we will go into detail later) encourage walking, and that these environmental factors are of greater importance to vulnerable populations with reduced capacity (Lawton, 1999). Furthermore, since changes in the environment are likely to impact travel decisions that vulnerable individuals might make, how planners and policy makers shape the built environment has a greater influence on these populations (Clarke and George, 2005).

A hierarchy of user needs for the street

These studies illustrate varying needs or demands that are placed on the street and it is clear that individual characteristics play a critical role in this. Therefore, it is important to define how these characteristics match up to the needs of the street and city, over which planners and policy makers have influence. For example, Figure 3.2 aims to build on the work of Alfonzo (2005) to differentiate these individual-level characteristics from quantifiable built-environment variables. These are scaled based on a pyramid of needs similar to Maslow's Hierarchy of Needs.

Figure 3.2: Travel behavior hierarchy

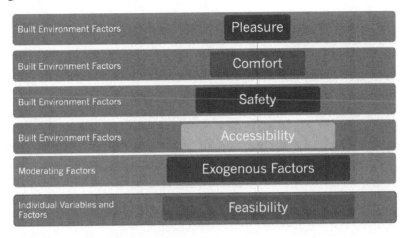

As displayed in the figure, the hierarchy emphasizes *feasibility* (related to individual characteristics such as age, race, health or physical mobility) as a baseline measure for walking behavior. It therefore sits at the bottom of the pyramid. Studies have shown walking behavior and activity levels can be tied to individual-level, socio-cultural factors such as race, crime or gender barriers (Jankowski, 1991; Scott et al., 2007). Some studies cite perceived risk and social networks or environment as additional factors contributing to walking and increased physical activity in this domain (Cromley and McLafferty, 2002; Wolch et al., 2005). These individual-level factors (related to age, race, income and so forth) form some of the primary variables that dictate preferences toward or against walking.

Moving up in the pyramid, a smaller domain sitting on top of feasibility is *exogenous* factors which affect decisions to travel via walking or cycling. These could be factors as random as how weather impacts travel (for instance when it rains you may not really enjoy cycling) or the quality of schools (perhaps when you may want to enroll your child in a better school that is not accessible via walking or biking).

After this come *accessibility, safety, comfort and pleasure* (for example benches and presence of trees). These factors can be attributed to what planners and architects refer to as the built environment which has continually been shown to influence whether someone walks or bikes on the street (Diez Roux, 2001; Macintyre et al., 2002; Oakes, 2004). Certain urban attributes could be associated with each tier is this hierarchy, for example topography and shade with comfort; crime and street grid density with safety; distance to various resources with accessibility; and physical capacity with feasibility. There is even some research that suggests the age of one's home serves as a proxy for walking behavior; presumably for its affiliation with more traditional-urban-center neighborhood design (Berrigan and Troiano, 2002).

Moving from behavior to design: answering questions

Now that we have this framework for human travel behavior, which is explored again later is this book when thinking about ways to reinvent this aspect of how cities work, it is important to explain other facets of the practice of transportation planning and engineering. As I mentioned in introducing this chapter, this is something that has been held as exclusive for many years but is not exactly rocket science. As I will discuss, it is simply making average assumptions that can be used to plan for traffic—usually of the auto variety.

Since I started my career as a transportation professional with many questions, I will use a question-based framework to guide us. In my view, there are often simple answers to these questions, but if something really interests you, then you can check out the notes I have provided following each topical question. This includes additional reading and resources that can help make these topics more relevant.

Q: What is trip generation and how does it work?

A: Trip generation is the first step of analysis in transportation planning. It is when planners and engineers try to anticipate the size of transportation at a system level and determine the number (or volume) of trips that occur within a particular area (Metropolitan Washington Council of Governments, 2016). This can be city wide or in a certain zone, and it can be to study current conditions or future trends.

Engineers define a "trip" as vehicle movement with either the origin or the destination (exiting or entering) of a location or study site (ITE Technical Committee, 1976). Each individual trip has two ends, which are usually referred to as an origin and a destination, and that trip is impacted by many things—just as Figure 3.2 shows. These include variables related to land use, population density, region, connectivity, roadway design and accessibility, to name a few. Trip generation models are also meant to consider the trips of pedestrians and cyclists, as well as motor vehicles. More often than not, the land use of whatever location being studied is one of the largest indicators of how many trips a place will produce or attract. Think of it in terms of gravity. For example, a residential zone will result in a different trip (usually lower) generation outcome than a commercial shopping center. Similarly, a zone with a high level of employment will be a highly attractive center for trips.

While these trips might be inferred from counting the number of trips at a location, for future, planning examples have to be determined. These examples usually these come from something called the ITE Manual, a book that shows a number of land uses alongside what the estimated trips for what those uses are. This is calculated by undertaking an assessment of many other places around the US and fitting the number of trips these locations yield into a statistical curve that allows them to be generalized and applied elsewhere.

If you are not comfortable with statistics, do not worry. The main thing you need to understand is that land use and project types vary widely, so statistics like this (which aggregate points) are only as good as the individual points. In some cases, you might experience projects that are much different than the norm and are not a good fit for these kind of models. For example, a lot of higher-density, mixed-use areas, where both residential and commercial land uses are combined, typically do not fit these linear analyses. These places tend to have fewer trips than engineering models estimate. The trips in mixed-use areas also tend to be shorter. Further, these zones also tend to create an environment where individuals can walk or bike instead of drive, which we sometimes refer to as "internal trip capture."[1] Based on this, planners and engineers sometimes have to adapt their analyses in these areas to estimate how much lower the number of trips might be. This is sometimes called "de-generation."

Q: What is level of service?

A: Level of service (LOS) refers to how a facility accommodates a form of transport or a "mode." In simpler terms, LOS is essentially how many vehicles can get through an intersection at one time or how much roadway capacity exists. Think of streets as pipes: how much can we fit through them? LOS is calculated using assumptions about speed and capacity, and roads are assigned a grade in how they are performing, either for current or future projects.

This rating system is broken down into six levels from best to worst: A, B, C, D, E and F. A rating of "A" is achieved on a roadway when traffic flows at the posted speed limit and cars can change lanes. Based on how much delay passengers experience in a vehicle, the grade moves from B to C and so on. An "F" could be equated with gridlock. Most transportation planners and engineers use LOS to plan for projects, but this has recently become controversial because it tends to focus solely on cars and roadway expansion. It also penalizes high-density projects which generate more trips. These trips get assigned or attached to local intersections and create calculated time delays—and therefore result in poor LOS.

However, higher-density projects with mixed uses actually result in less travel on the whole or less assessing vehicle miles traveled (VMT). Based on this, many have argued that professionals should move to assessing VMT as opposed to LOS (Cervero and Murakami, 2010; Litman, 2011).

The critique of LOS has been that it exacerbates sprawl and reduces space for pedestrians and cyclists. Further, it has been discussed that LOS ignores other indirect problems such as parking congestion, increased traffic accidents and increased pollution from emissions.[2]

Q: What is multi-modal level of service?

A: Multi-modal level of service refers to LOS analysis that includes multiple transport modes when evaluating a transport system. Historically, LOS analysis only evaluated motor vehicles with respect to congestion and traffic flow, but this automobile bias has led to urban sprawl and highway expansion. Multi-modal LOS is an improvement to standard LOS analysis because it encourages the development of cycling, walking and public transit systems.

Multi-modal LOS allows for a more balanced and comprehensive approach to analyzing existing roadways for smart growth and transportation demand management (TDM) planning. The LOS rating system helps planners to identify performance, diagnose problem areas and offer solutions. A multi-modal analysis gives planners the tools to help relieve congestion and inefficiency. With the opportunity to prioritize biking and walking, the LOS rating system provides a tool for a reduction in emissions and in traffic accidents with cyclists and pedestrians. Furthermore, the tradeoff of favoring safety and comfort of those biking and walking over increasing traffic capacity helps eliminate auto-dependency.

Factors in the multi-modal LOS rating include traffic protection, network connectivity, network quality, road crossing, topography, sense of security, cleanliness, wayfinding and marketing (Litman, 2011). Pedestrian safety, comfort, convenience and a sense of security are usually the top priorities for planners using this model. Cyclists are the next priority, followed by public transit, then carpool or ride share motor vehicles. Single-use motor vehicles are typically the last priority.

Since multi-modal planning prioritizes alternate modes of transportation, there will typically be a decrease in motor vehicle usage which has many direct and indirect benefits. There is a decrease in parking congestion, a decrease in pollution from emissions (a tool to help lower a city's carbon footprint) and a decrease in energy consumption. A decrease in traffic congestion and speed results in fewer crashes. Moreover, the indirect benefits from an increase in biking or walking results in healthier lives.

Multi-modal LOS dramatically differs from traditional LOS evaluation regarding vehicles. While the traditional seeks to increase roadway ratings, multi-modal LOS is more flexible and all-encompassing because it includes multiple transportation forms. For example, a decrease in the LOS intersection rating might be tolerable if there is a parallel increase in ratings for the bicycle or pedestrian LOS through bike lanes or wider sidewalks.[3]

Q: *What are some opportunities and constraints of multi-modal level of service?*

A: While multi-modal LOS has allowed for a more comprehensive approach to planning transportation systems, it remains limited as it still evaluates roadway users separately. For example, bicycle LOS and pedestrian LOS are treated as separate networks. This can sometimes be an obstacle to integrated streetscape planning, working in opposition to the idea that streets should become more livable. Roadway separation, therefore, is somewhat incompatible with the idea of shared streets, like that advanced by Dutch engineer and designer Hans Monderman. He advocates for streets that are "naked" and use driver uncertainty to increase driver and pedestrian safety. Typically, engineers in the US like to engineer driver certainty (think freeways, which are "certain" because they require no turn decisions). You can imagine this is not a small point of contention![4]

There are also examples of US cities gradually nudging this direction. In recent years, Chicago has taken great strides to build generous sidewalks for pedestrians, an extensive network for bikes and large multi-modal plazas, particularly along the lakefront. Along with Washington DC, they are experimenting with separation between bicycle and automotive traffic using soft low curbs that delineate bicycle lanes from drive lanes (Alpert, 2016; Spielman, 2021). These are common in Europe and are sometimes called "Copenhagen curbs" since they provide a way of setting aside bicycles and pedestrians from faster-moving drive lanes and providing protected travel along a street. They are usually small and rounded enough that vehicles can cross them but are designed to discourage this maneuver.

Q: *What are other ways planners measure walkability and bikeability?*

A: Walkability and bikeability describe the overall walking and biking conditions in an area. This means they reflect how conducive a place is for walking, not actual walking behavior (Riggs, 2015). There are many key variables to consider when analyzing a region or city's walkability or bikeability. For example, path and sidewalk quality, connectivity, universal design (such as handicap accessibility), land-use policies, cleanliness and how close buildings are to one another (Frank et al., 2009). A study by Ewing and Cervero (2010) indicates that street-grid connectivity may likely be the single strongest determinant of walking or cycling behavior among built environment variables. Most other studies identify residential density, street connectivity and land-use mix as most important.

Much of this method is based on two studies, one using land-use data from metro Atlanta as a part of SMARTRAQ (Strategies for Metropolitan

Atlanta's Regional Transportation and Air Quality) and the other from Seattle with the King County Land Use, Transportation, Air Quality, and Health Study (LUTAQH) (Frank et al., 2009, 2005). Both employ standardized "urban form" variables to establish an objective measure of walkability (Frank et al., 2004). These variables include: (1) net residential density (number of residential units per residential acre based on census block-group); (2) street connectivity (number of intersections per square kilometer); and (3) land-use mix (one kilometer, network-based street buffer). These measures are normalized, weighted and combined using Z-scores. These Z-scores simply provide a way of standardizing very different attributes to combine into a single indicator. Tools such as Walkscore.com build on these methods, using Google-indexed geo-locations to gather this data.

Other benchmarking tools have been developed but have not gained as much market traction. Some of these tools include the Irvine-Minnesota Inventory (IMI) and the Systematic Pedestrian and Cycling Environmental Scan (SPACES) which survey qualitative factors such as pleasurability, perceived safety from traffic, perceived safety from crime the Pedestrian Environmental Data Scan (PEDS) and the Workplace Walkability Audit Tool (WWAT) which evaluate elements of sidewalk, road and urban design improvements.[5]

Q: What is street suitability and how is it different from accessibility?

When planners mention accessibility, they are usually referencing the access of a location to goods, services and various types of land use. This is important because it is very different from the idea of suitability which usually equates with the quality of pleasurability and can be tied to the concept of livability. Factors influencing suitability include street width, number of lanes, safe speeds, bulb outs, crossing improvements and the presence of trees and are identified in many FHWA pedestrian level-of-service factors (Dowling et al., 2008). Suitability also includes perception issues with safety, such as fear of crime or heavy traffic, that some pedestrian audit tools attempt to uncover.

While these suitability factors are important for walking or cycling behavior, a large body of work suggests that they are subordinate to the idea of accessibility, the importance of destination and land-use and population characteristics (Ewing and Cervero, 2010). That said, counterpoints on suitability factors that improve the quality of the environment are abundant. Urban design literature emphasizes safety, quality of path and path context (Southworth, 2005) (Chin et al., 2008), and the notion that many routes may not be tied to rational decisions but to how much people like walking on certain streets.[6]

Figure 3.3: A diagram of a street with attributes designed to encourage users of all kinds

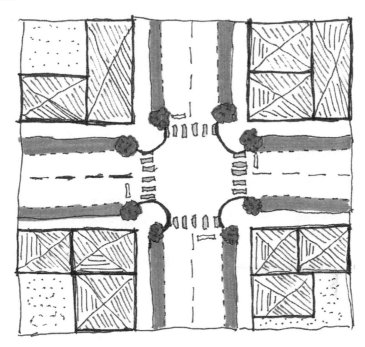

Figure 3.4: An aerial street view with features that support biking and walking, including bike lanes, sidewalks, bulb outs and crosswalks

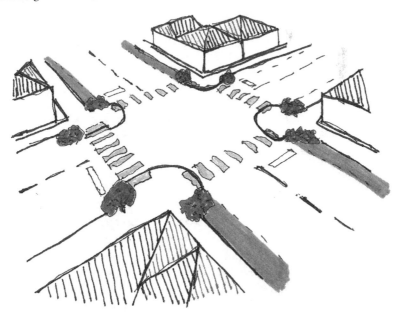

Q: What are common design treatments that facilitate biking and walking?

A: A simple factor that can facilitate walking and cycling is increasing the amount of roadway space for sidewalks and bicycle lanes. Dedicating roadway space to pedestrians and cyclists provides safety since it reduces sharing narrow spaces with motor vehicles, with the addition of buffered bike lanes promoting biking behaviors. Other treatments include adding bicycle signals and right-of-way markings at intersections that limit vehicle conflicts. Some unique treatments my students and I have looked at follow.

Bulb outs, pinch points and curb extensions

Bulb outs are used to maximize the amount of space between a vehicle and a pedestrian. It is essentially the widening of pedestrian pathways, making vehicles more aware of the pedestrian space. The expansion of the space calms traffic as vehicles must slow down for pedestrians. When occurring mid-block and not involving a crossing, curb extensions are referred to as "pinch points" since they constraint or "pinch" with width of the road and slow cars down.

In these locations, pedestrians are more visible to vehicles which not only promotes their activity but makes them feel safer. By taking away room that was originally reserved for the street thoroughfare, there is, consequently, more space for public gatherings and vegetation. This also leaves additional space that can be used for street lighting, urban street furniture or planters. These bulb outs help reduce blind spots for drivers. They make crosswalks more apparent to vehicles and encourage slower driving because of how the road becomes narrower and the crosswalk becomes a shorter distance to cross.

Sidewalk extension

With this technique, the sidewalk is extended into the parking lane or driving area. This leads to more pedestrian access and less automotive space but does not create an extension that is hazardous and not conducive to vehicles needing room for turning or safe navigation. It is used as a mitigation measure to slow traffic to create a more pedestrian-oriented area. Extensions increase flexibility in terms of how street space can be used. They offer an opportunity to create more sidewalk space for pedestrians but also opportunities for future bike lanes and bus stops, as well as alternative road layouts. Pedestrians have more visibility in locating vehicles because road space is less visually cluttered. Drivers in cars also have more visibility locating pedestrians. Furthermore, there is increased space for lighting and other amenities including benches, trees and landscaping, bike travel and parking and dining.

Figure 3.5: Concept diagram of sidewalk extension that uses physical barriers (indicated in dark gray) to separate pedestrian space from automotive space

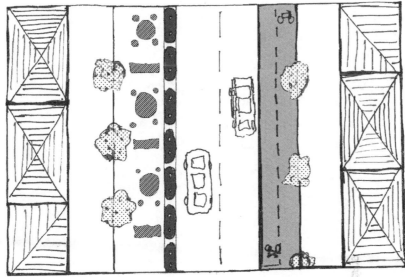

Note: The graphic also shows how a parking lane could be converted to a dedicated bikeway.

These extensions do not have to be permanent as the road can be narrowed and street space decreased by using hay bales or temporary sidewalk extensions with crates or other items. During the COVID-19 pandemic, many physical structures provided onsite dining that functioned in this capacity and formalized the extension of the sidewalk for other uses.

Chicane

A chicane is a permanent or temporary narrowing or curving of the road. It slows traffic speed and increases the amount of green or public space where the original road would have been. Places adjacent to the chicane location feel less threatened. In terms of its functionality, a chicane encourages public uses. Chicanes allow for excess space from the narrowing roadway to be used for bike parking, benches and other creative spaces. They visibly gesture a space designed for people and not cars. Chicanes can be permanent structures or created using more temporary objects—for example things like hay bales to temporarily guide the road a certain way.

Parklet

Parklets typically utilize parking spaces as a form of a sidewalk extension. As a roadway treatment, a parklet usually occupies the outer end of sidewalks

Figure 3.6 An example of a sidewalk extension in San Francisco

Source: San Francisco Planning Department https://www.flickr.com/photos/sfplanning/51017457052/

through the width of the parking space. Put simply, they provide more public or leisure space. People can enjoy this public space on their work breaks. Parklets provide a gathering or meeting space for people. Some would describe parklets as a small public park, though some do not serve park purposes, but rather are sitting or gathering spaces. They promote social interaction (enclosed space gives people comfort in communication within a parklet) and serve as a place of inspiration.

From a design perspective, parklets have minimal impact and are highly efficient from a people–capacity standpoint. Parklets usually take up minimal space (1–2 parking spots), equating to an average of 1–3 people occupying that space in 1–2 cars. Yet, once converted, the space can be used comfortably by 4–10 people (depending on the size). Pedestrians walking by can use it if tired or looking for a place to hang out. Bicyclists can park their bikes and take a break. Motorists parking close to the parklets can take a moment to sit down and enjoy the space due to its convenience.[7]

Woonerf

The idea of the woonerf is derived from street types in the Netherlands. The Dutch word, loosely defined as "living street," can be characterized as a street that supports and promotes human life. In his text *Livable Streets: Protected Neighborhoods* (1980), Appleyard identifies the two defining design features of woonerfs as:

Figure 3.7: A series of parklets with natural features and seating on Linden Lane in San Francisco promote gathering and socialization

Figure 3.8: A parklet in San Francisco with planters and a community gathering space

1. Sharing street space between vehicles and pedestrians and eliminating curb distinctions between the sidewalks and street pavement; and
2. Conveying the impression that the whole street space is usable by pedestrians with visible changes in direction and surfaces, plantings, and street furniture designed to be obstacles to vehicle travel and to create a residential atmosphere.

Woonerfs can be distinguished from other "complete street" design concepts in that they encourage the mixing of traffic (Appleyard et al., 1981). In essence, they encourage conflict between different kinds of travelers. While woonerfs and complete streets share a common purpose of multi-modal accommodation, the focus on complete streets is on modal separation—for example through protected bicycle lanes or separate public transit lanes.

Woonerfs, however, break down physical barriers between uses; they are intended to be user-friendly to all parties involved—automobile and bicycle operators, pedestrians, people who pursue the street as a destination and people who simply are using it as a channel to travel from point A to point B. But, as I mentioned before, they also invite conflict between modes.

Woonerfs are sometimes called *naked streets* which is a term stemming from the work of Dutch planner Hans Monderman. The streets don't have signage or directions and people traveling have to "broker" how they will interact with other people traveling around them. This kind of visual negotiation creates both a safe and slow environment. Ultimately, the idea is to dissolve the traditional barriers, physical or regulatory, that separates users. For example, woonerfs in Berlin, Malmo (Sweden) and Toronto accommodate many types of travelers without reserving space for anyone in particular.

This idea of this kind of naked space forms one of the biggest building blocks for this book, and one might assume that it is a practice limited to countries in Scandinavia or Europe.

True, some of the best examples remain in places like Amsterdam, Utrecht and Delft in the Netherlands, Freiberg in Germany and Exhibition Road in London. But there are many other examples around the world; one of the most successful US examples is in New York.[8]

The rebirth of the street as transport in New York

New York is a particularly good city to focus on because it has almost literally seen its street reborn. While the phrase "I love New York" is a bit of a cliché, like most American cities, New York has a lovely story to accompany its lovable diversity. The city was transformed by the automobile as a personal mode of transportation from streets that bustled with horses, trolleys and people on foot to efficient automobile routes. This shift led to many improvements in urban life but also resulted in increased pedestrian deaths, frequent vehicle collisions, unsustainable land use patterns and a decline in the social, civic, physical and economic activity on its streets.

Yet over the last 15 years there has been a revolution of the street in the city. New Yorkers have seen the development of successful strategies to support pedestrians, people on bikes, public transit and universal access in addition to automobile use. Through the creation of the *Street Design Manual*, which was originally published in 2009, New York developed a vision for its streets that reflected the principles of livable streets (New York City Department of Transportation, 2020). As a result, America's largest city is witnessing a street renaissance that has not been seen since the 1950s when Robert Moses and Jane Jacobs famously faced off over urban renewal and the construction of expressways through New York City neighborhoods. Transportation infrastructure and streetscape changes have been unveiled that encourage a wider variety of transportation choices and sustainable design to support public health and economic activity on the street. Examples of these street transformations can be seen at 9th Avenue, 14th Street and along Broadway.

14th Street

The 14th Street project is particularly interesting because the roadway runs underneath the West Side Elevated Highway. The West Side Highway was constructed between 1929 and 1951 and was one of the first urban freeways in the world. It closed in 1973 when part of it collapsed at 14th Street. It was demolished afterward but, since the closure, the city has grappled with how to support all forms of transportation in a very dense environment. Nonautomotive users faced difficulty navigating and brokering the space—for example, pedestrians were forced across a 120-foot-wide crosswalk.

The modification of the street transformed the space. It expanded pedestrian space and created a triangular plaza in the median on the north side. This new public space provided an area for people to gather and reduced the 120-foot crosswalk to two crossings of 24 and 34 feet. It also better defined the intersection for auto traffic. Furthermore, a protected bicycle lane was installed to serve cyclists. And, like many streetscape improvements around the world, this one began with temporary treatments or experiments. The project began with removable planters marking the edges of the plaza and inexpensive street furniture placed for public use. People occupied the space almost immediately and ultimately many of these changes became permanent.

Broadway

In addition to the 14th Street experiment, a design project on Broadway stands out. Broadway cuts diagonally from Union Square to the north end of Manhattan, passing Madison Square Park, Times Square and Central Park. This diagonal boulevard offers both challenges and opportunities as it crosses Manhattan's grid street system. This results in irregularly shaped and congested intersections. Over time, the corridor has had problems with traffic congestion and safe pedestrian movement with overcrowded sidewalks and chaotic street crossings. Yet, at the same time, this irregularity and heavy use also offers potential for unique public spaces.

Given this organic use, the city began experimenting with design changes along Broadway with temporary and inexpensive improvements, with a focus on reducing gridlock and improving pedestrian spaces. They put planters and tables on the former traffic lanes and preserved a wide bike lane as a start. This improvement to the pedestrian realm not only demonstrated better traffic flow and safety but it increased economic activity. Given this, the city decided to make these woonerf-like designs permanent. And the numbers seem to validate this approach. In 2015, New York had its lowest number of pedestrian fatalities since 1910.

Figure 3.9: Broadway Plaza in New York

Source: WikiCommons https://upload.wikimedia.org/wikipedia/commons/1/18/Broadway_ Plaza41_jeh.JPG

Simple solutions beyond New York

The design changes in places such as New York are things planners and engineers can do in neighborhoods anywhere, in big cities or small towns. For example, my students and I have found similar changes made in San Luis Obispo, California, a small town of roughly 50,000 people.

The city of San Luis Obispo installed bulb outs to calm traffic and made visual changes to the street to encourage vehicles to slow down when making turns through a crosswalk. My students and I found that these sidewalk and crosswalk treatments, done with yellow paint and red brick pavers, reinforced where pedestrians were allowed to be—improving the overall safety at crossings.

While the act of having a crosswalk is not novel, surfacing it or giving it visual delineation is. We will talk more about the psychology of this later, but anything a city can do to raise a driver's awareness of their surroundings can improve safety. Designing uncertainty into the driving experience as opposed to taking it out (what most engineers abhor) helps raise awareness and is good for cyclists and pedestrians. It is one of the things that makes woonerfs work, and it's also one of the reasons why people driver slower in places that they are not familiar with.

Some of my own research looks at how this happens when a street is converted from a one-way to a two-way street. What happens is that street gets safer. And why is this? People drive slower. Drivers don't experience a "freeway" effect and they experience uncertainty. They don't see multiple lanes going in one direction for them to go along with. They see oncoming traffic as well as travelers in the bikeways and on the sidewalks; and they have to cognitively respond to it. This is a flipped paradigm of designing streets to reinforce the cycling and walking experience as opposed to cars. Yet, it is important from a travel perspective because these newly designed streets can also have environmental benefit.

And, if the streets are well designed enough, it could be that the place a person is going stops mattering because there are so many destinations or places along the way. It's this transactional environment we will talk about next as we think about the street as an economic engine.

4

The Street as Economic Space

> Consider two human patterns. On the one hand, consider the
> fact that certain Greek village streets have a band of whitewash,
> four or five feet wide, outside every house, so that people can pull
> their chairs out into the street, into a realm which is half theirs,
> half street, and so contribute to the life around them.
>
> And on the other hand, consider the fact that cafes in Los
> Angeles are indoors, away from the sidewalk, in order to prevent
> food from being contaminated. Both these patterns have a
> purpose. One has the purpose of allowing people to contribute to
> the street life and to be part of it—to the extent they desire—by
> marking a domain which makes it possible. The other has the
> purpose of keeping people healthy, by making sure that they will
> not eat food that has dust particles on it. Yet one is alive; the
> other dead. (Alexander, 1979, p 119)

As quoted by Christopher Alexander, one street can be alive and one can
be dead. But what is it that makes a street thrive? Just like in the streets of
New York, San Luis Obispo or Anaheim, the thing that makes streets work
is that they are transactional. They are where exchange happens. And in
my mind this exchange comes in many forms: shopping, food and people
talking. They are all transactions and trade—things that are the core economic
elements of why cities ever formed. Hence, in this chapter, we focus on the
things that make the *street an economic space*.

We can likely all cite an example of what we think of as a "dead" street
versus one that is economically vibrant. Whether from an experience walking
down a road that is vacant and lonely, to the visions in post-apocalyptic
films such as *I Am Legend*, *Mad Max*, *The Day After Tomorrow*, *Wall-E* (you
get the picture), we intrinsically know what makes a street alive. (And I'll
note that there are a number of films with visions of great streets that are

not apocalyptic, favorites being Spike Lee's *Do the Right Thing* and Woody Allen's *Midnight in Paris*.)

For me, the vibrant streets in Louisville and Chicago provide great examples of how planners and policy makers can harness the power of the street. These are cities under-recognized compared to larger metropolitan areas such as New York City or San Francisco, yet rich in a history that is too often forgotten. For example, in the late 18th century, architect Daniel Burnham's Great White City in Chicago provided the pinnacle of walkable design along the Lake Michigan shorefront. Individuals attending the World Columbian Exhibition could walk along canals past buildings decorated with sculptures and take in the many innovations of the day, which included the original Ferris Wheel. Yet, when suburban expansion exploded, these shoreline walkable developments ceased.

As a child in the late 1970s and early 1980s, I remember sitting in highway traffic for hours while traveling to visit family on trips from Louisville to Chicago. I also recall hot summers in downtown Chicago on a barren waterfront where we were the only people on foot, looking at the beautiful urban skyline.

But from around 2015 onwards the shoreline experience has changed. Chicago has invested in being sustainable with downtown greens spaces, parks and residences. Urban Chicago is cool again, a fact that echoes throughout the Midwest. Investment in other cities such as Louisville, Indianapolis, Milwaukee and Minneapolis has created a string of pearls of Midwestern cities that are making changes to how they accommodate pedestrians and bikes in the public right-of-way. Louisville, for example, has focused on converting old train bridges to pedestrian and bike walkways and converted many multi-lane one-way streets to two-way, both of which have had profound economic regeneration implications.

Beyond the US, there are other cities ending roads and killing the traditional idea of the street. For example, London has always been a great city for walking and cycling even with the pressure to suburbanize after the World Wars, but since the late 2010s it has been doubling down on tying these forms of travel to economics. While the city has done traditional planning, it has also focused on the economics of traffic congestion, health, social inclusion, crime prevention and community enhancement in creating a more walkable and bikeable street. All three of these examples, Chicago, Louisville and London, are worth some discussion, and I will focus on them in this section as well as the lessons in the economic power of the street and how streets might be reshaped to capture this energy.

Chicago

I have many memories from my childhood in Chicago, particularly of being one of the few families walking the lakefront in the early 1980s, doing circles around Buckingham Fountain and exploring the places that were the foundation of the World's Fair or Great Columbian Exposition of 1893. Of course, this was almost 200 years after that event, but since learning about it I've always felt the legacy of people such as Daniel Burnham and Frederick Law Olmsted, who were instrumental in designing the Exposition and could be experienced walking in the "windy" city of Chicago. A lot of this nostalgia likely stems from stories my dad told.

My dad grew up in south Chicago in a house where they could only afford one set of water pipes, either warm or cold. They chose warm, which made for warm lemonade in the summertime and a sweaty toilet in the wintertime as water condensed on the warm porcelain. Chicago had many of the first-tier suburbs (like Berwyn, Oak Park and Riverside) which were designed to be walkable and bikeable in a different way than the central city—still positive and community building, yet different. My father told stories about walking and biking to the park with his four brothers and cousins causing trouble which almost always resulted in some form of destruction.

I was introduced to this environment through my great-grandmother's house where I have memories of walking to the park or the corner shop in Riverside, which was designed by Frederick Law Olmsted. We would eat dinner outside on warm summer evenings and then stroll down to the ice cream shop for a tasty treat. From there, it might be Shakespeare or some classical music in the park, or if the Cubs were playing, catching a baseball game back at home on the television. My great-grandmother, Edna Haley, was one of the oldest living fans when she died in 2000. I remember each year she would get a letter from Cubs management thanking her for her loyal patronage.

These memories of the Chicago suburbs illustrate the economic power of place. They were moderately dense with housing that was walkable and bikeable. You could walk to small downtowns and transact with many local businesses in a way that was not available in downtown Chicago at the time. Suburban expansion had left downtown empty of most residents, and retail establishments struggled. 1960s urban renewal efforts resulted in wide roadways and large super-blocks that concentrated affordable housing in infamous high-rise towers such as Cabrini-Green. Put succinctly, when I was a child downtown Chicago was hostile to walkers and cyclists. Yet Chicago has changed since the original complete streets plan in 2013. The city has built a new environment downtown—one with a walkable and bikeable urban core.

Chicago: economic regeneration through complete streets

Chicago first developed a complete streets policy in 2006 and renewed its commitment to designing streets for all users with the 2013 Complete Street

Chicago guide (City of Chicago, 2013). This 2013 document developed a pedestrian-first hierarchy for transportation projects and programs—followed by consideration for public transit, people on bicycles and, finally, automobile traffic. These efforts worked to improve the safety of streets for all users to meet the goals of 10 percent fewer automotive crashes and injuries each year, 50 percent fewer bicycle and pedestrian injuries by 2017 and an elimination of traffic fatalities by 2022.

While these goals are still an aspiration as of today, the document set a pathway for aggressively changing downtown roads to make them safer and economically prosperous. The guide established protocols for different types of streets and traffic and for identifying priority streets or intersections for complete street improvements. Using a data- and research-based approach, the document recognized the need for testing new ideas, the iteration of projects and the observation of impacts so that streets could meet user needs. The pedestrian-first model was expected to temporarily frustrate people who drive, but the city noted that there would be overall benefits to the public and to automobile users who drive safely and respectfully.

The design guide established the need on most streets for a pedestrian realm—or sidewalk—that includes space for frontage, a clear walkway, street infrastructure including trees, bike racks, streetlights, benches, signs, newspaper boxes and other features that brought activity to a sidewalk and buffer pedestrians from traffic. The interstitial area—or space between the pedestrian realm and the roadway—gave flexibility in design as the space along the curb could be adjusted to provide a bike lane, parkin or a right-turn lane. All of these were tied to increasing the possibility of economic activity on the street.

The Complete Street Chicago guide suggested flexible use of a median space that would provide landscaping, a pedestrian refuge, bus rapid transit (BRT), a protected bike lane or a left-turn lane. In general, the guide favored intersection design that was compact as opposed to complex, which included creating more intersections as opposed to having fewer, more complex junctions. Finally, the guide outlined opportunities to reduce excessive pavement at many intersections, which reduces vehicle speeds, enhances pedestrian safety and comfort and allows for the inclusion of green infrastructure. Shorter pedestrian crossings could be located where pedestrians naturally cross and where they were visible to drivers, and street crossing pavement treatments could reflect the size of the street and the level of traffic.

The Fullerton Avenue project is an example of a successful project that was implemented from the guide—yielding new spaces for travel, interaction and commerce. Railroad tracks were removed, sidewalks widened, street trees planted, lighting upgraded and narrower street crossings and bulb outs installed; bus stops were improved and the streets resurfaced. The economic thrust of the project was to spur economic development and improve connections between neighborhoods. These goals were met by doing things such as providing a better aesthetic environment for pedestrians, creating adequate space for people on bicycles, eliminating conflicts at bus stops, calming traffic and providing safer street crossings for the disabled.

Likewise, on Argyle Street, Chicago has experimented with the more transformative concept of shared streets. The three-block project in Chicago's Uptown neighborhood will allow pedestrians, people on bicycles and automobile traffic to share the space in an open, plaza-like corridor. By removing curbs, reducing the speed limit, integrating trees and planters into the street and using paving stones instead of asphalt, Argyle Street will allow all users to co-exist in a "living street" that can have plantings and seating but also allow for dining and shops in the roadway. The shared streets concept has demonstrated fewer accidents as users navigate the space more cautiously and through eye contact with others (Leber, 2014). The design changes also hope to attract more customers to nearby businesses and increase the vitality of the diverse immigrant community.

Given that former mayor of the city of Chicago, Rahm Emanuel, championed that "bicycling is an integral part of Chicago's transportation system," and made it a part of his economic revitalization plan for the Chicago lake front, there are also ample changes happening there (City of Chicago, 2012). For example, the Lakefront Trail is an 18-mile-long stretch of paved path where individuals can engage in active travel on Lake Michigan. The path connects many business establishments and neighborhoods throughout the city and is integrated with parks and gardens. It includes licensable and rentable recreation areas including beaches, playgrounds, soccer fields, volleyball nets and tennis courts. There are also many connecting amenities like washrooms, drinking fountains and concession stands that make this area a great place to visit, as well as to purchase a nice beverage.

This integration capitalizes on research that shows the astounding effects active transportation planning can have on economic growth in cities, from promoting healthier lifestyles to creating more economic capital in the city (Pivo and Fisher, 2011; Rauterkus and Miller, 2011). Street design can and does lead to an economic return on investment particularly for residential properties around interventions. For example, there are a number of studies which indicate that street patterns, improvements to city amenities and location to a transit station have positive effects on the value of residential properties nearby (Bartholomew and Ewing, 2011). These street-design efforts and patterns play a role in improving pedestrian activity which equates to more local business traffic. Neighborhoods that contain pedestrian-oriented features and have a more grid-like street system tend to have higher housing prices.

Likewise, homes with a pedestrian connection to commercial uses, mixed uses and bus stops within a quarter of a mile do have higher sale value. Sacramento homes with more well-designed streets had 4–15 percent higher sales than others. Homes in walkable neighborhoods command a sales premium of up to $34,000 more than homes is less walkable neighborhoods (Rauterkus and Miller, 2011). The same concept can be illustrated in Portland, Oregon and San Diego, California, where there is a premium for houses in areas that contain interconnected streets and smaller blocks (Bartholomew and Ewing, 2011). In one case in West Palm Beach, traffic circles, neckdowns and speed bumps were installed and property values jumped from $65,000 to $106,000 over a period of three years (Bartholomew and Ewing, 2011).

These traffic-calming measures that create a more pedestrian-friendly environment have an impact on urban economics—particularly on property values. Most research shows that efforts that make an area less desirable to vehicles and reduce car volume increases the value of local land. For example, in Portland, Oregon, researchers have found that street trees that were within 100 feet of the front of the residential property increased the value of the home by as much as $8,700 (Pivo and Fisher, 2011). Clearly, when cities invest in a new vision for streets, it can lead to real economic value for citizens.

Louisville: harnessing the economic power of the street

This notion of how economic value can be gained from calm and green streets is also represented in some of my own work. My research in Louisville has looked at converting old multi-lane, one-way streets to two-way corridors—trying to fuse urban design and complete-street philosophies. My work suggests that design and type of the street have a direct relation with traffic safety and neighborhood quality-of-life indicators including crime, housing values and economic growth and jobs (Riggs and Gilderbloom, 2015). The focus on the street itself as an approach to urban livability, as opposed to the surrounding accouterments, has been novel and is consistent with the main idea of this book—ending the preconceived notion of what a road is and seeing what a street can be.

My colleague John Gilderbloom and I spent about five years rethinking streets using Louisville as an example. We looked at the city as a case study of how it has used streets for economic regeneration. We tested street conversions where multi-lane, one-way streets were being converted to two-way. These conversions were happening throughout the US and internationally in places as diverse as Cincinnati, Ohio and Havana, Cuba, yet there was limited research on their quantifiable impacts—hence our work in Louisville.

Why Louisville? In addition to being my hometown, the city has built some of the same street transformations as places such as Chicago and other creative and hard-working Midwestern towns.[1] The city has been able to capitalize on the economic potential of the walkable and bikeable environment and makes a good case. Louisville is one of 148 American cities with a population over 50,000 not located within 20 miles of another mid-size city. The city went through a revolution between 1950 and 1960 when two-way streets were converted to one-way thoroughfares to spur suburban growth. Many inner-city neighborhoods suffered from neglect because of this development trend (Duany et al., 2001).

Despite that, however, the city has always been romantically walkable and bikeable with five Olmsted-designed parks coupled with traditional steel-framed, brick-faced buildings, and riverboat captain mansions all over its downtown. The city has more historic brick buildings than almost any place except New York, and you could almost pretend that you are a character in *The Great Gatsby* strolling down the main street to the Ohio River rather than where the book is set in New York (although the character Daisy was from Louisville). The river waterfront connects to a train bridge that has been converted to a pedestrian bridge. The Big Four train bridge spans the river between Kentucky and Indiana.

Walking the bridge, you can almost feel the strength of the iron that used to carry the locomotives across the waterway. The bridge is not too far from the first portage point where George Rogers Clark (of Lewis and Clark fame) came ashore as the two continued down the Mississippi River on their exploration west. The duo's famed great walk would ironically end up in the San Francisco Bay Area which we will visit in Chapter 5.

In thinking about Louisville's streets, Gilderbloom and I channeled Jane Jacobs who once wrote,

> The best place to look at first is the street … The street works harder than any other part of downtown. It is the nervous system; it communicates the flavor, the feel, the sights. It is the major point of transaction and communication. Users of downtown know very well that downtown needs not fewer streets, but more, especially for pedestrians. (Jacobs, 1958, p 127)

In 2014, we sought to test the impact and merit of one-way, multi-lane streets and to evaluate the benefits of converting one-way streets to two-way streets, something that was suggested as an economic regenerator by organizations such as the Urban Land Institute (Beyard et al., 2003; Dunphy et al., 2003). While studies have shown two-way streets may have safety benefits, and possibly help in placemaking, we saw a natural experiment happening in Louisville where some streets were being converted and other segments were unchanged, and what we found was astounding.

Property on one-way streets was half the value of property on two-ways—$64,681 compared to $152,629 in 2014 dollars. Total crime was almost double. Business traffic declined on one-way streets and increased on slower, two-way corridors. While this might sound a bit too good to be true, it is consistent with other work that suggests neighborhood accessibility, walking and biking, are good for a city's economy (Ewing and Cervero, 2010; Pivo, 2013; Gilderbloom et al., 2015). But we were also able to show even more— we showed that lives were saved. Neighborhoods with one-way streets had twice as many injuries from car accidents. Car collisions were two-thirds higher on one-way streets—126 more on average each year.

This data was sobering to us, but since we completed that work others have been finding similar things about how poorly designed streets pose an economic burden to many in our society. In Louisville, the worst streets were in minority neighborhoods where the poverty rate was three times higher than the rest of the city. The median income was less than half in neighborhoods with one-way streets than in neighborhoods with more efficient two-way streets ($27,311 versus $65,183). There is ample literature on cyclical poverty among minorities and the disparate impacts of urban blight on economic mobility (Corburn, 2005; Williams and Jackson, 2005; Brulle and Pellow, 2006; Mohai and Saha, 2006; Cutts et al., 2009; Hipp and Lakon, 2010). But this was happening in our own backyard—by changing streets we could potentially start to change economic outcomes for those who need it most.

Put simply, street design, or what I sometimes call typology, can impact housing prices, foreclosures, property improvements, collisions and crime along with economic mobility (Riggs and Gilderbloom, 2015). And while you may be skeptical about this, some of the street scenes we observed around Louisville told the story even better. They showed dilapidated and unmaintained housing on one-way streets and beautiful, well-cared-for homes on the slower two-way streets. They showed people walking and cycling and engaging with local business on two-way streets but not on their one-way counterparts.

What we found was that streets can kill, or they can heal, and design can make for a healing and economically productive street. Yet better design that leads to prosperity is not something that is only happening in Louisville. It is a global phenomenon. Literature shows that establishing a more walkable neighborhood can also give opportunities for people to save money they would usually spend on their car and invest it back into their house, thus raising their home's value even further (Konecny, 2011). Walkable and livable areas are valued by residents for their diversity and sense of community

(Brodsky, 1970; Pivo and Fisher, 2011), and studies have shown that over 80 percent of homebuyers are willing to pay more to live in a sustainable area with proximity to "neighborhood amenities." These transportation-efficient amenities can include schools, workplaces, hospitals or shops—all of which can drive job growth and market expansion (Tan, 2011).

And given this economic impact, you might ask why housing prices do not just keep going up for these locations, and what that means to the people who live there? Well, in short, economic growth does continue, but this growth can have some negative impacts. My work for the past 10 years clearly indicates that this value creation from complete streets can have a dark side if not mitigated. It can cause gentrification in places that have historically been affordable and lead to people being pushed out (what academics call displacement) or choosing to live elsewhere (self-displacement) (Riggs, 2016, 2011). While we will discuss this trend later, the idea of affordability is important to introduce here since it lends itself to think about how investments in streets impact housing choices.

Since the early 2000s, academics and policy makers have strongly argued that people who live in walkable, bikeable and transit-rich areas spend less money on travel and, therefore, have more to spend on housing. Planners and policy makers call this concept location efficiency, and it is one of the additional economic gains that more well-designed streets produce. As we have already discussed, housing prices reflected the transportation efficiency of the neighborhood. So, conceivably, if cities invest in location efficiency, they will see a return on this investment through increased prices. Yet as we have discussed, this puts pressure on affordability and as prices rise people can be displaced. What can cities do to maintain affordability in this situation?

One idea is to give people financial or monetary credit toward their housing for living in an area where they save money on transportation. This has been most commonly done through home mortgages, or what we call Location Efficient or Transportation Credit Mortgages. To do this, some cities have tried (in small pilots) to allow borrowers to get more money to buy homes in locations with higher population density and better transportation access. This can help with housing affordability by giving financial credits to people in low-to-median income levels (Riggs, 2017a). Likewise, other philanthropic and private sector entities are developing large investments funds to take down the cost of development and provide lower-cost housing for working families. In theory, these kinds of policies can help achieve broader societal benefits (say reducing driving emissions) while taking out a dent in the average American's budget for transport, ranging from 14 to 21 percent (Chatman, 2007).

This kind of financial experimentation may sound simple, but it has been rare in the US. Some of my recent work shows that there has been very little innovation in the way cities finance infrastructure and development

(Riggs and McDade, 2016). While I will talk more about these concepts later, an exciting example of experimentation in the economic and cultural rejuvenation of the street is coming from London.

London: moving to experimentation

If you're tired of London, you're tired of life. I remember this paraphrase of a 1777 Samuel Johnson statement from a college class. While I scoffed at this idea at first, years later, having worked there and completed research in the city, I could not agree more—London has become a truly livable city. While the city developed much of its walkable infrastructure during the industrial era, large portions of the city were destroyed and had to be rebuilt after WWII. The result of the reconstruction was not always supportive of the walkable environment. In the 21st century, however, London is truly a city of experimentation where they are working to reinvent walking and biking using many creative ideas. Walking there in 2022 is a different experience than it was even a few years before. Many of the old surfaces of cobblestone have been paired with new reflective safety delineators creating an extraordinarily pleasurable and safe experience. These are interspersed with hidden gardens where one can find children playing and laughing and adults holding parties.

And while organically built structures and uneven cobblestones and bricks can give an appearance of being unplanned, there is more of an intentionality that makes up the streets of London today. There is policy focused on solving the economics of transport—and doing so in a very multi-modal way. This investment can be seen in a simple jaunt through Hyde Park to the South Kensington area, or through the exemplary behavior of former Mayor Ken Livingstone who was an avid walker and transit rider. But most importantly they can be seen through focused financial strategy for investment in these areas that started with congestion pricing.

Congestion pricing and related investment

The London congestion charge policy came about as a way to encourage sustainable work-related travel in the central city, and it is something that has shaped the travel experience in the city. This policy-placed zone is an invisible barrier or zone around central London and (due to the success of the program) has been expanded beyond just the central city. If individuals pass through the barrier of the zone, they pay a fee. The fees are then used to fund bus, bike and pedestrian improvements throughout the city. Despite speculation that the policy would force jobs out of the central city during the early implementation, it has been a success for the economics of walking and biking in London—a windfall of more than £150 million per year (Broaddus, 2014).

Improvements for pedestrians include things such as increasing the number and widths of pedestrian crossings, installing ramps at crossing points, implementation of 20 mph zones, providing better routes and easier access to transit stations and commercial centers. From a cycling standpoint, the city has improved routes and safety—designing pathways for better interactions between bikes and cars. This has led to changes in travel. Transport for London, the agency that leads the policy, has documented an increase in walking and cycling by 50–60 percent that parallels the congestion zone and subsequent infrastructure investments (Transport for London, 2004). The street has changed and resulted in better places for everyone—with less traffic, more trees and more places to sit and eat (Greater London Authority, 2015).

One of the best examples of this change is Exhibition Road near Imperial College London. Studied in great depth by my colleague Borja Ruiz, the road embodies the notion that we need to kill the preconceived idea of what a street is and can be. The design of Exhibition Road is subtle: a street with one level, no curb, only delineated for travelers by variations in pavement, drains for runoff, signs and places to sit or gather. It fuses Monderman's naked street with modern engineering, putting pedestrians literally on level ground with cars for an incredible walking experience. There are no rules for you as a pedestrian or as a cyclist. The only indication that you walk left on the sidewalk is a small coloration difference on the ground. You can just go wherever you want.

Borja calls these kind of streets "lively" which probably characterizes them best (Ruiz-Apilanez et al., 2015). They are always active. Since there is no overt delineation between pedestrians and cyclists versus car space, pedestrians and cyclists can be observed going back and forth from one side of the street to another. This situation creates an environment of complexity but also caution. Drivers must be aware of crossings at any time or location, and this awareness results in a slower and safer environment. The design of the street builds a platform of mutual respect between bikes, pedestrians and automobiles on the street.

Figure 4.1: Multiple street surfacings on Exhibition Road in London

Figure 4.2: Streets for dining as economic activity on Exhibition Road in London

Figure 4.3: A pop-up flower shop occupies the road on Valencia Street in San Francisco

Source: San Francisco Planning Department https://www.flickr.com/photos/sfplanning/51016630913/

The streetscape is also ripe with regenerative economic activity. The design allows for the street to become a plaza for commercial activity. While walking it, you can stumble upon shops and restaurants extending beyond where the sidewalk would normally end—with no indication of where the street starts and someone's shop stops. This blend of economic and social wellness is worth noting. It is very plain to see how the streets are making London more vibrant when you look at the multicolored tables filled with people, and I think we've only seen this expand during the pandemic as streets have facilitated pop-up shops in outdoor areas that have kept our local economies strong.

Streets have also become social. And this social aspect of the street is what we will focus on next.

5

The Street as Social Space

The road belonged to us then; we sang in it, we argued in it, while
the horse-bus flowed softly by ... (Le Corbusier in Berman, 1983)

Singing, arguing, belonging; even Corbusier, who is sometimes derided for
his views on transportation, believed the street was home for many things
other than movement. Just as we saw with the case of Exhibition Road
in London, the idea of interaction between people on the street is very
important. Roadways of all kinds provide conduits that make cities work.
They provide activities, socialization, encounters and confrontations. And
I believe these are the kind of words (and ideas) that kill the traditional
definition of what a street can be. These words bring about images of people
singing, playing and connecting with one another, or even occupying streets
for protest.

For example, in 2010 and 2011 pedestrians occupied the streets in Cairo,
Egypt, shaping what would become the Arab Spring. I remember turning
on the news and being blown away by the massive crowds across Tahrir
Square. I thought "there is the power of the street." Likewise in the US, many
people fled to the street during the 2011 Occupy Wall Street movement and
for the commemoration of one of the most important events to happen on
the street—the 1965 "Bloody Sunday" march against segregation in Selma,
Alabama, where police brutalized protestors on the street during the Civil
Rights Movement. These activities have importance because they frame the
social action that is essential to democracy and a free society.

I like to think about the words of former US President Barack Obama
when considering this. In his 2015 speech commemorating the events in
Selma, he spoke about people who met near a bridge to take their message
to the street and changed the future of American society. He proclaimed,

"The Americans who crossed this bridge were not physically imposing.
But they gave courage to millions. They held no elected office. But they

led a nation. They marched as Americans who had endured hundreds of years of brutal violence, and countless daily indignities – but they didn't seek special treatment, just the equal treatment promised to them almost a century before …. they proved that nonviolent change is possible; that love and hope can conquer hate." (Obama, 2015)

It is fascinating to think about how streets have this kind of power. But planners, policy makers and engineers rarely consider this when designing their streets. They rarely consider how roadways can be places of gathering and how public assembly can change the world. It is clear that how we have designed cities works against us in this matter. Cities have expanded and separated people further from their centers and society has become more disengaged. What can be done to recreate the social ties that make up community? How can the street encourage dialogue and communication in a fractured society?

I often think about the family that moves from the inside of their homes to be in big cars without ever exposing themselves to the world around them. This is the relationship that Robert Putnam talks about in his classic text *Bowling Alone* in which he correlates the dawn of suburbia and urban sprawl with the decline in civic engagement and community cohesion (Putnam, 2001). Streets can be tied to the decline or acceleration of social cohesion, even down to their physical form.

Think about two different types of streets: one with multiple fast-moving lanes of traffic and the other with one or two narrow lanes, generous sidewalks, trees and slow-moving vehicles. Can you guess which is more inviting for automotive users and more inviting for people who want to walk or bike?

The answer likely seems simple: we instinctively want to walk or bike on the slower street. But there is a hidden trick here. Your perspective may be different when you are behind the wheel of a car or when you are walking down a busy street. A lot of someone's perspective on safety and comfort is framed by individual biases and what you are thinking about at a given time (this is called availability heuristic which we will talk about later in this book). Take, for example, the fact that you are reading a book about ending the idea of the street for autos. This predisposes you to think in a more hostile way towards vehicles. You are already primed to think of yourself as a walker or cyclist. At the same time, you might think much differently while driving or riding in a car.

This dynamic was clearly depicted in a recent study showing people videos of different street types (Riggs, 2017b). I divided roughly 500 individuals into two groups: people who would think of experiencing the street as if they were driving a car, and people who would experience it as if they were cyclists. I then asked the members of each group to respond with to how comfortable they would be on different kinds of streets. Consistent with what you might expect, those who were thinking about driving a car perceived wide streets as being more comfortable. Those who saw the street from the cyclist's perspective wanted narrower streets. They felt that wider lanes and streets with multiple lanes were less safe for themselves and for their children.

So, what does this have to do with the social aspects of streets? Everything. Many of the social factors that have been identified with great streets— including economic transaction, conversation and casual strolling—only happen in a comfortable environment. Great streets embrace an environment of confrontation. They facilitate encounters with wide sidewalks trees, bike lanes and benches—things that bring people to the street.

This environment of encounter, as opposed to one of confrontation, is important to consider as many streets have grown wider, yet plazas and civic spaces have grown smaller. These places for exchange and encounter get us out of our homes and help us interact and relate with one another. Take for example the design typologies below which are based loosely on a diagram by Don Appleyard from the 1970s. In the example of the shared street and pocket park streets, the form of the street provides a place for gathering. It can be an extension of adjacent housing, challenging people to come out into the public realm and engage with one another.

The road diet can also encourage encounter by constraining automotive space with wider sidewalks, bulb-outs, bike lanes, pinch-points, chicanes or other interventions. Parking can also be configured in a manner that calms rather than induces traffic. The idea of a shared street takes advantage of a portfolio of interventions—dedicating the urban right-of-way for humans rather than vehicles. This can also be achieved through creative means such as mid-block parks and play spaces that prevent cut-through traffic, or the creation of informal streets modeled on Dutch (woonerf) design—places where interaction and play can truly end the idea that the street is simply a road.

The first time I was exposed to streets that challenge what is vehicular space and what is human space was when I was a student at the University of Oxford, in the months following the Achilles injury I referred to in Chapter 1 of this book. While at Oxford, I was struck not only by the narrow, cobbled streets but how pedestrians challenged the roadway space. Since I was still recovering from my injury and had just begun to jog again, I felt this "full access" to the street was provocative. I could choose to cross the road within the traffic lane in most cases with little risk to my safety. I could also travel the many informal footpaths that combined trails with sidewalks and roads—a network that I found fascinating and unlike anything I had ever experienced in the US.

One of the strongest (and perhaps regular) memories was how pub life was often not constrained to the pub. I remember many days when my

Figure 5.1: A continuum of livable street designs

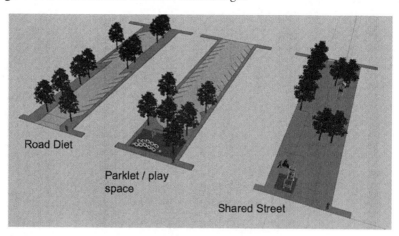

Road Diet

Parklet / play space

Shared Street

friends would sit on the curb in front of the Bodleian library having a pint, a Shandy or a Pimms and lemonade. At the time, I thought these were just the joy-filled exploits of a group of college students, but in retrospect this experience crystallized an appreciation for the same type of street that Appleyard was pushing for—a street that moves beyond the status quo and is a place where friends could drink and converse, children could play, politicians could proselytize and organizers could protest.

My interest in this power of the street to transform public expression has grown in recent years as I have seen it empower social movements which draw formal power from informal structure. Again, these include events such as the Arab Spring, Occupy Wall Street and Black Lives Matter. They reflect an informal spirit in streets that is different from the more formally designed roads of London or Chicago but more akin to the street in places such Delhi—where the street is both social and beautifully chaotic.

Delhi, India

Delhi, India, provides an amazing example of how the street can be social. Streets in Delhi are informal, yet this informality is a thing of beauty. These kinds of places and experiences might have been considered exotic and not normative for a long time, but I believe they now provide lessons that many engineers and planners in the West can emulate—trying to pedestrianize and reinstall casual encounters in the core of some of our large cities.

Indian cities have been experiencing dramatic growth in recent years, most notably Delhi and Mumbai in their Western-like exurbs and suburban areas leading to dramatic changes in transportation needs. While this might be an opportunity to evaluate transportation sustainability, most of this development relies on autos (Shirgaokar, 2012). At the same time, these cities have a rich tradition of streets dominated by bustling traffic, pedestrian activity, commerce and even cows.

According to my father-in-law, Dr. Surendra Sethi (dad), this informality can be characterized by the concept of *gulis* (English spelling of the Urdu word meaning crowded alleys), of which India has a rich tradition in its large cities. An immigrant from Punjab, Dr. Sethi fondly describes the streets in his home country built without the need for cars. These include places near his family home in Patel Nagar, which was an original residential area that used the British town-site framework (Hall, 1996). As shown in the figures below, they were informal things of beauty so often appreciated in Western cities, such as the narrow streets in the North End of Boston or the streets of pre-Haussmann Paris.[1]

Dr. Sethi talks about the historic open marketplaces such as Chandni Chowk, Karol Bagh and Connaught Place in his hometown and how he now sees many cities around the world developing urban streets very similar to these Indian settings. While some of this is just "the Indian way," he notes that much of this happened after the 1947 partition of India and Pakistan. The population swelled by over a million people almost overnight, with the migration creating dense villages where there had been an imposed colonial order to the streets. It established a "new" paradigm of streets that

Figure 5.2: Chandni Chowk streetscape

had existed for centuries in India but was not consistent with Western design (Bhan, 2009).

Yet there have been recent moves by the international development community to correct the nonlinear streets in many Indian neighborhoods with more formal grid and suburban layouts. This aligns with a more traditional approach to transportation engineering that focuses away from the social aspects of streets. I sometimes like to call this the "engineering effect." In that sense, I mean that we engineer uncertainty, spontaneity and fun out of our streets and transportation experiences. This creates less safe and more boring environments for people. If you walk or bike on a street that is not designed for interaction, you do not get the same social experience from the world around you.

But how can we integrate experience of that place? How can we design streets that latch on to the concept of the flâneur that was discussed earlier in this book? In most places, this kind of imaginative social space is not possible. We rely heavily on engineering when designing our streets and cities, and this is only increasing as technology firms experiment with an optimization-and-efficiency-oriented city. As planners and engineers try to classify the factors that make streets awesome—mainly so they have rules for implementation—the social aspects of streets become deprioritized. These social and humanistic aspects of streets are hard to quantify. They fail our attempts to measure, thus making us unable to benchmark their benefit. And while some may insist that we measure their benefit, for many of the same reasons that technology firms want to optimize the city and make it more efficient, quantification of the social aspects of the street may limit the experience of it. Planners and policy makers may become limited by focusing on such rigid rules.

A parallel example of this can be found in the limitations of the hierarchical logic systems of local zoning. As Sonia Hirt suggests in her book *Zoned in the USA*, most US cities insist on rigid zoning (Hirt, 2015), and that may cause difficulty when adapting to new uses in housing or workplaces that do not fit this model. Flexible land uses may not fit. Planners and engineers may have trouble balancing and weighting the multiple land use as well as the social and physical aspects of cities.

Let's look at Delhi again. While a rules-based approach can be good for implementation, in the global south it presents difficulty, particularly when much of the urban core of these cities is, in fact, highly urban and walkable, yet in an informal and hard to quantify way. From a quantifiable standpoint using Western benchmarks of walkability and bikeability, one might suggest that Indian cities need more sidewalks to support pedestrians and cyclists (CAI-Asia, 2011; Bergen, 2013). Yet in most of these places shared streets have been the norm for years. They have highly interactive non-automotive forms of travel. So, should the physical attributes of streets in India change to be more like the US? I would suggest not.

Given that the streets of Delhi already support the lingering and social interaction attributed to "great streets," perhaps they should be discussed as a good example. Some physical design attributes from the West—such as formal sidewalks and benches—might be effective at calming traffic, but this can also be accomplished by more organic means. Traffic calming can happen by having shops spilling into the streets or rugs placed in the roads for seating. While these designs elements are informal and organic, they are effective at generating pedestrian traffic and creating lingering and social interaction. So, in my view, they should be embraced. The attributes that create this social interaction are cross cultural and worth consideration in other locations. To detail them, they include things such as:

- activation of streetscape for commerce
- creation of visible interest
- uncontrolled signage and organic beatification
- mixed or unregulated flow
- slow speeds or heavy traffic
- informal passages.

These ideas should not surprise anyone because they are not dissimilar to items found in traditional urban design literature. They may just have less quantitative "oomph" behind them in engineering circles. They are hard to quantify in terms of benefits, yet if the scenes from near my father-in-law's old home in Delhi are any indication, they have value and are worth exploring. The streets of India may not match our traditional traffic modeling or engineering frameworks (Western norms), but they may better match social fabric (Lo, 2009a, 2009b, 2011) and the diverse ways in which all of us are slightly odd and nontraditional (Nussbaum, 1986; Sen, 1999).

While embracing informal streets may sound reckless, it has an academic merit and should be seen as refreshing and energizing. Citizens, policy makers and planners do not have to reinvent the wheel to evolve thinking about what a street is and can be. We might establish a new way of conceptualizing streets that emphasizes the social and informal at the same time as the physical and use that to inform our planning and design. This way of contemplating streets might take two perspectives: (1) an engineering and modeling perspective and (2) a more socially conscious implementation and personal narrative perspective.

From an engineering perspective, we might think of new ways to model or quantify social factors and prioritize them. We might highlight the physical design and social aspects of streets just as much or more than land-use factors. From an implementation and narrative perspective that paralleled this model, we might explore informal ways to implement more lively streets. In saying this, I mean we might find creative ways to make

Figure 5.3: Streets with shopping, Delhi, India

safer and more social streets that supersede the built environment and create social encounters and lingering experiences. And we can do this in much the same way as the safe and social streets that came to life during the COVID-19 pandemic.

An example of this approach toward the social street comes from my experience as a parent. When I became a professor and my wife, two children and I first moved to San Luis Obispo, we lived in condominium complex that was very dense but had wide streets with blind turns. Like many kids, my children loved to ride bikes, scooters, play with balls—you name it; they were in the street. The potential for an accident frightened me, so I would do the best I could with the resources at hand. Each day when I got home and before the kids went out to play I would throw our bright red and blue coolers into the center of the street. These became not only obstacles to slow traffic but social magnets. At first, people just came and talked to me about what I was doing. Then the kids started to congregate around them. Before long, neighboring parents would come out to share a beer and watch our kids play. It was the perfect example of how something based on the informal overcame, and counterbalanced, engineering.

But this was not something new to me. I knew what I was doing having already spent some time experimenting with these kinds of tactical solutions. I am almost always the planner and engineer who wants "do something" rather than just talk about it, and this was just another example. On many

Figure 5.4: A slow street in San Francisco during the COVID-19 pandemic

Source: San Francisco Planning Department https://www.flickr.com/photos/sfplanning/50568735692/

occasions during my professional career I was the one advocating for doing pilots and testing. I was always the one to advocate for throwing a hay bale into a street to see how traffic reacts to it, shutting down parking or closing a street to traffic for a period of time.

This spirit of experimentation was energized by many of the stories I heard about streets and neighborhoods during the late 2000s, and these are worth exploring next since they underscore the social fabric of how streets support strong and sustainable neighborhoods. As many of these were defined by my research in San Francisco, I will start with some examples from there before discussing other locations.

San Francisco: defining walkable places and culture

San Francisco has been a city that has experimented for a long time with what makes a place important for walking and cycling. When I first moved to the city, I thought that these factors would be simple to define, measurable, fixed and visible to the naked eye. I thought you would be able to measure the street, count the trees and number the safe crossings, and voila! Clearly, while I am exaggerating slightly, I did have a textbook knowledge of how the built environment could be assessed. Yet despite significant efforts to define the most important variables for walking (Ewing and Cervero, 2010), many items were hard to qualify and measure.

For example, aesthetics are difficult to measure. What is beautiful to some is not to others; one person's idea of a nice shady tree is very different that another person's idea of a nice shady tree. Yet there is an impact of beauty on the experience of walking that is very different. While there are studies that indicate trees and beatification amenities may attract more people, reduce heat island effect and have environmental benefit, there is only limited (and some contrary) information about their value to walking behavior. But that is not cause for dismissing the idea that aesthetics can frame a more welcoming and social environment for walking and cycling.

Metrics exist which factor in type, quality and presence of sidewalks, but there are few tools to measure the social quality of these attributes and why people choose to use them. People make choices to walk or bike based on complex, and sometimes a bit irrational, worldviews, and the social construct matters. As one planner I talked to in the San Francisco Bay Area put it:

> "It's complex. It's not just physical, it's also social. What is the existing walking, pedestrian infrastructure to the degree that a person can easily make the decision to walk? It has to be easy, and sidewalks have to exist. Then there's the social aspect. This woman who I interviewed in southeast San Diego who lives in a Latino neighborhood ... said the neighborhood is controlled by Latino gangs. She literally said, 'If I have to go to the grocery store, which is only two blocks away, I'll drive my car.' So that's a walkability issue that doesn't have anything to do with the infrastructure. The social conditions are such that she fears for her safety, so she's not going to walk two blocks." (Interview)

And crime and safety are only a small portion of socio-cultural factors that affect walking and biking choices. Some would argue that the US has a social resistance to traveling on foot or bike. For example, in Europe there are strong cultural or historical roots tied to walking and cycling. In another interview, a planner described this historic context by offering examples of two different cities in which he had recently spent time.

> "For instance, in Torino (Italy) one of the historical architectural traits are porticos, or beautiful covered sidewalks. They were designed because the king wanted to be able to walk from one part of the castle and go strolling without getting wet. So, he had this giant covered sidewalk built and that became the general style of any nice building on the boulevard. And so, there are eleven miles of walkable (covered) sidewalks in the historical part of town. They are about twenty feet wide and pretty, with shopping storefronts, and restaurants. And it

forms a city that is based on walking; with flea markets and cafés in these porticos. So, even though the whole rest of the city might not be like that you can still have this cultural history tied to walking.

And then switching completely to Spain where there is a cultural practice to go out for a walk in the evening—and to go out to dinner or else just to go to the square and walk around. Madrid is one of the most crowded cities for pedestrians I've ever seen, outside of maybe a busy Saturday night in Greenwich Village. It's just that everybody is out walking. So, that's just one basic thing—you have people … (Another thing) is how Spanish people want to be together whereas American people want to have their privacy.

So, you have an essential question of do people even want to be walking near other people … is there a cultural reference for that? That's something I don't usually think about. I'm usually focused on the physical safety and the sidewalk character. But that's the weird thing—in Europe it just seems like people do their best to get along and not worry about conflict or safety. And we have an American viewpoint that there is absolutely going to be conflict, assuming bike, pedestrian and auto conflict." (Interview)

While this observation may not be earthshattering, it does underscore the core reliance on engineering and optimization. In the US, we engineer-out uncertainty for drivers to make streets safer, but by doing this we lower driver awareness and may make roads less safe for bikes and pedestrians. The idea of the freeway or highway illustrates this idea. In concept, we have engineered out the uncertainty of stops and turns on these roads, and therefore minimized the number of decision points and related driver mistakes.

This, however, creates for a less-aware operator and potential points of conflict. Take, for example, highway on-ramps. They are key places where drivers are mentally shifting into autopilot. Drivers are assuming they are entering a certain environment. Yet, if you were to integrate bicycles and pedestrians into more-certain environments such as on-ramps, it would be quite dangerous. They would have trouble trying to find a break to merge into traffic as drivers become less aware of their surroundings based on the simpler rules and decisions around them.

While these locations (highway on-ramps) are engineering challenges in themselves, the issues represent the idea that streets can be designed to be both physically safer and to create environments for social and uncertain encounters—even if it is just waving at the neighbor who is driving by. One example of this kind of design in San Francisco is Lombard Street. Similar to the Dutch living street or "woonerf" concept, the street evokes imagery of fanciful thoroughfares that comes to life almost like an amusement park ride. It has unpredictable topography, colorful landscaping and design and is a departure from mainstream comfort. It is inviting to some and frightening to others.

While Lombard Street is popular, exciting, potentially dangerous and seemingly alive next to its counterparts, there are examples of how San Francisco has thought to reinvent streets in both an organic and socially constructive way. One example has been through its recent focus on alleys as a part of the pedestrian network. This is an area where my former students

Figure 5.5: Lombard Street, San Francisco

Source: https://commons.wikimedia.org/wiki/File:Lombard_street_in_San_Francisco_
Americas_crookedest_street.jpg

and I have invested a lot of time and energy (Riggs and Gross, 2017). Put simply, alleys can function in a way that supports the social function of cities, be both destinations and passages and, when properly planned, generate a safe and effective space. All those features can be seen on display in some of the really cool alleys of San Francisco.

But before we dive into details, a bit more about alleys in general. Most alleys in the US that were created after the invention of the automobile were designed for providing service access for garbage collection, firefighting and emergency vehicles, or parking for both bicycles and autos. They are generally narrow and have low auto traffic volumes. These valuable attributes have been attractive in recent years since many cities have explored converting these spaces to community assets.

I liken these conversions and the idea of using the coziness of the alley to the writings of Jacobs, who wrote many volumes about harnessing the power of streets to create (and interact with) community. Given that many alleys have the most intimate relationship with housing units, they provide a natural way for urban life to spill out onto the street and blur the lines between public and private space and street and yard, while still functioning as networks. London, for example, has been exploring using alleys and low-volume streets as "quiet-ways" to encourage non-automotive travel.

Furthermore, alleys can become destinations, providing access to shops and community resources close to residences. My friend Denver Igarta, who leads the complete street program in Portland, Oregon, suggests that alleys support a sojourn function—providing people with space to sit, observe or be active. People are drawn in, whether by business, unique attributes or signage. Their unique wayfinding features create curiosity and wonder. In doing so, individuals connect with other people and with the surrounding built environment, including connections with art and natural green space. These pathways can provide a cool microclimate with space for planting. Treatments that some cities have explored include vertical plant walls, planter boxes, ground plants and trees—all of which reinforce the pedestrian and bicycle environment. Bioswales (rain gardens) and permeable pavements have also been installed in these kind of spaces, most notably in Chicago, which established a specific "Green Alley Program" (City of Chicago, 2010).

So, what about San Francisco? Well, my students and I were fascinated with a handful of alleys in the city, particularly Linden Lane and Ames Alley. Both are part of a rich and somewhat hidden network and recently became part of the City of San Francisco's program to activate these spaces as "living alleys" (Rocha, 2007; Kuchar, 2013).

The idea of the living alley was quite simple—the small street could serve more than just cars—that it could be designed "primarily for pedestrians and bicyclists as well as space for social uses. Vehicles are typically still allowed access but with reduced speeds." (San Francisco Planning Department, 2015a).

My students loved Linden Lane because it has a great coffee shop, the first Blue Bottle coffee shop. I also had affection for these kinds of roads stemming from living in San Francisco's Mission District. The alleys in the Mission were rich with Latino-influenced murals indicative of the area's large immigrant population. They were usually full of kids out playing soccer. My wife and I owned a condo that entered onto Ames Alley, and one of our strongest memories was watching a group of kids participate in a quinceañera that our neighbors hosted in the street. The visual of young teens dressed in their Sunday best and dancing in our alley is etched in my memory.

Given these affections, my students and I were curious about what made these backstreet paths work. So, to figure that out, we reviewed alley plans internationally. We then ran surveys of people using them, particularly focusing on Linden Lane and an adjacent alley called Ivy.

What we found was not earth-shattering, but it was important: people love activated or living alleys. We found many "alley plans" across the world in places as diverse as Melbourne, Australia and Bozeman, Montana, and almost all had a focus on community creation and socialization, even if they had other stated interests in green infrastructure or encouraging active travel via walking and biking. This focus was confirmed when in San Francisco we asked people in these less formal pathways why they were there. The most frequent response was "the amenities." While people did use these small streets because they were a part of their route, other factors such as landscaping, street art, open space and coffee made them prioritize the alley as a path. They were social routes.

My grandmother might have call these "lollygag" streets because they seemed to reinforce social activity, but the alleys we studied were not preserved by San Francisco in isolation. They were part of a bigger plan to change how people traveled and reinforce the power of the street for social aspects of a city. For example, the San Francisco Bicycle Plan established a proposal for the redesign of the Market Street corridor that had art and experiences across it (Roth, 2010). The Better Market Street project intended to change the nature of the central street that ran the length of the downtown and make it car-free but also highly social (San Francisco Planning Department, 2015b). With the goal of improving San Francisco's civic and commercial core—and the busiest corridor for pedestrians, bicycles and transit—the Better Market Street project is focusing on supporting improved pedestrian and bicycle safety and comfort as well as public spaces that attract a diversity of people and users.

The project also provides an example of the shifting mindset in San Francisco toward streets that balance the needs of all users while lessening impacts on the natural environment. The highly visible case of Market Street demonstrates the commitment of numerous city agencies, residents and neighborhood partners to streets that enhance mobility, safety and economic vitality. And this kind of transformational project is important as it creates trust and institutional investment in the social cohesion of the community over the long term.

The project is something that numerous people I spoke to in San Francisco clamored for. Many talked about how this was an investment in the social forces that make up the city. Some highlighted how it is very aligned with a cultural reinvention of the street as social space, that has been present in South America and Europe for centuries. They discussed the street being an extension of the home, saying that around the world "there is a cultural practice to go out for a walk in the evening—and to go out to dinner or else just to go to the square and walk around." San Francisco's efforts to reinvent alleys and streets are just a small piece of work relating to these international trends to reinvent the street, yet these efforts may not go far enough at revolutionizing streets and cities around the globe.

Beyond San Francisco

It is important extend beyond examples such as San Francisco. Elsewhere, we can see exemplary cities that are rethinking the idea of the of street and social city, particularly exploring the idea of the woonerf for all. Two good case studies are Bell Street Park in Seattle, Washington, and Freiberg, Germany. Both provide excellent examples of successful planning and implementation and have shaped more social and shared streets in the same ways that many of the people who I talked to in San Francisco wanted to see.

Bell Street Park, Seattle, Washington

Bell Street Park was openly and deliberately designed as a woonerf in 2014 (City of Seattle, 2021). It is 56,000 square feet in area and includes the essential components of a woonerf. "Vehicle lanes [are] not separated from the pedestrians by a curb," creating an impression that the space should be shared (Curbed Staff, 2013). When the park first opened it instantly changed the perception of the area from a seedier spot to a more inviting location. It has one lane of traffic and wide landscaping highlighting the potential for successful woonerf implementation.

Before the introduction of the woonerf design, Seattle residents did not tout the area around Bell Street Park as one of the city's more attractive places. As one local writer noted, "Bell Street was one of those streets that you avoided due to low-level crime, drug-dealing, etc." (Gaydos, 2014). The area is home to a number of bars and clubs. Problems on the street arose not when the bars were open, but after they closed. According to a Seattle Policy Department spokesperson,

It's the kind of phenomena we experience as the bars close, and they announce last call and then people start exiting at 1:30 or 1:45. There is this mass exodus out of the different venues. The sidewalks can't accommodate them and they start spilling out into the streets. We don't want people hit by a car. (Lacitis, 2013)

Prior to the woonerf, the police would address the problem by closing off streets to traffic until the crowds dissipated. Perhaps as a marketing strategy that recognized the pre-existing perception of the area, city officials opted to name their new woonerf as a "park." This label did create some confusion according to one local business owner:

> I think there's a disconnect from the community's perspective as when you look at it, it does not look like a park. It looks like a boulevard. We've had folks come up to Local 360 who will ask, 'Do you know where Bell Street Park is?' We say, 'it's right here!' (Gaydos, 2014)

Despite the dissonance in nomenclature, the inviting nature of the woonerf design in Bell Street Park is credited with creating more visibility and decreasing illegal activities. Users take longer and more social visits to the woonerf now, so much so that some have expressed a need for restrooms. At the same time, it is important to note that drivers of cars struggle to comprehend the rules of the park. This is not necessarily a bad thing and is something that relates back to an idea I have talked about with my colleague Anurag Pande—that drivers have become accustomed to certainty. Introducing uncertainty causes pain.

For example, one citizen accused Bell Street Park as operating as an intentional "speed trap" to generate revenue from traffic tickets. "On some afternoons … police could have ticketed nearly 100 percent of the drivers, who obviously don't understand how to navigate" the site (Westneat, 2015). While clearly these new street designs can be expected to cause some pain and take some getting used to, they challenge the notion that we planners and engineers can kill the notion of the street in the US and make it match models such as the woonerf to increase both safety and socialization.

Freiburg, Germany

Freiburg, Germany, extends the idea of the social and shared woonerf even further. Experimenting with streets completely dedicated to non-automotive traffic, this city of over 200,000 residents in the southwest corner of Germany is situated at the edge of the Black Forest and in close proximity to France and Switzerland. While this university city may not be a popular tourist destination, it is increasingly grabbing the attention of the world for its sustainability initiatives, including leadership in integrating alternative transportation into new development. It is sometimes called

Germany's ecological—or environmental—capital and was named the European City of the Year in 2010 by The Academy of Urbanism, in part because of efforts over the years to position itself as a sustainability leader (Eberlein, 2011a, 2011b).

Much of this focus on urban greening has to do with the city's transportation footprint and how it was rebuilt following World War II (Lennard and Lennard, 1995). I find it fascinating that the city leaders consciously decided to rebuild based on its medieval street plan with narrow, pedestrian-oriented corridors as opposed to following the modern planning concepts that was in favor at the time—wide, straight and auto-oriented street networks largely derived from Corbusian logic. To put it in context, at that time, the auto was seen as the next great advance in city design, and designers such as Corbusier were saying "Hey, let's kill our idea of the street, and make our cities work better." But he was actually redefining the street for automotive travel. What designers did not understand at that time was how this would cause cities to expand and change and how the emissions from these vehicles would ultimately become an environmental problem.

The decision to design streets around human interactions and socialization in Freiberg was unique. It differed from many European cities in similar situations and has proven to be a catalyst for a thriving city center and a model for sustainable urbanism. This decision has been followed by decades of bold and creative ideas for developing a green and livable community. After the controversial rebuild of the city center, Freiburg began using planning to prioritize dense, affordable and zero-energy homes while incorporating car-free streets, public transit hubs and the idea of "access by proximity" (Eberlein, 2011b). Concerns about affordable housing, energy waste and the inefficient use of land inspired the innovative Reiselfeld neighborhood, which was built to address a housing shortage in the 1980s and 90s.

Planners focused on three main goals for the new development: to build a real neighborhood, make it compact with everything needed proximate and provide easy access to transit to reduce vehicle use (Broaddus, 2010). The result was a masterplan that prioritized pedestrians, bicyclists and transit through effective design with limited residential parking often located below ground; easy access to a tram with direct service to downtown; slow speed limits on streets (18 mph/30 kph); a wide range of community services and essential shops located within the neighborhood.

Another opportunity for sustainable development presented itself after the Cold War when Freiburg transformed a decommissioned French air base into a neighborhood. The main goal for this new neighborhood was to reduce car use as much as possible by building a district of "short distances" to necessities, easy access to transit, narrow roads primarily used for access, limited parking times, off-site parking garages, small city blocks and relatively high density. The result was a district with less than 100 vehicles for every 1,000 residents; below the national average of over 500 and the Freiburg average of 430 (Eberlein, 2011b).

Meanwhile the city center continued to build upon the medieval street network by building a pedestrian-focused district. Although cars were banned from a few city streets in the downtown as early as 1949, the pedestrian zone was not fully implemented until the 1970s when a ring road was constructed and the city center was dedicated to walking. To reduce traffic and bring activity to a downtown area struggling to compete with larger retailers on the city's periphery, the pedestrian zone was implemented as an experiment before being widely accepted in 1986.

Parking was centralized in off-site garages to serve residents and visitors; downtown streets were closed to traffic and repaved with natural stone and these pedestrian promenades were activated by trees, fountains, seating, lighting and art installations. During this transformation the city elected to treat the streets as the city's "carpet," paving with natural and local stone often arranged into geometric designs, and historic, cultural and commercial symbols. Finally, the streams that flowed from the nearby mountains and previously buried below the city's streets were integrated into the streetscape. The result of these efforts has been very popular with residents and local businesses (Lennard and Lennard, 1995).

Public transit naturally became more desirable and popular after the closure of the city center to automobiles. Combined with efforts to coordinate transportation planning with development to limit the need for personal vehicles, Freiburg extended the public transit system, increased parking costs while reducing parking availability, implemented traffic calming measures and reduced speed limits, channelized automobile traffic and actively promoted cycling. Additionally, transit fares were reduced through passes, local transit was integrated with the regional and national train network and various transit authorities were consolidated. Further, separate paths and lanes for bicycles were created and expanded, bike parking was increased and bicycles were even banned from some streets to increase pedestrian safety and comfort.

The case of Freiburg, and the successes of other European cities in transitioning to streets that prioritized social cohesion and social equity by emphasizing bicycles and pedestrians, is much different than almost any American city but can serve as a blueprint for transformation over time. By embracing the informality of places such as Delhi and the notion of uncertainty, the planners and policymakers have created a more equitable streetscape that erodes the idea of what the street can actually be.

These places embrace the idea that a street can serve people first and cars second—perhaps even functioning to create joy and reinforce positive culture. And this is something worth talking more about as we think about culture and other functions of streets, turning our attention back to California.

6

The Street as Cultural Space

Let me live in a house by the side of the road
Where the race of men go by —
The men who are good and the men who are bad,
As good and as bad as I.
I would not sit in the scorner's seat
Nor hurl the cynic's ban; —
Let me live in a house by the side of the road
And be a friend to man. (Foss, 1897, p 11)

In the previous chapters I've discussed many ways that we can create more environmentally, economically and socially sustainable streets, but I believe streets can also be a cultural space. They can create culture. They can facilitate activities and cultural capital that form the "glue" or cohesion of communities that people think makes them durable and resilient in the face of challenges. If you're skeptical, consider the last time you saw kids playing in the street in front of your home. They are forging life-long memories and social bonds that will last a lifetime. They are with other children who may be of different races or economic backgrounds. Or consider the last time you went to a house with a front porch facing a neighborhood street, where people were passing by or were interacting with the street. They may have been exercising or going to and from work and have offered a wave, a smile or nod. These simple interactions and gestures are small things that create culture and one-ness of community.

   This idea of the front porch has special significance in my mind. The front porch was one of the defining features of my great grandmother's home in the hills of Kentucky. It was a space that provided a place for cultural experience and engagement. This was where they would sit on rocking chairs, talk to neighbors and watch "the race of men go by," just as the quote from Sam Walter Foss' poem suggests. And this is one of things that built a street that creates (and supports) culture—where a porch on the front of the house can be a catalyst for watching, engaging in and experiencing the road in front of it.

In a larger context, this social pastime of sitting on the porch is not an anomaly. Many of us have experienced congregating in front of a home. Residential stoops or entrances also serve the same function—providing space for engagement, community and social cohesion. As one of my students recently diagrammed in his work for me, porches and stoops can provide the opportunity for homes to have a quasi-public outdoor space between the sidewalk and their front door. This space can be "sit-able" and can transform the front of a home to a place where activity occurs, whether it be playing, resting on the steps after a walk or work or hosting a neighborhood barbecue.

Perhaps this is the reason why the classic children's television show *Sesame Street* is set in a neighborhood in New York. It is similar to the Greenwich Village/Hudson St. neighborhood where Jane Jacobs fought to protect the native values of connecting buildings with street. This is the place that those of us who used to watch the show might remember Bert, Ernie, Oscar the Grouch or Snufflupagus inhabiting—a city where one could have a beautiful home, great parks and good job all connected by livable and sustainable streets.

Is that too much of a cultural phenomenon to ask for? I hope not because, for me, the idea, or perhaps the feeling, is tied to more places than just *Sesame Street*. It reminds me of the streets in cities ranging from London to San Luis Obispo, where a culture of cycling, walking and transit has taken hold.

The visual picture of *Sesame Street* also reminds me of the phrase written across one of the buildings I used to work in at UC Berkeley, Hilgard Hall, about "the native values of rural life." The origin of the phrase is vague but to some degree it frames California's culture, which is having one foot in an innovative future and one in a deep tradition focused on natural resources and agriculture (Howard, 1902).

Consistent with this, many of the cities focused on building a culture of streets for cycling, walking and transit have implemented solutions that do not stem from complicated engineering design or novel technology. They have built solutions that harness the intrinsic value of their unique identity as a city—for example taking advantage of existing assets as well as the power of people. Given this, I believe there are several examples worth exploring. The description of social activity in Delhi illustrated in the prior chapter provides one, but in the US the idea of encouraging play and cooking and eating food in the street are becoming key aspects in the cultural transformations of roadway space. I mean quite literally that you're playing and having BBQs on the street, and one of the best examples of this has filtered from Latin America in the form of ciclovía.

Ciclovía and a culture of cycling

Ciclovía is a Spanish term that translates to "cycleway." Simply put, ciclovía occurs when certain streets on a temporary or permanent basis are banned to automobiles and opened exclusively for cyclist and pedestrian use. In practice, however, it is a cultural event that celebrates street activity and play. This practice originates from Colombia and dates back to 1974 (Gómez et al., 2015; Abolghasem et al., 2018). Certain main streets of Bogota (for example Cali and Medellin) were—and still are—blocked off every Sunday from 7am to 2pm while many activities take place. Miles and miles of car-free streets are then packed with cyclists, runners and walkers.

These events attract nearly a quarter of the city's population and are a desired activity within the community. The appeal of the ciclovía is seen worldwide, making it one of the largest recreational events globally—the idea being that the convergence of the people engaged in a cultural event creates paved parks and drives a culture of health. It is also something that has gradually filtered into cities including San Francisco, Los Angeles and San Diego (Wilson et al., 2012; Zieff et al., 2013; Engelberg et al., 2014; Cohen et al., 2016). Ciclovía-inspired events in these cities exemplify an urban city transforming its public streets into cultural spaces for outdoor recreation. Through their public appeal, ciclovías have the ability to improve the overall health of both the city and its people as well as promote business opportunities for those supporting the event.

In San Francisco, for example, the ciclovía practice is known as Sunday Streets, with large components of the Golden Gate Park and various neighborhood commercial districts being closed to traffic completely. One of its goals is to "inspire people to think differently about their streets as public spaces." (City of San Francisco, n.d.). The event inspires people to think of the street as not only made for the automobile but made for the people as well. It promotes and encourages residents to replace automobile trips with public transportation, bicycling or walking—thus creating a culture of active transportation.

The original intent of Sunday Streets was to provide a temporary park for the people, a space designated for outdoor activity as well as all the benefits associated with parks. Sunday Streets does this by providing a temporary linear park, 2 to 5 miles in length, that offers opportunities to both pedestrians and bicyclists. Yet the practice has had other impacts.

The shutting down of these major streets can be seen as a temporary shift in the aspects of public life that city streets support; it brings the focus to the people. Sunday Streets has promoted an increase in park use; the San Francisco County Transportation Authority states that 2.7 million more people now use parks on an annual basis. This initiative was supported by a 2006 study that indicated 116 percent more people use the park on Sundays than on Saturdays (Wilson et al., 2012). Also, associated with the ciclovía is a variety of benefits for the environment and the community, potentially decreasing air pollution as well as reducing street noise.

Furthermore, ciclovía is also a way to unite different neighborhoods with historical divisions. In other words, the event brings together neighborhoods that do not normally socialize or interact, thus promoting a sense of community. During the ciclovía, many local businesses and community organizations offer free activities such as, but not limited to, tai chi, yoga, roller disco, rowing, dog walking and dancing. Many participants at the event said that they were motivated to attend because of the safe opportunities to participate in outdoor recreation.

There are also positive business impacts. In analyzing the aftermath of Sunday Streets, researchers have shown that 68.4 percent of participants visit commercial districts for the events and 65 percent purchase a meal (Zieff et al., 2013). This means that these events provide increased opportunities for restaurants and retailers. In comparing non-event Sundays with event Sundays, the researchers found that merchants who actively participated in the events perceived to benefit more compared to those who did not.

Los Angeles put the "LA" in CicLAvia. There the event is said to "catalyze vibrant public spaces, active transportation, and good health through car-free streets ... [and] transform our relationship with our communities and with each other" (City of Los Angeles, n.d.). With the streets now car-free, we can see public spaces for their full potential and thus can utilize the space accordingly to nurture our relationship with the community and therefore with each other. Removing the cars provides a safer environment for building community, social identity and social engagement. In LA, the event has impacted local and regional transportation policies related to pedestrians and bicyclists.

CicLAvia is said to have improved the air quality by reducing ultrafine particles in the air by over 20 percent and yielding up to 263,000 MET-hours of energy expenditure (Cohen et al., 2016). In surveying participants, 40 percent said that if they were not at CicLAvia they would have been physically active elsewhere—meaning that the vast majority of the people, 60 percent, would have been inactive without the event.

This a unique opportunity to create a culture of health on the streets worthy of significant effort to attend. As a result, the events have continued to gain traction in shaping the culture of play and activity on public roads. Yet these are not the only kinds of events that can happen in the roadway. One of the other great examples is that of farmers' markets—and one of the best is in San Luis Obispo, California.

San Luis Obispo Farmers' Market

San Luis Obispo (SLO) Farmers' Market is a cultural phenomenon that turns a street in the US—yes, in the US—into an open market. The event is held every Thursday evening on five city blocks of Higuera Street, shutting the street down to cars and opening it up to throngs of people. The event has grown significantly since its inception in the early 1980s, and today includes a variety of vendors ranging from farmers and artists to restauranteurs and activists. There is even a bicycle valet service available to people who choose to bike to the event.

But what really does this mean? How does the street transform people? How does it shape their view of society and culture? Perhaps this role of the street in San Luis Obispo can be best summed up by some of my former students, who remembered,

"The smell of tri tip and kettle corn permeated the air as I walked down Higuera Street on Thursday night. Vendors, merchants, and musicians lined the streets while a seemingly endless stream of people made its way up and down the busy street. Everything from fresh produce to burgers to flowers were for sale and for a teen-aged high schooler visiting a college for the first time, this was sensory overload. Yet, I took it all in and couldn't get enough ..."

"I felt at home here. I don't remember all the details of that first day in San Luis Obispo, but the Farmers Market is my earliest memory of the place that I would come to call my home for four years of my life in college. The San Luis Obispo Farmers' Market changed the way I viewed farmers' markets. Prior to experiencing the "World Famous" farmers' market in San Luis Obispo, my idea of a farmers' market was a couple of tents pitched in an empty parking lot with a few venders offering some produce at an obscure location no one visited."

"The SLO Farmer's Market was different. It was something that everyone knew about and made a conscious effort to attend. It was fun and went beyond simply buying produce – it was an experience that brought together all walks of life in the community from college students to tourists to young families. Thursday nights just felt like the start of the weekend ..."

My students' sentiment is not unique. Most of my other students, friends and colleagues felt the same way: the SLO Farmers' Market was a cultural fixture. It tied people to the land in a way that other street events that I have been to have not, perhaps in a way that harkens back to that quote from Hilgard Hall at UC Berkeley—"harnessing the native cultural values of rural life in an urban setting."

But the SLO Farmers' Market was not always the great success that it is today. In fact, it came about in response to the need to reclaim the streets for pedestrian foot traffic. In the 1970s, downtown businesses broke from tradition and began staying open after 5 pm on Thursdays (Colhouer, 2015). (Sounds a bit crazy to think about now, I know.)

This gave residents an opportunity to run errands and do shopping that they wouldn't normally have been able to do. On Thursdays, people from all over the county would visit downtown SLO, which became alive and thriving with these new hours. Shortly after this initial success, many high school and college-aged kids began driving their cars up and down the main street, Higuera Street, literally taking over the area (Middlecamp, 2010). Downtown SLO became the meeting place for the local youth to compare their cars and ride around.

This was a deterrent to the local population and caused individuals to stop shopping downtown on Thursdays. (I'm sure there was a bit of drama due to the "rabblerousing" by all those young people.) But in response something magical happened in the early 1980s. The Downtown Association barricaded off several blocks of downtown to vehicles in an attempt to bring back the shoppers and foot traffic. While this effectively ended the "cruising" scene, initially it did not do a great job in bringing back shoppers, but at the same time there was a cultural movement at place that focused on local, seasonal and sustainable food. Led by those such as Alice Waters of Chez Panisse in Berkeley, the California food movement began reshaping how food was connected to local culture. In 1983, the city shut down a street for a rib cookoff which brought approximately 700 people downtown. The following week, the first farmers' market was held on Higuera Street where it continues to this day, attracting thousands of people each week.

Since then, while the downtown has changed, the farmers' market has not. Businesses have come and gone but it continues to thrive. People don't bother driving downtown on Thursday evenings anymore because the farmers' market has become such an institution. And for many, the farmers' market symbolizes the city: a small college town on the central coast of California known for gently rolling hills, wineries and nearby beaches.

I taught at Cal Poly, San Luis Obispo, not too long after this period, and I'm sure you could imagine why I had trouble leaving SLO to move back to San Francisco and why Oprah calls the city one of the happiest on the planet. But one might ask "was it really just shutting down the street and connecting people with farm-to-table food?"—I doubt it. The history that shaped much of the farmers' market event does not take into account much of its impact—particularly helping to revitalize the downtown and building on the local agricultural strengths. That said, the city has capitalized on these strengths and achieved the benefits of sustainable local businesses and desirable real estate within close proximity to downtown. Can you imagine being able to walk or bike to such an event? How lucky!

These experiments in the culture of food in San Luis Obispo have only been built on by many cities across the globe throughout the pandemic where streets have become a place for dining, socialization and community. San Francisco was one of the places experimenting with alternative uses of the street over time. The city was one of the first to embrace the celebration of LBGTQ communities with a huge parade each year celebrating Pride. The event occupied all of Market Street and provided a day of festivities and culture that championed freedom of love and tolerance.

The city of San Francisco has built on this powerfully throughout the pandemic. While they were experimenting with parklets and on-street dining even before COVID-19, the city has been an example of where food, art and music can reinforce the culture of a city.

But there have fantastic examples of how the streets have been tied to culture beyond California and across the globe. A centuries-old example heels from the Christian and pagan traditions of Carnival. In both Europe and South America, there have been long traditions of the pedestrianization of streets to celebrate culture, dressing up to celebrate these days. These are colorful events full of music and costumes, but one of the more interesting permanent installations where streets have shaped and been shaped by the art community is Paseo Bandera in Santiago, Chile.

Reinforcing the artistic culture of a city: the case of Santiago, Chile

Paseo Bandera is an amazing example of how streets can be shaped by and tied to the artistic culture in a community. Santiago has long had a rich community of artists and history of street art. When I recently traveled there, even after a series of violent protests, the evidence of murals and a lively arts community was visible on the street. Street musicians and bands still occupied intersections and created a lively celebration of Chilean culture.

This was tied to food, drink and shopping in many locations, though much of the downtown of Santiago was becoming increasingly auto-oriented. That changed with a significant artistic thrust with the re-creation of Paseo Bandera (Taggart, 2018). Led by artist Dasic Fernández in 2013, there was a push to remake the street more appealing to pedestrians in only 30 days, creating a series of vivid art installations across four blocks in the central city. This was one of the richest cultural centers in the downtown.

With strong support from the community, Fernández used paint and sculpture art in the street to create installations that were reminiscent of the strong artistic identity of the city, ranging from visual and musical arts to poetry and literature. There has long been a strong culture of street art in Santiago dating back to the days when Pablo Neruda was promoting social democracy before the 1973 military coup (Smith, 2017).

The result was an amazing success. Pedestrian traffic and economic vibrancy only increased. The original idea was that the installation would

Figure 6.1: Paseo Bandera

be temporary. But in 2018 the city decided the cultural intervention would remain permanent. This made Paseo Bandera in Santiago one of the first cities in the new millennium to begin exploring fully pedestrianized corridors.

A community decision to celebrate the street

Clearly, this celebration of the street, whether it be for art, a market or a ciclovía-type-event, illustrates that the power the idea of harnessing roadways to support local traditions and customs. In these cases, the communities decided to use the street for culture and it made a difference—it was the decision to end the way the road was being used and take it back from automobiles. And that is something that still resonates today. In both cases, the community decided that pedestrians would get priority over automobiles and would celebrate the street in different ways. They could have done the events in a parking lot but chose not to—now those places have become housing and storefronts that serve to reinforce the same community decisions.

Put simply, they created culture in the street that reflected community values and interests. And while you might think "that's not the novel," think again. It is pretty amazing that these communities have the foresight to get this done—and in the case of SLO, sustaining it for almost 40 years. Imagine the obstacles that they faced over that time, let alone the tension with other competing city priorities. Harnessing the power of place and culture is important, no matter what you do in the street, but it is a challenge and that is important to acknowledge. We will talk about some of those challenges, from both a practical and policy perspective, in Chapter 8, particularly focusing on a key interest of mine—keeping people from moving or being pushed out of cities as we invest in walkable, biking and transit friendly streets—but before we do so let's consider how our roadways can become more natural spaces.

7

The Street as a Natural Space

> I sum up that in 50 years nobody has systematically looked after a good urban habitat for Homo sapiens. We have written very few books about it. There's been very little research done. We definitely know more about good habitats for mountain gorillas, Siberian tigers, or panda bears than we do know about a good urban habitat for Homo sapiens. (Jan Gehl in ASLA, 2021)

Streets should be for people. But as illustrated in the introductory quote from Jan Gehl, streets can support and enhance the human condition as well as the broader urban ecosystem. Roadways need not be limited to the transport, cultural and social aspects of the city. They can also be a part of the natural experience.

This idea is not new. It has a lot of connection to some of the original thinking from many of the individuals we discussed earlier in this book, from Jacob Riis to Ebenezer Howard. And new scientific studies are telling us how many of the places where we have engineered greenery out of our buildings and cities (something that became particularly acute in some 1960s brutalist architecture) is unhealthy.

In 2001, a story about noted psychologist couple Steve and Rachel Kaplan appeared in the *Monitor on Psychology* (Clay, 2001). The article entitled "Green is Good For You" was a story about the husband-and-wife team's research into the restorative properties of nature. While both Steve and Rachel had done significant research on the topic, they did not realize the strong personal implications of their work until Rachel, a professor of psychology at the University of Michigan, switched to a new office.

While her old office had looked out onto a "barren courtyard," the new one offered a "tree-top view with lush green trees, birds and squirrels (Clay, 2001)." Despite the convincing nature of her own research Kaplan, was surprised at how good she felt in her new office. "My previous office was harder on me than I realized," she said. "I have to admit I was more convinced of my own work after I changed offices. I realized that all of our results were right."

This testimonial by a pre-eminent researcher gives inspiration to practitioners in fields such as planning, architecture, design and development to produce more physiologically and physically healthy cities and streets. A 2006 article in the *New York Times* chronicled the stories of many people seeking to bring nature into their homes and improve environmental design (Sole-Smith, 2006). It documented people who have started companies that produce "living walls" of plants such as ficus, hibiscus and orchids. These walls can clean air and provide a more natural environment so that humans can realize the benefits of biophilia in their cities.

Biophilia and biophilic design

Biophilia is essentially the idea that access to the natural world is essential for humans—that being near green space improves both physical and mental health. Put simply, green environments have clear restorative properties. Almost everyone can say they enjoy either taking a weekend hike or stroll in the park, the grass and leaves glimmering in the sheen of a summer day or the breeze whisking past your face on an autumn afternoon. The experience of natural beauty can help escape the daily routine of work. It can be rejuvenating to both the mind and body, but in reality has more to do with our physical health than we regularly recognize. The availability of community green spaces can have positive health-related benefits from both the mental and physical perspectives.

For years, scientists have been curious about the relationship between the environment and humans. Early data theorized a "biophilia hypothesis" suggesting that humans have an innate need to interact with other organisms and the natural environment to fully develop. The hypothesis further suggested that, devoid of this interaction with nature, living in a "denatured environment" led "to a society of childish adults" (Dekay and O'Brien, 2001, p 20). Other scientific research has found that when we think about the natural environment the brain is relieved of "excess" circulation (or activity) and nervous system activity is reduced, thus reducing stress (Maller et al., 2006). Subsequent research involving people in hospital environments, prisons, office spaces, military camps and even people after horror films has indicated that in many cases those exposed to, or immersed in, green spaces have better health on the whole (Frumkin et al., 2004).

The research of Roger Ulrich was particularly unique as he dealt with hospitalized patients who were physically ill (Ulrich, 1984; Ulrich et al., 1991). Ulrich was a physician interested in patient recovery within the natural settings. He initiated a study evaluating the recovery of patients after gallbladder surgery, finding that those with a natural view recovered faster, with less time in the hospital, than those who looked at an urban scene.

Ulrich found that patients with rooms facing a park had a 10 percent faster recovery and needed 50 percent less pain-relieving medication compared to patients in rooms facing a building wall.

An additional study published in 2002 illustrated this fact for elderly individuals (Takano et al., 2002). In the course of the study, over 3,000 senior citizens from similar age cohorts in Tokyo were evaluated over a five-year period. The residents were studied according to whether or not "the factor of walkable green streets and spaces near the residence" influenced lifespan. At the conclusion of research, the study confirmed that living in areas with walkable green spaces positively influenced the longevity of life. It recommended that future development plans consider the green environment as essential for senior residences, concluding that,

> The availability of space near your own residence for taking a stroll is believed to increase the chances of walking outside of the residence, which helps to maintain a high physical functional status. The results with the factor of walkable green streets and spaces that are independent of personal characteristics suggested that the value of parks and tree lined streets near residences is particularly high in densely populated urban areas ... (Takano et al., 2002, p 916)

This research has been expanded upon and used as a justification for architects to redesign hospitals with integrated green spaces, zen gardens and courtyards, and the research has been confirmed by psychologists. This includes Stephen and Rachel Kaplan from the University of Michigan. They have showed that workers having window views of trees and flowers felt their jobs were not as stressful (Kaplan, 1989). These workers were altogether more satisfied when they had a view of trees and flowers than their colleagues who could see only urban environments. They had fewer physical ailments, including reported illness and headaches—a fact that gives credence and physical justification to every worker who has ever desired the "corner office with a view."

Kaplan and Kaplan have done more research into the physiological benefits and restorative effects of nature. Based on their studies they have found the four basic elements that make an environment "restorative" to be:

(1) an effortless fascination or an attention-grabbing property
(2) a sense of escape, getting away and possibly risk
(3) the sense of being a part of a something larger
(4) the power for individual choices and creativity of purposes

In sum, evidence shows that people who are closer to the natural environment are altogether healthier and happier. Designing for nature or biophilic response is good for human health. As Roger Ulrich has said,

Nature is powerfully relaxing ... We evolved to recognize the kind of natural setting where we could let our guard down because there was water available, sunlight and views to help us spot predators, and refuge to protect us. So when we recognize those elements today, even if we're highly stressed or sick, our blood pressure lowers, our immune system functions better and we feel less stressed. (Sole-Smith, 2006)

Integrating nature into city streets

However, these studies do not take into account the fact that many communities are without such green space and have limited access to the natural world. The Rand Corporation undertook an in-depth study of park use in Los Angeles and found that, on the whole, the majority of the city population was underserved by the park system and did not necessarily access to parks to maintain physical activity (Cohen et al., 2006). The study showed that over 80 percent of users lived within one mile of the park and data showed that proximity to the park was related to both the extent of use and the amount of exercise. While the majority of users were young males playing organized sports, this illustrated an opportunity for organized programs for females and seniors.

The study also pointed out a critical design flaw of several natural spaces. Many of the parks did not have areas for moderate and vigorous exercise, including places like running, walking paths and trails. These are some of the most-used facilities by seniors and adults. Most people at the parks were sedentary, with the most common activity being sitting. The study recommended encouraging more locations for walking and moderate-to-vigorous physical activity, which would result in more active patrons and neighborhood residents. But urban parks need not just be limited to wide open spaces.

In my mind, streets can serve this role. They can provide what Jan Gehl refers to as a "soft edge" that provides a natural seam between personal and public space (ASLA, 2021). And this is a seam that can have purpose. Soft and natural streets can encourage bicycle and pedestrian travel by having easily accessed doors and windows, places to set, rest, dwell and encounter others. These soft edges can be play places where children can build forts or climb trees. They can even provide nourishment in the very plantings that occur on them—whether through fruit trees or vegetable gardens with kale and tomatoes.

Just think about the simple act of planting street trees. Research shows that trees and vegetation can not only have traffic-calming benefits but can help improve water and air quality and lower urban temperatures. Vegetation can help deal with watershed issues, offset emissions and reduce the heat gain in cities from the pavement—what we call the urban heat island effect. In that aspect, "green-complete streets" have benefit, not only in terms of a transportation mode shift, but for water quality, water volume and flood control. These streets are also likely to affect other aspects of a community including the social use of space, public health (via increased pedestrian activity and improved air quality), property value and crime rates or public safety.

My students and I have captured some good examples in a recent plan in Anaheim and Paso Robles, California. In Anaheim, the landscaping was designed not only to create a comfortable walking environment but also for ecological benefit. Streetscapes had systems that dealt with runoff storm water. They incorporated bioswales, or vegetative retention basins, that can hold and slowly release storm water back into the ground. This is far more advantageous than letting water run off streets into gutters and eventually out to the ocean, since it cleans and filters water before it soaks into the ground.

Simultaneously, these green infrastructure improvements made streetscapes more interesting and comfortable. The street provided clear soft, natural edges that facilitated a healthier environment. They provided destinations along the route, be they benches or parklets. To create a livelier urban environment, they used sidewalks for other activities, including sidewalk cafés and seating. Seating provided opportunities to sit, relax and people watch, making streets more leisurely and friendly to visitors. We sometimes call these environmental "co-benefits" meaning that we could benefit people and travel goals at the same time as the environment. In essence, the physical space becomes transactional in that people exchange relationships with the environment in the same time that they are walking to their destination.

In Paso Robles, there are similar set-ups that combine both green stormwater infrastructure with the attributes of a complete street. Local planners wanted to deal with a seasonal creek that had been paved over and undergrounded. Over time, due to the lack of ability for water to permeate the soil, the amount of stormwater on the street had increased. This caused flooding and contributed to pollution in the nearby Salinas River where the

Figure 7.1: The natural streets of Paso Robles

Figure 7.2: A process to make streets more natural might include building infrastructure and lane thinning, followed by efforts to remove parking and think shared

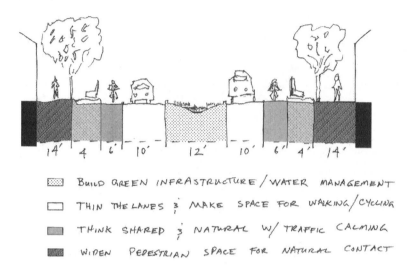

creek historically emptied. At the same time, planners wanted to improve bicycling and pedestrian infrastructure.

To address this, the city of Paso Robles installed green infrastructure improvements that made streetscapes more interesting and comfortable. They first invested in green infrastructure and large water filtration culverts down the center median; they then thinned driving lanes to provide more shared multi-modal infrastructure for cycling and walking.

The concept of greening streets has also had significant benefits in more wet cities like Portland and Philadelphia. Portland began implementing projects in 2003 with the primary purpose to focus on health and stormwater treatment, using primarily bioswales and water retention areas (City of Portland, 2021). Philadelphia has developed a comparable plan to use curb extensions, permeable pavements, rain gardens, rain barrels and green roofs to reduce flooding, sewage overflow and recharge groundwater levels, while improving bicycle and pedestrian safety.

Urban greening in China and Australia

But what about examples outside of the west? Cities in China specifically have been taking urban greening quite seriously. Green rooftops, rain gardens and replacing concrete sidewalks and pavements with wetlands helps stormwater get absorbed back underground, making water a friend for the city as opposed to a foe. Referred to as "sponge city infrastructure," the

Lingang district of Shanghai has been transforming its streets from concrete to green streets one by one (Roxburgh, 2017). The pavements in the Lingang district have been lined with beautiful gardens and public squares are filled with plant beds and trees. Between the construction sites and cranes, there are buildings designed with water features that help manage stormwater runoff through streams and ponds. As the "sponge city" of Shanghai, the district shows that streets can not only become more natural but can provide solutions for coastal cities at risk of sea rise and flooding. The government is taking note at the national level.

Large cities in China such as Beijing have continually been cast as unhealthy and having poor air quality. This reputation for high levels of pollution and the associated health problems have led the country to think of quick actions that can be taken—much of which involves rethinking about sustainability, architecture, urban design and street infrastructure (UBS, 2019). China builds about two billion square meters of buildings on a yearly basis, and more recently these construction projects are mandated to adhere to rigid environmental regulations. The government in China has stated that 50 percent of urban buildings being built must be certified as sustainable (UBS, 2019). The country's Green Building Action Plan makes it mandatory for public buildings such as hospitals and schools to meet the sustainable standards of the building as set by the three-star rating system known as the Green Building Evaluation Label. There are six basic categories that are taken into consideration, including water, energy, resource efficiency, operational management, indoor environment quality and land.

The Leadership in Energy and Environmental Design system, which has been linked to green street initiatives in the US, also has a notable presence in China. In the year 2015, buildings certified as Grade A office buildings comprised 28 percent of the complete market. With efforts such as Vertical Forests and Forest cities underway alongside their "sponge city" streets, China is proving that it is possible for economic growth and sustainability to go hand in hand.

Similar transitions to more sustainable and soft-edged streets are happening in Australia where Melbourne's "green laneways" program has incentivized the naturalization of streets (Cabanek et al., 2020). The city has built an interactive online map to illustrate streets that could be greened (City of Melbourne, 2021). The goal was to encourage citizens to transform their own roads so that they would become "leafy, green and useable spaces for everyone to enjoy." Residents could click and find their street to see what kind of greening they were allowed to do and then work with the city to plant trees, build parklets or construct vertical plantings.

The program was huge success and not only created biophilic value but reinforced culture, social and transportation values. In one location near popular bars and restaurants, a large vertical wall was constructed and planted with over 1,000 plants of over 80 different species. In other places in the city, planters broke up the street and provided traffic calming measures. Planter boxes with lush greenery provides places of visual interest underneath windows and alongside doors. This was connected to a larger urban revitalization project that was designed to create a more lively and active downtown environment in the city (NACTO, 2021).

Starting at the beginning

If we were to summarize what these global cities are realizing, we might say that cites are re-educating themselves on historic roots. We are starting at the beginning and remembering that natural streets are good for us. As mentioned in the introduction to this piece, early architects, designers, naturalists—even politicians such as Ebenezer Howard, Fredrick Olmstead, Daniel Burnham, John Muir and Theodore Roosevelt—understood the need for a connection between urban design and nature. Roosevelt (1910) was quoted as saying, "Leave it as it is. The ages have been at work on it and man can only mar it." Thus, it is not surprising that many of our most cherished places, that some of these men labored on, have a more natural feel, with parks, vistas, a town square and community facilities all within walking or cycling distance for residents.

The World Health Organization's (WHO) Ottawa Charter for Health Promotion supported the re-integration of these green, sustainable practices, advocating that the protection of natural and built environments and conservation of natural resources remain essential for human health (Thompson et al., 2018). It suggested these items as upstream prevention measures for a healthier city. Supporting actions aligned with this strategy through the built environment may be the start of resolving the health crises we see in America today.

What is the best non-drug way to treat depression? Exercise and social connectedness. What is the best non-drug way to treat Type 2 diabetes? Exercise and weight loss. What is one of the most safe and accessible forms exercise? Walking. What are the most fuel-efficient and least-polluting ways to commute? Walking and biking. These sound like simple suggestions but sadly our current development model which encourages wide streets and sacrifices pedestrian and cyclist safety does not make them achievable. However, through the promotion of sustainable development that encourages and allows access to exercise and socialization, we can begin to improve our physical and mental fitness through the built environment.

There is a basic human need for interaction with the green environment. The data may never be absolutely conclusive because of differences in race, gender and choice, but the actual results are intuitive to the naked eye. The senior can have a leisurely walk in the park, and the worker can have a better view from their desk. Green cities with sustainable environments become filled with people who are on the whole healthier because of their walking, cycling, socialization and contact with nature.

We can conclusively say that living near and having access to environments, including walking trails, bike routes and green space, gives people access to exercise more. We know that use is more prevalent when these areas are safe. We can say that community gatherings encourage more human interaction, a basic building block for mental health. We know that people who exercise more are healthier and less susceptible to chronic health or mental health issues. The more physically and mentally fit an individual is, the less monetary burden that person is likely to have on society. Conversely, we can also assume that a citizen of a green society has greater personal contribution. Knowing that is powerful but doing it is not without challenges. And challenges are what we will talk about next.

8

Challenges to Ending the Road

Let me live in my house by the side of the road,
Where the race of men go by,
They are good, they are bad, they are weak, they are strong,
Wise, foolish – so am I,
Let me live in my house by the side of the road
And be a friend to man. (Foss, 1897, p 12)

The ideas discussed in the last two chapters are not a panacea. The notion of making streets more livable through culture and urban greening is tied not only to local economic development but to the sentiment of the Sam Walter Foss poem my grandmother used to read to me. The idea of creating livable streets is built on concepts that have been around since the earliest cities—following the same logic that most modernist architects (such as Corbusier) would embrace—that form should support function. And I believe that the form of the street can support an intentional function of cities today to address climate change and support light forms of transport that are greener and have less emissions than driving.

Yet, at the same time, this future is not one that everyone has or will have. As a part of my long-standing research on walkability and housing choice, I have found that, while people may want to live in these of places where they can engage in green travel, they may not be able to. Neighborhoods that are less walkable and bikeable are also significantly more likely to be poor and minority. I have also observed a trend of minority flight to the suburbs, where the poor, low income and minority populations have concentrated in more auto-centric locations—leading to a litany of potential health and social disparities. This trend is a huge challenge to the future of streets—and it brings up the question: could someone actually afford that *home* "by the side of the road?"

The reference to a *home* links to how people are moving around urban areas to find housing. These migration trends are tied to many factors—but one of the most documented is the idea of flight from the urban core, often called displacement. The idea of displacement starts with a mismatch between housing and jobs. Urban neighborhoods increasingly face pressure to meet both housing and employment demands. In doing this, they can become either housing or job rich, and many neighborhoods continuously grapple with related imbalances in the supply of either housing or jobs.

While this can be mitigated by policy, policy that concentrates jobs or housing in one place but limits it elsewhere can have unintended effects. Likewise, economic development and community investment strategies can lead to decisions that push people out of walkable, bikeable locations, or have them choosing to cash out and move elsewhere. While planners and engineers used to talk about the rise of property values and more economic gentrification with these kind of community investments, these ideas now carry a more negative connotation (Gilderbloom, 2016)—one more likely to be associated with displacement and loss of community.

I used the term displacement cautiously since it is broadly used and rarely specifically defined. It is an environmental justice issue with many facets. The term can be related to the idea of housing, jobs or individuals. Displacement can occur in many forms. It can mean slum relocation or the loss of traditional mom-and-pop businesses because of the infusion of larger chain stores.

For example, as a part of the environmental clean-up and redevelopment of toxic (brownfield) sites, mayors have looked to bolster their tax base and increase economic vitality by attracting middle- and upper-class residents back into the urban core. This has resulted in a loss of minorities from those locations (Essoka, 2010). Conversely, in other cases, minority residents have chosen to "cash out" when market conditions reached a point where they could afford to buy a place elsewhere (Riggs, 2014b). Likewise, as many consumers balance housing and transportation costs, they have chosen cheaper housing in suburbs and given the ease and relative low cost of driving. This has led to suburban growth and the rise of what some have referred to as "ethnoburbs," that is suburban locations where displaced urban minority residents cluster (Li, 2009).

These are the kinds of examples I was seeing in 2010 in the San Francisco Bay Area, as many individuals began to cash out of places such as San Francisco and move to the outer suburbs. Affordability of housing was becoming an issue and people of color were moving out of walkable and bikeable neighborhoods. Pockets of racial minorities were become more concentrated in areas where driving was the main transportation option. I was observing minority clusters beginning to form in less walkable and bikeable areas of Oakland and Richmond across the bay from San Francisco as well as in some isolated pockets of San Francisco.

We still see this happening in cities. The same neighborhoods that are less walkable and bikeable are the same neighborhoods that have a high concentration of minorities. The question is why, and how we can work to slow down or eliminate this phenomenon—which is more than simply a housing affordability issue. The culprits are not solely economic. The reality is that travel preferences and housing location are much more complicated and deeply embedded into culture and history—a challenge that we will explore by looking at some of the history of the San Francisco Bay Area and neighborhoods in Oakland, Richmond and San Francisco.

A brief Bay Area history: Oakland, Richmond and San Francisco

Oakland, Richmond and San Francisco have different walkable environments but they developed similarly. All three had areas originally developed to provide housing for workers, immigrants, and the military. From the early 1900s to the 1950s, real estate developers used a model that included public infrastructure investment to transform rural districts into suburban neighborhoods and provide housing for military service members and workers affiliated with war efforts during the period (Loeb, 2001).

As inner suburbs, Oakland and Richmond developed based on a need to accommodate workers and immigrants, especially during World War II. Early in the 20th century, some East Bay communities provided summer respite to affluent San Franciscans who wanted to get away from the coastal fog. As more people moved, a thriving downtown developed. Oakland particularly had a booming downtown and train system (the Key System) to support travel to shops, restaurants, theaters and nightclubs. The city represented this trend of pre-WWII leisure in the US. The East Bay was the terminus for the Santa Fe and Southern Pacific Rail lines and represented a hotbed of both white- and blue-collar employment (Johnson, 1991). This prosperity put pressure on the housing market and created shortages even at that time.

As a result of these shortages and the legacy of wartime production, many minority-concentrated neighborhoods developed—particularly around locations with a focus on shipbuilding that had experienced an increased immigrant population. As Marilynn Johnson put it in an article in the Pacific Historical Review,

> Both cities ... experienced some of the greatest population gains on the West Coast-over twenty percent for Oakland between 1940 and 1944 and nearly four hundred percent for the smaller town of Richmond. Both cities hosted major shipyard operations, including the Kaiser and Permanente corporations in Richmond and Moore Dry-dock in Oakland, as well as a variety of other defense contractors and major military supply centers. (Johnson, 1991, p 285)

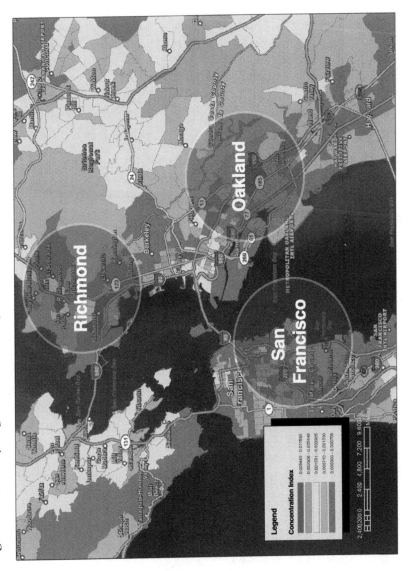

Figure 8.1: Minority neighborhood clustering in less walkable areas

Up to 60 percent of the population in these areas was migrant-based during the War and post-War era, and many of these migrants were southern Black people.

For example, the Black population in Richmond increased over 2,000 percent from 1940 to 1944, creating what were called "shipyard ghettos" which geographically separated newcomers from older residents (Brown, 1973). This segregation of sorts was coupled with new housing shortages in which residents were quoted to be "sleeping nightly on outdoor benches in public parks, in chairs at all night restaurants, in theatres, in halls of rooming houses, in automobiles, even in City Hall corridors" (Johnson, 1991, p 289).

The Black population, again largely from the southern US, concentrated themselves in less walkable and connected areas in West Oakland and east Richmond that were affordable.

> Barred from inland areas by resistant white residents, black migrants flooded into multiracial lowland neighborhoods. As black migrants moved into these areas, white ethnic residents became a relatively smaller and less visible part of the community. In West Oakland, for example, the percentage of blacks in the total population increased from twenty-four percent in 1940 to sixty-seven percent by 1950. (Johnson, 1991, p 293)

Furthermore, many of these minority residents continued to raise concern about the fracturing of their community, as if it was a loss of family.

> One long-time East Bay resident felt that the area had changed for the worse during the war. Her neighborhood, she said, "used to be like a big family. Everybody seemed to get along nicely together because I think everybody owned something … and we had pride in what we owned." The newcomers, she said, "just didn't understand … [and] they didn't have a pride like we had in our little city." This view suggests the importance of home ownership among pre-war blacks and reveals a sense of class distinction between old-timers and newcomers that persists to this day. (Johnson, 1991, p 294)

This influx of newcomers bundled with discriminatory practices led to massive construction projects by the Federal Housing Authority of close to 30,000 housing units, followed in subsequent years by multiple affordable-housing programs. For example, in 1967 the city of Oakland was one of the first communities to participate in the federal-leased housing program (Melkonian and Whitman, 1968). At the same time, many White people fled both Oakland and Richmond to new neighborhood communities and developing suburbs over the East Bay hills (Spencer, 2005).

Cities like Oakland and Richmond have since struggled with blight and urban disinvestment. Less walkable and high-minority-concentrated areas have seen little public funding. While downtown Oakland experienced a renaissance of development in the 1990s and 2000s, blight remained. The investment included new state buildings and a civic center project in the more walkable downtown (Howard, 2006). It was paralleled by Mayor Jerry Brown's initiatives to build 10,000 housing units in the downtown and to redevelop historic assets such as the Fox Theater. However, many minorities continued to live in less walkable areas such as East Oakland and Richmond, neither of which saw equitable growth or investment. There were continued complaints of gentrification and of neighborhood polarization in these locations, with blue collar, working class and minority residents segregated from the urban white-collar residents in the Oakland hills and downtown (Diaz, 2011).

And this was not a trend that was exclusive to Oakland. Service-class ethnoburbs have formed in places such as New Jersey and Los Angeles (Li, 1998; Li, 2009), relating to the idea of the suburban American dream and romanticized "individualism" (Archer, 2009). Yet few of these locations have dreams that can be realized and they have sometimes been called "slumburbia" (Quastel, 2009; Schafran, 2009). In these places, residents experience housing disinvestment, long car commutes and social isolation—something much different than the experience they had wished for. In many locations there is chronic joblessness and an increasing amount of crime.

This trend is highly acute in Paris, for example. Lower-class minorities have become concentrated in enclaves on the outside of central cities. These exterior parts of the city have become the new slums and resulted in deep cultural rifts in the community—rifts that have been revealed through the 2019–2020 yellow vest protests. These locations have issues with crime and frequent rioting, often based on workforce issues. Housing does not connect to jobs. Concentrations of service-sector employees are unable to live in the city and are poorly served by transit, yet these employees are often too poor to own a car.

This trend of displacement from central cities is also present in US locations such as San Francisco. For example, the Ingleside district had been a location with a concentrated minority population that developed in walkable areas. In 2022, it has many features that make the environment more walkable including street art, high-visibility cross-walks and pedestrian bulb outs. And while the district had originally been an example of cultural diversity in a walkable and bikeable area, it is challenged in this way today. Due to trends in gentrification, forced displacement and self-displacement, it is not as multi-cultural.

Historically, the area developed around the idea of providing middle-class, worker housing around transit. Developers Baldwin and Howell began work on the area after the 1906 earthquake using portions of a 4500-acre ranch sold by the heirs of Adolf Sutro. Little public infrastructure existed in the rural district. A toll road (modern-day Portola Drive) that connected Twin Peaks and Mt. Davidson existed as the area's main connective artery. The planning involved the extension of public transit from downtown San Francisco to west of Twin Peaks, and this became critical to the success of new residential developments such as Westwood Highlands (as it did with Oakland's Key System).

These new developments did not sell well until this transit was complete, and it reduced a trip from downtown to the new neighborhoods from one hour to twenty minutes. Transit made the neighborhood viable for first-generation-immigrant residents to easily commute to downtown San Francisco and local roadways promoted interconnectivity for pedestrian trips. While the physical traits of these city extensions were somewhat less walkable than their downtown counterparts (including curvilinear street grids that followed the topography and lots that were larger and more single-family-home oriented than what was normally found in other parts of the city) they were served by a commercial district along Ocean Avenue within walking distance of the development.[1]

Despite a framework that was receptive to minorities, Baldwin and Howell embedded discriminatory practice in their methods. They used price restrictions to concentrate socio-economic groups in the new neighborhoods (Loeb, 2001). This was based on their idea that they could bolster the aesthetic and socio-economic "standards" in the adjacent Westwood Highlands neighborhood. The new sub-divisions were divided into "price areas." Higher-priced properties were further away from the streetcar and from the Ocean Avenue shopping district. This, in turn, made the affordability of more walkable and bikeable housing a challenge for working class and minority residents. As a result, concentrations of those who could not afford more in the less-walkable areas of an urban environment formed. This idea of "worker housing," segregated by economic capacity, paralleled the placement of public housing projects to the east near the port and maritime facilities in less connected areas on the Bay. Barracks from WWII were reused as housing projects and these locations became full of a poorer, and largely Black, population.

Displacement and neighborhood change

Fast forward to 2022, and what has happened? Urban disinvestment in public housing and discriminatory developer policies have made it ever harder for minorities to live in walkable and bikeable places in San Francisco. Put simply, if you are a minority or poor, things are worse for you and you are likely finding it harder to afford to live in a walkable or bikeable area. For

Black people specifically, US Census data shows a trend of moving from central cities to the suburbs for more affordable homes. They have been leaving more walkable locations such as San Francisco in record numbers. According to 2019 estimates, Black people accounted for only 5.6 percent of the San Francisco population. This is down from 6.5 percent of the San Francisco population in 2005, and a high of 13.4 percent in 1970. This has been the steepest decline of any major US city according to the Census Bureau and the flight from parts of Oakland and Richmond has been equally dismal (Farrell, 2009).

What are some reasons for this phenomenon? Some experts say that, while poorer minorities occupy public housing, it is middle-class minorities who are cashing out or who have children, and are:

> ... vanishing from the social and cultural fabric, priced out and marginalized by the urban redevelopment policies of the past half century ... (fleeing) to northern California cities such as Stockton or Antioch ... (and killing) the life and spirit of the (urban) community. (Farrell, 2009)

A 2009 task force by then-San Francisco Mayor Gavin Newsom found that "very-low-income households made up more than two-thirds of the black population" in San Francisco—up from roughly one half in 1990 (Farrell, 2009). The assessment argued that middle-class Black families are moving across San Francisco Bay to Oakland and other cities in the eastern Bay Area. They are also contributing to a decrease in the population of children in the city. From 1990 to 2000, San Francisco lost 45 percent of its Black children. From 2000 to 2004, an additional 15 percent left the city, bringing the total population for African-American children to fewer than 10,000 for the first time in decades (Pomfret, 2006).

This trend of parents moving away from central cities in search of better schools and opportunities has long been dialogued. Middle-class individuals (of all ethnic groups) are drawn to the suburbs based on a variety of push and pull factors that are not just financial—from schools to a desire for green space. Yet the notion of minorities using the value of their housing to "cash out" of a city and move to cheaper and more auto-centric environments is something new. As stated in a San Francisco State University publication, an "increase in economic status has enabled many African-American homeowners to sell their houses and take the profits to the suburbs" (Ginwright and Akom, 2007, p 3). This supports the idea that more affluent minorities have newfound residential mobility to choose housing outside of the central city, which is not bad in itself but it suggests that many of these people may be concentrating in less-walkable inner or outer suburbs.

Curious about these factors, I conducted interviews and focus groups in these neighborhoods to obtain a better sense of why people were choosing neighborhoods where they had to drive as opposed to being in a place where they could walk or bike. What I found was not that surprising. Pull factors included better schools and more green space. Push factors involved things such as less crime or being forced out because of housing price increases. Many would talk about the desire for more "space" and "a yard." They would talk about getting a larger house in the suburbs than they could get in an area more accessible and suitable for walking in the central city, implying a trade-off between certain housing styles and neighborhood walkability. Street design, walkability or bikeability were never mentioned as something that they thought about.

The price of a home and the amount of space in it were of utmost importance, as were cultural and social factors. Many individuals mentioned price first, but then spent more time talking about social places such as churches, barbershops and salons than they did price—even if these locations were located 20 miles away in the original place they had moved. For those who had moved from San Francisco to distal and not walkable areas, many individuals talked about how they drove back to the city for church or to spend time with friends. These discussions included mentions of relationships and community and imply that, while the cost or price of housing may be the underlying factor, many minorities choosing more auto-dominated areas value socio factors more than the idea of walkability or bikeability.

I felt like this was something important for planners and designers to hear—since many assume that if you build walkable and bikeable infrastructure then people will use it. But that is likely just a "Field of Dreams" myth—the idea that if you build they will come. Getting people to value living in a walkable or bikeable area is complicated—let alone getting them to engage in walking or cycling behavior. Table 8.1 summarizes many of the reasons people said that they made these decisions. Most relate to either affordability or socio-cultural preferences and not reduced car dependency, walking or cycling. Assuming these reasons are valid, it is likely that many places are experiencing a clustering of minorities who might otherwise choose to live in a more walkable or bikeable environment but are unable to do so. They want the culture and accessibility of the central city but not the expense.

Where are these individuals going? In some places, such as in southeastern San Francisco, East Oakland and North Richmond, there has been rapid growth in the concentration of minorities—particularly in the Black population. Maps produced using Census Neighborhood Change Database (NCDB) data illustrate that these neighborhoods have grown to be over 60 percent Black (GeoLytics, 2010).

In San Francisco's Ingleside and Bayview neighborhoods, even with affordable public housing projects, many individuals I talked to expressed

Table 8.1: Snapshot of reasons described for housing choice

Reasons cited by minorities concentration in less walkable areas

---

Affordability / Price-related
- Lower price / was more affordable
- Desire to be in a larger home / more space
- Being 'forced out' of walkable areas or 'stuck in' or staying in less walkable areas
- Staying in place as locations become less walkable

Individual / Social / Cultural Preferences
- Desire for less crime and a safer environment
- Space for kids and schools
- Perception of less walkable places as the American dream (to own a car and not walk as a source of pride)
- Tendency to stay near their family or friends, especially for recent immigrants
- Looking for diversity or a multicultural environment

Figure 8.2: Concentrated Black neighborhoods that are less walkable and bikeable in San Francisco

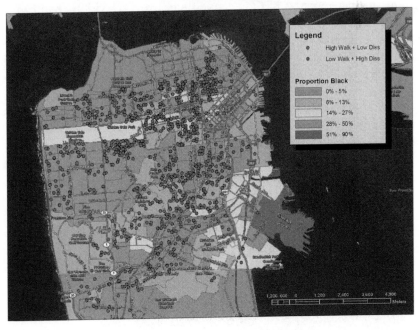

pressure from increased prices and were facing (or had faced) decisions to relocate based on price. Residents described these places as being filled with minorities in the past. One neighbor described the southern portion of San Francisco as "almost an (entirely) Black community in the 1960s" where "people could afford homes and raise a family." He claimed this was based on the collective culture, price and preferences, such as proximity to the ocean.

Another resident, who characterized his current neighbors as primarily Asian, spoke about how his "people" (his friends) were "forced" to move to Brentwood, Suisun City and Vallejo primarily because of the cost of living. In order to emphasize how expensive it was to live in San Francisco, he noted that his house that cost $30,000 to $50,000 years ago now costs $600,000 to $800,000. He stated that he had stayed in the neighborhood because he loved the cool weather, proximity to the beach and his church, and that the majority of Black individuals had stayed for similar reasons, but that this number was dwindling. He claimed that the Black community specifically could not afford the neighborhood, saying:

> "San Francisco is expensive to live in, especially if you want to own a house … My kids are grown and gone (because of the price). When I came it was easy to buy a house, but that has changed. It's not half as expensive (now) as it was two years ago but it is still not achievable for most normal folks (to buy a house)." (Interview)

Other former residents of the neighborhood we were visiting confirmed that they had moved away because of housing affordability, cashing out for other locations with presumably less access to walkable amenities. Some expressed that they had lived and owned their homes in the neighborhood for generations, walking everywhere, but then chose to relocate elsewhere because the community is unaffordable to minorities.

This choice is driven by factors such as "more space," living near like-minded individuals, desire for a yard, the idea of or pride in owning a car and a single-family home. Many of those interviewed loved the ideas that kids could "walk to school" and that you could "walk to church" or to the barbershop but these were not significant enough to keep them from purchasing further out—they could always drive in for these activities.

Another Black individual said that, in addition to lower prices and less crime, living in a more suburban location and owning a house and car was associated with status, saying:

> "… the American dream is definitely to own a car, not to walk … there is some level of pride or accomplishment with owning a car." (Interview)

Once this happens, a minority male described how the trend continues based on individual desires to live near like people, and the concentration effect is compounded.

> "… (they) tend to stay near their family or friends, especially in the case of recent immigration. Usually a city is too large and full of many new

obstacles: language, cultural, economic, etc. and families will select areas near family and good friends. The culture lends itself to spending lots of time with family and you see many extended families living within the same block (if not the same house) as their relatives." (Interview)

That said, as one mixed-race interviewee described, this trend of migration is not limited to the suburbs. It also happens when individuals move to concentrated areas in the urban core that have not had investment (in streets, sidewalks, lights, parks, etc) such as the Bayview. These are places that have very "crappy development rules." She felt that minorities tended:

> "... to have lower income jobs, forcing them to live in lower-income housing in also a lower-income neighborhood. Few city dollars are allocated to these areas for maintaining streets, sidewalks, parks and playgrounds. Furthermore, higher crime rates in these neighborhoods (due to financial disparities, lower education, opportunities and so forth.) dissuade people from wanting to be outdoors at all—especially parents with kids. Businesses such as restaurants, grocery stores, coffee shops, boutique shops (that thrive on walkability) also do not locate in these areas because inhabitants don't have the disposable income to support a local business. Also, as gas prices increase and US cities start to face the inevitable reality that seems so obvious when you look at European nations, that it is expensive to live in the suburbs and transportation costs actually aren't completely inelastic, more people move from the suburbs into the city, raising the prices of inner city living and also displacing lower income neighborhoods into less convenient areas of town." (Interview)

For example, Oakland and Richmond have drawn in individuals moving to and concentrating in less-walkable areas that are experiencing disinvestment, and when questioned, many individuals expressed frustration that they could not achieve the American dream.[2] When interviewed, they talk about why they lived in a less walkable area in a manner that was dismissive of price—as if they were resigned to the harsh reality they had no choice at all to stay in more walkable and bikeable areas. They would say:

"We moved here because ... (It's) just the best, cheapest place we could find."
"I feel like it's overpriced and you get very little for what you pay for."
"It was not necessarily affordable for us."
"We looked down there, but the homes were too expensive for us."

A few young minorities relayed that having children shaped their housing choice, saying things such as: "We had a daughter; we moved because of that"

Figure 8.3: Concentrated Black neighborhoods that are less walkable and bikeable in Oakland and Richmond

and "We were interested in the schools." In Richmond, while almost all said they looked for diversity or a multi-cultural environment in housing, most said they had not wanted to move to there and did it because they had to.

Of all the people I talked to in my research, only one said that staying close to friends ("buddies") was a primary motivator in how they chose their housing. The overwhelming majority felt price was the primary factor, that they might have selected otherwise if they had the choice. Many felt the concentrated areas that they had ended up in were less diverse than where they had been before, but that there was little reason to stay in more walkable or bikeable urban neighborhoods because more suburban areas were "cheaper."

This is consistent with discussions with Black residents in more walkable areas and was reflected by interviewees who would say things such as: "I wish I could afford more (in order) to live in the city, but what I have works"; "My housing choice had tradeoffs and here (in a less walkable location) I could get more for less, have a garden and some land"; "If money were no object ... we would live somewhere else."

Among other factors, the Black individuals I interviewed talked about a "need for space" and "yard." They spoke about being able to buy more than they could get elsewhere in terms of square feet. This implied that walking or cycling in such locations was less important than space (square footage) and that, from a health-resource standpoint, the most walkable or bikeable neighborhood was not available in locations where they had the financial ability to move. One woman said:

> "We went to look to buy a house. Well, little, raggedy, 2-bedroom, 1-bath, I-wouldn't-live-in-it kind of houses, were like $600,000 or $700,000 dollars. And I thought, you people are crazy! And so we moved to where we live now in Richmond up by Hilltop Mall. And we have a nice big house with a yard and a garden ..." (Interview)

One individual I spoke to talked about the disconnect between transportation, housing and schools, and how cars helped make up the differences in choosing a less walkable and bikeable neighborhood over a more highly connected neighborhood where one did not have to drive all the time. Another reinforced this experience, saying that it was important that they could get a bigger house in Richmond, even though they could not walk or bike to get goods and services. They related that driving made up the difference—that at least you could drive to areas that were "a little greener" or "a little easier for kids to walk to school." These were all trips that had been made previously by walking. Yes, "The transportation maybe could be a little better for the school kids ..." but the car made up the difference.

In East Oakland, at a fairly walkable location, I interviewed one person who noted "a surprising amount of traffic." He observed that it was hard to get to services because they were spread out in pockets. He felt that he would walk if there were more amenities and local services and described the idea of "deserts"—where there were places that might be connected by the street network but lacked amenities that would serve local residents. He said there was a racial difference in the people living there, especially when compared to more "upscale" locations "with amenities" that people could walk or bike to.

Yet there is a price premium with these walkable and bikeable locations— and these prices are compounded by the lack of supply and housing production—external factors that further complicate the choices people have in walkable and bikeable locations.

Combined with the legacy of historic discriminatory practices, this has created a situation where social and racial barriers can become magnified and there is no access to healthy, green locations where people can commute in carbon-free ways.[3] The trend: as parts of central cities are abandoned, with minorities unable to afford housing or choosing not to live there, they are relegated to more car-dependent suburban locations. Those who do remain in central cities are squeezed into areas that are less walkable and bikeable because of the increase in prices based on the sales from those who have left, but also because of chronic underproduction of housing that has kept the supply far below demand in many large cities across the US.

Why does this matter? What can we do about it?

Why does this dialogue on housing choice matter in a book about reinventing streets? Because the street is about more than just the pavement or things that drive, roll or tread on it. It is about the people, community and neighborhood that shape it. And as neighborhoods go, many times so do streets. In San Francisco, as the neighborhood has become less minority concentrated, many of the cultural institutions patronized by friends and family have started to dry up. As people have chosen to leave and businesses have closed or changed hands, the community has started to fracture. Neighborhoods have become more homogenous and issues between them more divisive—with differences of opinion on issues ranging from traffic and growth controls to crime and school funding.

One person I talked to framed this trend toward division in terms of "community loss," yearning for things to be how they were 50 or 60 years ago and complaining because so many friends of his friends had moved.

> "Back in the 1950s it was integrated; it was everybody. It wasn't like black, white, this, that or the other. Every class (at the local school)

had Asian, Black and White. It was very diversified. It was fun. It was clean." (Interview)

Others articulate that neighborhood visions made them the target of displacement from more affluent individuals seeking to redevelop their communities. They expressed latent anger that they were not able to live in the neighborhood where they had grown up—in the walkable and bikeable urban core. They made references to how other races now dominated what they had once considered their own social enclave—sometimes targeting other immigrant or ethnic groups as the culprits. They would say things such as:

"Many Chinese are coming from communist China and are used to paying nothing. Everything is free, you don't pay anything; no gratuity. So it is part of the mentality ... In the neighborhoods, when the houses go up for sale, you will see one Asian family that wants to buy that house and they buy in cash (and) put all their money together ... (or) get a loan under the table ... and they buy a house, and everybody lives there ... and they do that until they own every house on the block ... Blacks (won't do that) ... we're too proud." (Interview)

This complex view of race, income tension and being forced out is made more acute by recent increases in race-related crimes, which have been on the rise since 2010. (Smith, 2021; Zhang, Zhang and Benton, 2021). There have been numerous reports of Black-on-Asian crime, something that gives credence to the idea of urban balkanization and the formation of ethnoburbs. This has been the trend in many European cities as well, with cultural enclaves forming on the fringes of the urban core. It is a vicious cycle when gentrification occurs in poor urban neighborhoods that get improved through private investment, forcing a move to a new less-walkable, ex-urban, suburban neighborhood which will be subsequently gentrified.

What can be done to stop this cycle? I talked to numerous real estate professionals, urban planners and designers to get their take. Every one of them agreed that, generally, more walkable and bikeable neighborhoods were important even if they were not a top priority in housing purchases. They point the finger squarely at the issues of housing affordability and price—since the most desirable housing seems to be becoming less achievable for many minorities and those with less money or lending capacity.

From the real estate point of view, the solutions articulated are simple. They include nuts and bolts kind of urban planning, such as being creative with planning codes and housing tools and providing more financial tools for buyers and developers.

Almost all of the real estate professionals I spoke to recognized that the low supply of walkable and bikeable urban housing was driving gentrification and increases in housing price. One said simply, "a neighborhood 'works better' (but costs more) if you can walk in it." Some claimed that this was tied to retirees increasingly wanting to move to the urban core where they would not be as auto-reliant. One agent unable to live in the city of San Francisco complained that price was the ultimate driver for clustering, saying:

> "I would love to live in the city and be able to walk and bike everywhere … but it's too expensive … The city is awesome, I love it. It's just too expensive." (Interview)

A planner echoed these feelings about price and connected this to clustering when she said:

> "I believe that walkability increases property values significantly. This would keep out groups that tend to have lower incomes like minorities." (Interview)

A real estate broker who deals with property transactions across the San Francisco Bay Area added general context to this and why people pay more for walkability saying:

> "Of course it factors into real estate decisions. I wouldn't say it is the top deciding factor but it does weigh heavily on younger and older buyers. In many cases I'd say these buyers are more affluent, so price and price per square foot is no object; and we know that here in the Bay Area, many times you pay a premium for the hip urban homes. So they are getting a little less home? No matter. I think they see the city as an extension of their home." (Interview)

The realtor went on to talk about how he has seen fewer transactions lately as a result of the great recession of the late 2000s and how very few of these have been middle- or lower-income individuals. He didn't think it was a race issue but more a class issue, or "people who have money." He attributed part of the slowdown to not only the changing rules of the banking industry but also the *continued lack of available units* in the most desirable (and walkable) locations.

His assertion that one would pay a premium for walkability is consistent with an analysis of 94,000 real estate transactions in 15 major US markets showing walkability as directly linked to higher home values (Cortright, 2009). A one-point increase in walkability index was associated with $700 to $3,000 increased housing value. As one professional put it:

"Even in a turbulent economy, we know that walkability adds value to residential property just as additional square footage, bedrooms, bathrooms, and other amenities do. It's clear that consumers assign a tangible value to the convenience factor of living in more walkable places with access to a variety of destinations." (Interview)

Another added to this idea, saying that, while price may be dictating location decisions, at lot of places are becoming less and less walkable and bikeable. They have fewer places to go:

"... other than (to) liquor stores and in some cases the streetscape has not been invested in. There aren't good sidewalks, crossings, etc., and that is coupled with the crime associated with generational poverty." (Interview)

Although some claimed that they had not seen conclusive data on this issue, most planners agreed that affordability in walkable neighborhoods and disinvestment in locations that would otherwise be walkable were "emerging if not already an issue." As one urban planner said, cost and distance are two primary issues:

"If you could afford to design a walkable life for yourself (and to) map out wherever the nail salon should go, the grocery store go, and where your neighbors and friends would be ... it might not be too different from the suburbs, it just wouldn't be so far away ... and this stuff would really need to be two hundred yards away or five hundred yards away (to encourage walking). It can't be any more than that, or it's not just somewhere to dash down to (in order to) get your milk. It can't be like walking a mile to the grocery store." (Interview)

Similarly, others were forgiving to early suburbs and development tracts which they felt turned out well. Houses were small and close together, and, as one developer interviewed said, they:

"... were actually quite congenial places as opposed to the current, mass-produced, late dinosaur stage suburban tract model." (Interview)

Most professionals connected issues with the affordability of the walkable community to three key factors: restrictive zoning and planning codes, problems with housing models and delivery and limited financial tools for buyers and developers.

When talking about zoning, one academic focused on restrictive building codes as the single most onerous factor in the affordability of walkable urban housing units. In his opinion, the number of units was far too low and zoning code far too restrictive to encourage more units and therefore impact the housing market. One example cited was the limitations of use on single-room occupancy-zoned units in many cities. He noted that, while this posed a challenge to unit creation, some creative developers in San Francisco and New York were using the concept of the "micro-unit" condominiums to overcome this and work around zoning restrictions.

Another planner related the issue of codes to the topic of density, saying:

> "The single biggest difference (around the world) that you see everywhere is density. Even in small towns out in green fields the housing is all five stories high and all in apartment blocks with mixed-use below ... (Even in) the absolute cookie cutter standard of good housing ... is this basic density assumption—which means there's almost always some transit and always something to walk to. And so you get the bars on the street with the cafes, but you also get the grocery stores and smaller retail. There are big grocery stores, but there are just a lot more small stores because they serve the (dense) apartment building that they're located in." (Interview)

On the topic of providing dense affordable housing, a project manager for the US Department of Housing and Urban Development (HUD) said:

> "True federal public housing has not and is not being built ... you have people using various tax credits, but this provides a housing type that doesn't meet the true need." (Interview)

He went on to explain that many "grants" are used more as "loans" to secure more financing. This funding is only a small component of what makes a project work, yet it can restrict the size or type of housing unit produced. This funding-based restriction can exasperate the balance between rental vs. owned and whether or not the units can be accessible to those in the workforce who many need "middle income" housing but may not qualify for traditional affordable units. In this light, public housing or dedicated affordable units can create unit types or unit mixes that do not match the market. Communities can become saturated with lower-income rentals with no opportunity for ownership and only limited thought given to the long-term neighborhood fabric.

Some individuals I talked to lamented how government programs can cause projects to become more focused on green building technology than on site-related or walkability issues. While they may not be wholly a bad thing, as the HUD project manager described, the federal government:

"... has more interest on the energy performance than it does on where you eat or what you can walk to." (Interview)

A board member for a non-profit housing provider confirmed this, stating that since federal projects develop slowly the provider has worked to find other creative ways to build affordable housing. The organization has tried to develop many projects that turned out not to be financially viable because of the expense, noting that "just assembling parcels as an affordable housing project does not always work even if the parcel or block is donated." In the board member's opinion, the resulting complications in finance have changed the role of being affordable housing providers to that of a profit-based housing developer.

Again, while this is perhaps not a bad thing itself, it underscores some of the tension in providing affordable inclusive, and complete-street-supportive housing. And these are tensions that have only become more acute as homelessness and the fragility of shelter has increased in our large cities—only to be exasperated by market shocks and recessions. It also underscores the notion that we may need to change or kill off more than just street design to make our cities more walkable and bikeable. We will come back to this as well as the key ideas of reinventing zoning, housing delivery and financial tools—all places where I have some ideas. But before we do, there is an elephant in the room. We have not talked about decisions and behavior, and clearly that's an oversight. So, let's jump there now.

9

Beyond Streets:
Integrating Behavior

> Habit is habit, and not to be flung out of the window by any man, but coaxed down-stairs a step at a time.
>
> Nothing so needs reforming as other people's habits. (Mark Twain, 1894, p 44, 130)

Economic choices are what guide many of our urban experiences. As Mark Twain described, many of the habits that we have that need "reforming" need "coaxing" and those push and pull forces are the basic forces of supply and demand that many of us learn about in introductory economics courses. I sometimes describe those economic choices to my students as being something akin to "the Force" from the *Star Wars* movies—they are all around us and bind the galaxy together. Almost everything we do can be tied to an economic decision—ranging from where you purchase a house, work or do your shopping to how you choose to travel.

Traditionally, city planners and policymakers have framed these choices based on economic concepts from classic texts such as *The Wealth of Nations* by Adam Smith (1776). These kinds of books assume that we, as individuals, make rational choices that suit our own self-interests, engage in markets to balance scarcity issues related to supply and demand and that governments sometimes need to step in to make markets better. (Envision how your local farmer's market creates a place for people to sell vegetables.) While that is a bit of a simplification, what an economist might say would be more candid: simple travel choices are damn complicated.

Think of the choices you make every day and the trade-offs for traveling via walking and biking. For example, have you ever driven less than a mile for an errand even though you could have done it more quickly cycling? Likewise, have you ever idled your car and waited for a parking space (or continued hunting for a parking space in a full garage) when there are parking spaces just a short walking distance away?

I am always surprised when I catch myself behaving these ways because they illustrate that simply creating a marketplace for transportation is not enough. Our decisions are not the most rational when we travel. We are faced with many choices that influence both our health and the environment, and as a result they overshadow what traditional rational economic approaches can explain (Batty, 2007). Travel decisions present wicked problems in that most of us do not have all the information we need to make a good decision (Rittel and Webber, 1973), or may not be able to disentangle ideas or issues in our minds clearly enough to do the "right" thing (Batty and Torrens, 2001; Ariely, 2008; Palermo and Ponzini, 2010).

Essentially, we all face this kind of decision-making trouble. We have bias and conflicting ideas in our heads that make it hard to make decisions and we frame our choices and perceptions on our own experiences. Given this, it is important to emphasize the difficulty travel choices present to many people. In this context, I would argue that simply building better, safer, more shared and more awesome streets will not result in people choosing to get out of cars.

Getting people to choose to walk or bike is not an infrastructure decision—it is one that involves behavior. I realize that if you're reading this book, you may think that building bike lanes or sidewalks is the single most important thing cities can do to make travel more sustainable, but I think it starts with psychology and behavior. If you are skeptical, that's fair, but I would challenge you to take a step back and empathize. Put yourself in someone else's shoes who may have more complicated travel choices. Do you think that your own "bicycle bias" or walking behavior may predispose you to think that the choice not to drive is easier than it really is for some people?

Consider some of the people you heard from in the last few chapters; people who may be reading this book. If you are a member of a historically disadvantaged community, living in a distant suburb and have to be up at an ungodly hour to be at your job at the downtown hair salon, do you have the luxury to bike 15 minutes to the not-so-convenient transit? Or do you just get in the car and drive the whole way? Also consider your own commute. You may live in a highly connected, dense urban environment and have access to a bicycle or a good pair of walking shoes but don't necessarily have the time to walk 20 blocks to work every day.

Think about those who may rely on a service-oriented job at a restaurant or grocery store. Do you risk losing your job for being late when the bus didn't arrive on time? Do you risk exposure to sickness on a crowded train, for example during the COVID-19 pandemic? Likewise, consider that you may need to supplement your income by driving for Uber or Lyft. Why would you not drive given that you could make money with your car before and after your workday?

Some of you reading may have some of these obstacles in your life, and I think it is important to recognize that it is hard to see the health or financial benefits of engaging in a physically active commuting when you are dealing with other life pressures. In many ways, we all deal with complicated travel choices in our lives. I know that I find myself grappling with them all the time with my two boys. I'm usually the one who takes them to school and every morning it is a rush. When we're running late and I'm hurrying to get their lunches packed, clothes laid out, plan dinner, while somehow finding time get dressed myself, it can be easy to decide to forgo the half-mile walk to school and jump in the car. I know it is best for me and the kids to walk but the complications become insurmountable and the car is so easy.

These are the kinds of small choices that make travel behavior so complicated. Our lives become complex so we choose simplicity. But this is not something unique to busy people. We all make small choices that either enable or keep us from walking or cycling—just having a safely designed place to walk or bike alone is not a "silver bullet" to getting us to move away from driving (Forsyth et al., 2008; Riggs, 2014a). And ultimately that's why I believe it is important to focus on behavior and decisions at the same time that we are reimagining street design.

In this chapter, I will talk about some experiments that I have run on travel behavior and psychology. These relate to how we can rethink travel decisions and the things that cities can do to change how people think about their trips—what transportation planners usually call transportation demand management or TDM programs. While I will focus on this a bit later in this chapter, first, it is important to understand the basic economics of travel decisions. Then we will dive a bit deeper into how we can reshuffle travel decisions in our own lives and environments.

A basic introduction to travel choice and economics

In thinking about travel decisions, it is not wrong to consider them as market-based choices. Travelers face a set of options that we academics sometimes refer to as a "choice set." This suite of choices frame the "market" for your individual travel. You may live near a bus stop and own a car but live over five miles from where you work. So, in this scenario you might be disinclined to travel via walking or biking based on how far away your job is. But all things considered, your clear choice set is between transit and your car.

Moreover, people think at the margins, meaning that they think about the differences and the tradeoffs between one thing and another. For example, your car might be the simpler decision. You could get in it, turn the key and take a quick trip to your place of employment, rather than walking a quarter mile to the bus stop, taking a rather long bus ride and then walking to your place of employment. The economic trade off in this case is time, but there are other forces at play and externalities that are not visible here to you, being the consumer and key decision maker. These could include the cost of fuel and environmental impact of driving. When one is behind the wheel, already full of fuel and driving somewhere, it becomes harder to think that every mile is an expenditure, not just of time but of gasoline and related emissions. It is an even greater cognitive stretch for the same individual to consider the social benefit they might experience had they taken the bus, or the health benefit from the walk to the bus stop.

This is a typical scenario in which traditional economic theory breaks down. We expect rationality based on the way we are taught to think about economics. But since all of the information to make a decision is not clear or available, it becomes difficult to decide the best option. In all likelihood, you might choose something slightly irrational when you considered the full costs of your trips—such as when I drive my kids a few blocks to school. This kind of decision would be consistent with the work of my colleague Dan Ariely (2008) from Duke University, who refers to them as "predictably irrational." Rather than consider the full cost of driving and ancillary benefits of taking transit, choice is limited by the clarity of the information presented.

A broad swath of research now shows that we humans are not as good at decision making as we give ourselves credit for. Instead, we are "subjectively probabilistic," and many times use rules of thumb and relationships to guide complex decisions rather than actual data (Tversky and Kahneman, 1992, 1973). In essence, we are selective about the data we see and we see and prioritize the choices that we want to see.

But what if planners and government agencies could step in and correct these decisions? Another basic principle of economics is that markets are imperfect and sometimes intervention by the government is required. In the case of transportation, this is an opportunity for experts to intervene and make choices more equal or visible to people when they are facing travel tradeoffs. Here, I want to emphasize two words that transportation planners think a lot about in doing TDM: price and incentives.

Price, incentives and monetary vs. social norms

Why price and incentives? Research shows that transportation choices are tied to both of these factors from a monetary as well as a social standpoint (Brock and Durlauf, 2003; Dugundji and Walker, 2005; Marchal and Nagel, 2005). Yet these aspects of travel, along with the incentives and competition or gamification of travel, are often overlooked by urban designers and civil engineers designing streets. But planners know that policies and incentives can encourage or deter driving and influence auto ownership (Shoup, 2005; Weinberger et al., 2008; Guo, 2013). For example, pricing is one of the key factors that either hides or helps people to understand the social and environmental costs of driving (Willson and Shoup, 1990; Shoup, 1997, 2005; Deakin, 2001).

Price is a standard tool for managing travel habits and behavior. Examples include pricing things such as gas through taxes, the pricing of low-occupancy vehicles or prioritization of high-occupancy policy, the geo-spatial congestion zones or cordons and, of course, parking fees. For example, keeping parking rates low or requiring a fee for parking can encourage increased driving and GHG emissions (Ewing and Cervero, 2001). Conversely, if parking prices can be bundled with incentives such as free transit passes or cash back to encourage alternatives to auto travel ("cash-out" programs), driving can go down (Bianco, 2000; Hamilton, 2008). This is where the term TDM comes from and I love it because it really focuses on the idea of creative incentives to change the way people think about their trips.

In general, these incentives can be financial or social. There have been many successful financial programs, particularly those at large employers (Ferguson, 2000), yet some work suggests that social factors play an equal or paramount role to fiscal levers (Jariyasunant et al., 2012, 2015; Riggs and Kuo, 2015). Other work suggests that social nudge programs can be highly effective in facilitating travel changes but it also details that mixing social and financial nudges can pose problems (Jariyasunant et al., 2012; Riggs, 2017c).

Most notably, many incentive programs help to break down redefined mental models (also called heuristics) related to availability and fearing loss (loss aversion) and can augment decision-making (Kahneman et al., 1991). Moreover, work in the field of marketing shows that mixing financial norms (such as parking price) with social norms (such as a free bus pass as an incentive) can cause confusion so that individuals default to price and disregard the social incentive (Heyman and Ariely, 2004; Amir et al., 2005; Ariely, 2008).

Enter behavioral economics

So, how does this relate to ending the traditional idea of a road? In my mind, it means that we also need to recognize and begin to experiment with all the factors that shape behavior and perception. To begin exploring this, I will discuss three recent experiments I ran that address some of these issues. All three occurred in San Luis Obispo where I used to be a professor, so let me provide some context.

The city of San Luis Obispo has roughly 50,000 people; it was already well-positioned in facilitating sustainable travel with some mature transportation programs, decent street infrastructure to support walking and biking and a Mediterranean climate. The city received a Gold Award from the League of American Bicyclists (Bowles et al., 2006), and the county works hard to give attention and priority to the cycling community. The city, other local agencies and cycling advocates regularly host workshops, lessons, school assemblies and community events to continue to promote cycling as a form of recreation and transportation. For example, a local non-profit organization (Bike SLO), headquartered in San Luis Obispo, is offering bike-oriented education and outreach for residents and visitors. Furthermore, the city has a bicycle club. The San Luis Obispo Bicycle Club was founded in 1971 and promotes safe and legal riding for recreation and transportation in the city. All of these factors result in a ready ecosystem for cycling.

It is also worth noting that the community has a large university where a lot of people drive to work. California Polytechnic State University (Cal Poly) is the largest employer in the region and occupies a major share of the land near the center of town. As such, it could be likened to either a distinct neighborhood, development or a corporate campus within a bigger city with unique transportation needs. The campus a is vibrant place of intellectual exchange and innovation, but it also generates a lot of trips. These trips, particularly those that are made in cars, pose land use, sustainability and cost challenges, especially as the campus is an urban environment with space and budget constraints. For example, what happens to surface parking when there is a need for new things such as offices and student housing? What would happen as the number of jobs on the campus increases and traffic grows beyond the road infrastructure?

These are the kind of housing and traffic challenges that most urban campuses deal with. They present a need to experiment with alternative strategies and programs to get people out of cars. The monthly permit system at these institutions might be priced below market rate, as it was at Cal Poly, and since prices are low, demand is high. This encourages behavior such as "hunting" or "circling" for a parking space or parking in residential neighborhoods, something planners refer to as spillover. This was I started testing at Cal Poly. I wanted to explore new transportation programs that employers and institutions could implement to address complicated travel issues. I felt the campus provided a great opportunity for new, creative transportation ideas, so I began to run three experiments.

Experiment 1

In the first experiment, I wanted to compare how equal groups would respond to different incentives—something we academics call a planned comparison experimental design. As opposed to a stated preference-choice experiment that is normally used in travel studies (where all survey respondents are given the same options and asked to state how they might behave or travel), a planned contrast experiment evaluates how similarly assigned (equal) cohorts respond to different scenarios or incentives. Economists would call this a single-shot market option.

In this sense, I ran a survey that offered each person who drove one of four different incentives to bike, walk or take transit instead. The incentives were either financial or social (or a combination of both) and were randomly assigned. They included: (1) a $5 monetary incentive; (2) a gift of a free cup of coffee or juice; (3) a $2 free cup of coffee or juice (note the specified value of $2 which represents a monetized gift); and (4) a social request not to drive to help the environment (which was framed as a socially altruistic option). With these incentives, we were trying to tap into a previously identified environmental ethos or bias, which is why we asked participants to do the socially acceptable thing and help benefit the environment by not driving.

The survey revealed that people on our campus responded to social requests at a higher rate than to monetary incentives to bike or walk, a factor that may be unique to the socially and environmentally conscious nature of many college campuses, yet is highly significant. The idea of doing something good for the environment was successful 39 percent of the time as opposed to only 30 percent when the experiment tried to give people money not to drive. Put in an external context, social incentives can be effective at changing behavior. We showed that money is not everything.

However, that was not the most interesting finding. We also showed something else—that in transportation, rational and irrational forces collide. When we mixed financial and social incentives and asked if people would consider a $2 gift of a cup of coffee or juice, they were far less likely to take that offer as opposed to any other alternative. That said, when we offered them the same gift without mentioning the monetary value, they took it.

This paired contrast illustrates that when you mix messages, when you blend gifts and social nudges with financial ones, they become less effective. I usually like to talk about this using the example of how you might be attending a BBQ. Maybe you bring a nice a bottle of wine or case of beer to the host, but then upon arrival you start blabbering about how you got a great deal and it only cost you $10. That is clearly not cool, but it also ruins the value of your nice gesture.

Experiment 2

As a second experiment, I looked at the perceived cycling comfort of different types of cyclists on different kinds of streets. The idea was that people tend to think about their own commutes based, in part, on how they think about or perceive the environment as safe (Collins and Chambers, 2005; Ben-Elia et al., 2008). Generally speaking, adults are less likely to walk or bike in an environment they perceive as unsafe (Akar and Clifton, 2009; Dumbaugh and Rae, 2009). Given my background researching two-way versus one-way streets, I thought that cyclists might feel less safe on some types of roads than they did on others; for example a multi-lane, one-way with fast traffic or a slower two-way, bidirectional street (Chiu et al., 2007; Dowling et al., 2008; Gayah and Daganzo, 2012).

To do this, I used a "moving camera" approach to simulate the experience of riding through various intersections. This simply means I videotaped or recorded the street. This is something that researchers for other studies have used to understand the experience of travel. But to simplify, we filmed the experience of traveling on the street for cyclists and cars, and then we allowed people to watch that film and tell us what they thought about how safe it was. I did this for multiple kinds of streets including a one-way street with multiple lanes and two-way streets with both one lane in both directions as well as multiple lanes.

What happened when people were asked about their perception of safety and speed? I found that perceptions of safety are very important when making decisions to engage in walking or cycling. Consistent with many other studies, the experiment showed that, while dense and accessible environments and predispositions toward cycling are connected to travel decision, individual biases also play a large role. The results showed that how safe a person feels is directly connected to how a road is designed or the roadway typology. Just changing the number of lanes, the width of the visible roadway or the direction of traffic had a big impact on how safe people felt on their bikes.

People were 13 percent more likely to consider (and prefer) a single lane, two-way street than they were a multi-lane, one-way street (Riggs, 2019). They were 30 percent more likely to think a single lane, two-way street was safe than they were a multi-lane, two-way street. While these stats may sound pithy, the basic principle is simple. Roads that are wider, with more lanes in one direction, tend to be perceived as less safe—something that can keep people off their bikes.

Experiment 3

In a third experiment, I wanted to test if events that bring cyclists together (for example group rides, bike nights, critical mass events, etc.) had an impact on encouraging non-regular cyclists to bike. I wondered if these kinds of events had an impact on encouraging non-regular cyclists to bicycle or if they were just targeting people already comfortable with biking. For six months, my student Amanda Ross and I surveyed participants before and after monthly group cycling events. We asked participants what their motivations were for attending the event and if it reflected their everyday travel.

We found that, on the whole, event participants were already active users of bicycles. The majority (53 percent) were already cycling on a regular basis. The bulk of the rest took transit or walked most of the time. Further analysis confirmed that the majority of participants were not only active cyclists but also highly confident in their cycling abilities. Interviews and focus groups showed that the main reason people participated was social—they wanted to be a part of a community that they identified with.

While this social aspect of cycling may itself be an important goal for events, for me, it brought up a critical thought: did these events focus too much on users who would bike or walk anyway? Since they focused on active cyclists, were they just preaching to the choir? If the goal of transportation programs is to reduce driving, then perhaps events like this should be less important. The users benefiting from them may not be those who need the most help. They may not be the ones struggling with dropping kids off at school or feeling unsafe on a bike.

A new way of thinking about bias and rationality

This kind of critical thought is important to include in a book about rethinking streets and transportation practice. Why? Because we all have bias and find it hard to empathize with people who lead different lives than we do. My regular fear as an academic and consultant is that I have a "bike bias" or default to liking more dense locations, where people have easy access to cycling and walking, and in doing so ignore alternative viewpoints of city design.

Theories of behavioral psychology would suggest that this feeling of familiarity and comfort can lead to cognitive errors and poor decision-making (Tversky and Kahneman, 1973). In essence, you see what you want to see, what is most "available" to you mentally. Without careful attention, one can let their affinity for walking, cycling or transit get in the way of an objective evaluation of a situation—be it a bike program or the way you think about allocating space on the street. It might be possible, therefore, that a passion or excitement for promoting bicycles and streets for walking could get in the way of other factors that need consideration in the way we arrange space and facilitate travel in cities.

For example, the prevailing practice in city programs that try to encourage transit, walking and cycling has been to focus on monetary incentives, but as I discussed previously social factors, perceptions, fears and other non-monetary factors also influence travel choices. These social and cultural values are underemphasized in our current thinking about travel. And as we think about future travel and street design, it is important to focus on them. Perceptions and biases matter in how individuals make travel decisions. Overcoming the biases that shroud our travel decisions is an important step for individuals, as well as city engineers, planners and policy makers.

Recognizing uncertainty is also an important next step. While engineers recognize the complexity of travel behaviors in advanced mode choice models, it is possible that even these models might mislead and overestimate how humans behave. In the realm of theory, there are "dark-side" thinkers who argue that individual behavior is in a constant state of change

(DiClemente and Prochaska, 1998). Theorists such as Flyvbjerg and Yiftachel might suggest that this level of irrationality poses a limit to how certain planners can be about the future (Flyvbjerg, 2001; Yiftachel, 2001, 1998). If this kind of complexity is not recognized, it can lead to overestimating positive versus negative outcomes, for example assuming a street design will result in a vast reduction in auto trips and related emissions.

This kind of overconfidence could be framed by popular idioms such as seeing "the glass half full," and could manifest itself in subtle ways. Take, for example, a graphic illustrating a bird flying. Consider if it might encourage greater levels of walking behavior. The graphic in Figure 9.1 was designed to encourage people to engage in sustainable travel, but one would have to wonder if the person designing it was somewhat blinded by their own way of thinking. Would a potential customer be able to make a direct cognitive relationship between a flock of birds and sustainable commuting?

Behavioral theory would tell us, based on availability bias, that it might be hard for someone to associate a photo of birds with travel and commuting. Individuals tend to frame things based on what they have experienced—and very few individuals have experience flying by their own means!

So, a photo of birds may not have been the best choice to get people thinking about their travel habits, but there are many other ways that citizens, planners, engineers and policy makers respond to the environment around them. Take, for example, the case of a parking meter. When planners impose a 2-hour parking limit as opposed to a 90-minute limit, what does that tell consumers? Research from the business world suggests that people are willing to pay more just by seeing a higher number. Based on this theory, people seeing the number 2 (as in two hours) as opposed 90 minutes for an hour and half would actually be willing to pay more for less time. You would be willing to pay more per minute for your parking just because you saw a higher number.

Figure 9.1: A banner with birds attempting to relay commute information

127

Figure 9.2: Based on numeric anchoring, individuals are more likely to pay more for 90 minutes of parking as opposed to 2 hours

Some of my recent work confirms exactly this (Riggs and Yudowitz, 2021). When you are presented with a number, that number provides a mental "anchor" in your head and you become primed with that information. If I gave bunch of people in a room random numbers and ask what they would willing to pay for various items, the people with the higher numbers would be primed to pay me more for anything because they'd been shown a higher number. They would have been anchored to the idea of a high number. I call these "snap judgements" and they offer an area for planners and policy makers to shape programs that encourage people to put more value on scarce natural and civic resources and make more environmentally sound decisions.

Likewise, when presented with humorous information about going bald or killing unicorns if you violate parking rules, you may not care what the numbers say because of the inherent social norm. If you were presented with a sandwich board that relayed this information, you might ignore the price information and "anchor" to (and likely abide by) the social norm. While it may sound funny to create a non-monetary (and funny) social contract, these kinds of engagements activate deeper psychological motivations that are harder to break. Many times we do things because there are personal, cultural or collective expectations, and as a result it is just mentally and emotionally harder to violate a social contract or agreement.

Just consider the frenzy when Starbucks announced its viral Unicorn Frappuccino drink in 2017—it sold through the roof despite tasking like "a naughty child's birthday party" (Maynard, 2017). How many people just purchased the drink out of curiosity or because everyone was doing it? It

Figure 9.3: Parking messaging in Portland, OR

Source: Igarta (2017a); used and modified with permission

was a cultural experience where engagement was a rite of passage. The same could be said for programs that related to hand washing and staying at home during the early days of COVID-19. There was a social contract where non-conforming behavior was shamed, where we were all "in this together" and "together at home" in order to "bend the curve." In that light, it is not a stretch to say that people make decisions based on other factors than merely financial ones, such as avoiding shame, interest or sheer fun.

Though I don't believe that economic rationality is a thing of the past, more research and integration of behavioral norms and social contracts is needed in transportation. I believe that these ideas offer a new way of looking at travel behavior, decisions and policy. Our rationality is bounded and has limits, many times framed by our cognitive limitations—or, as Tversky would put it, our "natural stupidity" (Sunstein and Thaler, 2016). And, of course, there are many bright teams that are looking into these trends. It may be time for planners to recognize these limitations and rethink the future of how we engage travelers.

We may become bold enough that our employers will take a certain portion of pay away every time someone drives and people will walk or cycle to avoid loss (a form of loss aversion). Conversely, we may see experiments in mild public shaming where employee ID badges are designed to change color based on how someone commuted; it might turn red if you drove and stays white if you biked, walked or took transit. Similar programs have been used for handwashing and mask wearing during pandemics. Perhaps a comparable program would be effective if applied to transport.

Either way, it may be time to look for even more ways to reinvent travel and end roads— and a focus on behavior is a part of that. So, to conclude this chapter with another *Star Wars* reference, in the words of Yoda, there is no try. We must simply take action and "coax" ourselves into new travel behaviors with economic push and pull factors—and we must do so in an era of new vehicles and new streets. Chapter 10 thinks about these new forms of transportation and talks about how we can make great streets and sustainable travel a reality in the future—from design to the behavior—in light of the many innovations and disruptions our transportation systems are experiencing.

A Window into the Future: New Vehicles, New Streets

Neither a wise man nor a brave man lies down on the tracks
of history to wait for the train of the future to run over him.
(Dwight D. Eisenhower, 1952)

From 2012–2013, Google ran an automated driving pilot with its fledging
autonomous driving unit (Krafnic, 2019). The company emailed employees
to see who might want a Lexus that would drive itself to work for them
and were overwhelmed with responses. People wanted to be driven. The 60
best candidates were chosen for the program and given the car that would
drive them to work.

The technology was good. On the freeways, the participants could turn
on "autopilot" and not have to steer the vehicle nor pay as much attention.
It was a hit, but after about a month people were so comfortable that they
were really not paying attention. Instead, they were gaming, sending text
messages, putting on makeup and even sleeping.

Clearly this was a turning point on the "tracks of history." Google
discontinued the program given what was happening in the vehicles. But the
software had clearly surpassed the attentiveness of the humans in the vehicle.
For the first time, a software based on high-level visual recognition and
machine learning had operated in a way that allowed humans to disengage
from the driving act; driving decisions could be made by software.

This new era of disruption and distraction is now fully upon us and I am
both excited and frightened by the possibilities. Since 2013, Google has spun
off its self-driving division as Waymo and an entire industry has developed
around self-driving cars and automation of the driving act. Other companies
with self-driving vehicles include Cruise Automation, Aurora and Tesla.
As of 2019, there were 66 companies developing self-driving technology
in California alone. Most are pursuing what engineers classify as level-4
technology, or the ability to drive in most conditions without assistance.

The idea for level 4 technology comes from levels of classification established by the Society of Automotive Engineers (SAE). Automated activities are classified from 1 to 5, with 1 being the lowest and 5 being the highest. Levels 1 and 2 are some of the most basic forms of automation, for example automatic headlights, windshield wipers or adaptive cruise control. Level 3, or L3, gets to situations where the car can take limited control of itself in certain situations such as highway driving. L4 and L5 are classifications for fully autonomous driving. Level 4 vehicles can be fully autonomous in limited operational situations. Level 5 vehicles, or L5 computerized drivers, can in theory travel anywhere at any time in any condition. However, most companies believe L5 is not realistic, since even humans have limitations on when it is safe to drive—think the mountains during a winter snowstorm. In a June 11, 2019, talk, John Krafcik, CEO of Waymo, said "L5 is a myth."

I believe that automated vehicles have the potential to reshape driving, roads and cities, with next-generation cars improving safety inside and outside the vehicle.[1] According to the World Health Organization, over 1.35 million global deaths are attributed to vehicle crashes each year; about 3,700 people are killed each day (WHO, 2018). Furthermore, the US National Highway Traffic Safety Administration (NHTSA) has estimated that crashes costs US consumers almost $1 billion a day for things such as vehicle damage and medical costs, in addition to increasing congestion delay and emissions (Blincoe et al., 2015). Given this, the potential savings in terms of lives and lost property are immense. Vehicles will drive themselves in most but not all situations and are designed to facilitate other activities in vehicles—for example recreating, sleep and so on. And in this light, I think it may be easier to think about the future of the car in terms of what these companies designing—digital drivers who can know and respond to the environment around them. Companies are not building a future car but rather a future driver.

If I were to summarize how this digital driver generally works, I would start with unique parts in a car. The autonomous driver uses sensors to understand and grasp the world around the car. This is complimented by digital maps to frame and contextualize this world, and onboard computers to process this information. Finally, this "brain" conducts the driving act— actuating calipers, pushing the brakes, making turns and so forth. Research has shown that autonomation may result in great operational efficiencies, both reducing congestion and collisions (Anderson et al., 2014; Fagnant and Kockelman, 2014). As drivers, these robots can and will be able to respond to many of the things around it in a much different and more detailed way than human drivers can (Riggs, 2019).

In this sense, from a design standpoint, automated vehicles do not require special roadways in order to operate. Yet despite all of this, they are not the only thing disrupting the transportation sector. There are other new forms of transportation (be it shuttles, skateboards or scooters) and other experiences that are redefining how we can access travel. What do these all mean to the street? What do we do to plan and engineer roadways for pick and drop off alongside bikes, scooters and pedestrians? How do we design streets so as not to get "run over" by "the train of the future"? Perhaps the general answer is nothing new and everything old.

I sometimes joke that the best things transportation planners and engineers can do is focus on signs, lines and potholes. But that is not really a joke. While that may sound very boring and analog, as if there were some type of smart technology cities should pursue, these issues are very actionable and frame the perspective in this chapter: that we already have many of the tools we need to plan for the future.

I like to think of this in terms of simplification, distilling the idea down to thinking about streets for people, or as my colleague Julian Agyeman would say both humane and human streets (Agyeman et al., 2012). Famed founder of Apple, Steve Jobs frequently barrowed from the statement often attributed to Leonardo De Vinci, "Simplicity is the ultimate sophistication" (Isaacson, 2011). He used the phrase in the early Mac manual and, quite clearly, the ethos of this was seen in much of his work. Jobs harnessed the idea to mastermind products such as the iPod and iPhone so they could be intuitive—usable without the pain of a manual and integrated into daily life tasks.

Future transportation should be the same: humanized and integrated. Using this notion of simplicity, I think planners and engineers can develop an ethic for how to move street design forward in an era of autonomy and other forms of mobility. How do we do this as well as reinforce the way policy makers, planners and citizens simplify aspects of humanity that make cities vibrant—for example eating, shopping, playing and living in relationship to the street?

Perhaps the answer is to focus on its individual components and spatial arrangement first. The vision for a human street is fairly optimistic and not what we see in most of our global cities, let alone what we discussed in the case of San Francisco. I have hope in the new future of humanizing global mobility, as through the safe streets programs we saw emerge through the COVID-19 pandemic, but there are also many challenges with disruptive transport and the future of multi-modal street design. Perhaps the two most acute are the increasing complexity of our transportation choices and travel behavior, and spatially building (or designing) the multi-modal street. We focused on behavior in the Chapter 9 and will continue that focus here, particularly since the way we travel has changed so much since the 2010s. Then we'll pivot to street design, which, along with the travel nudge programs we discussed in prior chapters, can help frame how we behave.

The challenges of new mobility and disruptive transport: the future is complex and multi-modal

Historically, transportation options in the US have been limited and often required driving a private vehicle. Yet our demographic and automotive trends have been leading away from this for a long while. Since 2010, consumers have trended away from using just one mode of travel. While many factors have shaped the "perfect storm" for this trend, including rapid mobile technology growth with the introduction of the iPhone in 2007 and the sudden rush of the ridesharing industry, the trend away from singular modality was likely underway before that as many younger adults migrated to or stayed in urban centers.

Both baby boomers (those born between 1946 and 1964) and millennials (those born between 1981 and 1997) are more likely to live in urban centers than other segments of the population (Myers, 2016). Many are practicing "car-shedding," and are less likely to own a car in the first place (US PIRG, 2014). Across the board, young people move from central cities to suburbs less and are increasingly choosing alternatives to driving—be it traveling via scooter, bike, walking, rideshare or transit. The percentage of US high school students with driver's licenses dropped from 85 percent in 1996 to 73 percent in 2010 (US PIRG, 2014).

Some of my colleagues such as Richard Florida have discussed walkability and bikeability being at the core of the needs of the urban "creative class" (Florida, 2003, 2002). Data tends to support this. The US *National Household Travel Survey* has shown that in recent years young people have decreased their number of miles traveled in a car by 23 percent, while increasing walking trips by 16 percent and transit trips by 27 percent (Davis et al., 2012). Yet to make the story only about biking, walking or transit is wrong. Lately, we have seen an increase in both commute diversity and trip complexity. As a traveler, you may leave your house and walk to a shuttle station, connect to a train and take a scooter for the final leg of your trip. On the other hand, if you plan to go out for drinks on an evening, you may opt to take a rideshare service rather than driving. If you have children, you may drive on some of these segments, dropping kids at school or various extra-curricular activities. The idea of a simple point-to-point trip is not as straightforward as it used to be. We are traveling more and have more complicated commutes but are also finding it easier to access transportation, as if it was like turning on the tap to get a glass of water.

This vision of "mobility-as-running-water" with options that you can choose whenever you want sounds wonderful but we should probably not glamorize it. Our transportation systems are far from integrated or perfect. And increasingly, we see spiking vehicle miles traveled due to these new services—services that can be primarily attributed to the emergence of the ridesharing industry with companies such as Lyft, Scoop, Uber, Waze and many more. Sometimes called transportation network companies (also referred to as TNCs and sometimes as ride sourcing companies) because they use technology to harness a network of riders and source optimized trips, they have the capacity to fill gaps in the transport network.

But they also raise questions because apps are awesome until they aren't. Based on many of the features of these apps, from improved reliability, convenience and safety to the simple idea of dropping a pin and being able to go to that location, cities have seen large increases in congestion and miles traveled (Clewlow and Mishra, 2017; Schaller, 2017). There have also been challenges with establishing policy for this kind of mobility—one of the most acute examples of was "scootergedden" in 2018, when many cities chose to dramatically restrict urban scooter companies that had almost overnight dropped hundreds of scooters in many cities, and there was a ton of debate about who should yield to whom. Does a bike yield to a scooter and a scooter to a pedestrian? Can scooters and pedestrians mix on the sidewalk? Can bikes and scooters coexist in a bike lane?

Further confounding this brave new world, it is important to note that these quasi-shared private companies are both responding to and triggering new travel behaviors. While ridesharing originated based on the desire for cheap, convenient and reliable transportation, given how easy shared services have made it to access reliable and convenient mobility, they may supplant other healthier or sustainable forms of travel. A person who would have otherwise made their trip by biking, walking, transit or taxi may opt for a rideshare service (Shaheen and Chan, 2016; Hall et al., 2018; Gehrke et al., 2019). Conversely, those who might have walked a quarter-mile or a half-mile might lose the health benefit of that walk and jump on an electric scooter. Automated vehicles could exaggerate these behaviors even further by providing the ease and convenience of driving with even less friction. Most researchers speculate that this will lead to more automotive travel and more congestion and, in the absence of widespread emission-less vehicles, more pollution. Yet we know very little about this for now since no truly self-driving vehicles exist.

What we do know is that the future of transportation and mobility-as-a-service is not without costs and that some of those costs will be environmental (Slowik and Kamakaté, 2017). A handful of studies have attempted to model the potential environmental impacts of fully autonomous or semi-autonomous vehicles, and they are cause for concern. In one study, various metrics were analyzed, such as driving efficiency, routing, travel by the underserved, time spent looking for parking, speed of travel and overall travel (Brown et al., 2014). The study found that, without intervention, almost 50 percent more energy would be required to transport people in a shared autonomous environment due to vehicles circling around and hunting for riders—what we call "ghost trips" or "ghost vehicles." The results were the same even with simple assumptions of the way autonomous drivers might rest at times.

That analysis alone warrants the scrutiny of planners, engineers and concerned citizens but it does not even start to address changes in urban development. In a June 2016 article, journalist Christopher Mimms predicted changes in urban growth patterns with more cities sprawling beyond their bounds, resulting in a "new class of exurbs" (Mims, 2016). Author Rebecca Solnit has also argued against autonomous vehicles, saying that they will "poach from transit and kill the walkable city" (Solnit, 2016). Many others have also discussed potential social ills, such as ethical dilemmas and the "penning-in" of pedestrians and cyclists into cordoned areas. While many of these concerns are based on assumptions of behavior and how automakers deploy their cars (for example whether they are owned or shared), they form the basis for policy action that can mitigate impacts now.

Many of my colleagues suggest that we must increase the number of shared vehicles as well as electrifying vehicles as part of this transition (Fulton et al., 2017; Sperling, 2018)—yet I think we also need to transform behavior regarding how we think about travel and cities. As I have mentioned before, our cities might rethink their travel incentive or transportation demand management programs. Cities could also look at urban land use and growth, for example developing parking lots and auto servicing real estate into new uses, implementing suburban growth controls or encouraging dense downtown development. Or perhaps they might prioritize housing on former roadway parcels to help address the housing crunch that many cities face. They might set up standards to ensure transportation accessibility at all socio-economic levels or even establish their own form of autonomous transit.[2]

Most significantly, cities and citizens alike can focus on streets, kill old ideas and norms about what a street can be and then they can humanize them. Just think: an autonomous street could be one that is not only optimized for bicycles and pedestrians but involves allocation of road space for other uses such as gardens, playgrounds and barbecues. They could offer space for small units of housing or simple ways to tear up concrete and create a better way to filter water. While this may be on the verge of a pastoral version of the street, the COVID-19 pandemic taught us it was possible. The streets can be places where people take ownership of their neighborhood streets and claim for life as they sheltered in place—and I believe that the street can do a better job of disappearing into the landscape and likewise the landscape do a better job confronting the street.

My academic colleagues have critiqued me for calling this "landscape urbanism," which is apparently a phrase first used by Charles Waldheim (2012). In theory, the idea to let landscape inform urbanism is good. But it also may have limited applications—the New York High Line being an example. According to my colleagues, the High Line has at times been used for lower-density development that favored preserving the horizon line (that is the horizontal ground plane) over bigger and more dense buildings (building mass). Still, I like the term and the feeling it conveys. The phrase evokes images of people out in the streets claiming them for their kids, or the stories I hear from my friends in Boston of immigrants using streets as open spaces for cultural food production. In my opinion, if we can focus on these threads of humanity first, we can likely best use technology to focus on the existing strengths of our streets and the infrastructure assets that already exist to physically transform streets. And perhaps we can change those simple aspects of form with assistance from technology.

Using technology to rethink the street

We can use technology to rethink design, particularly as we think more and more about cars that can drive themselves (Larco, 2017). As autonomous vehicles get smarter, there are clear opportunities to reshape cities and improve our streets (Lipson and Kurman, 2016). Using a tool that Mike Boswell and I created with our friend Ryder Ross called ReStreet (app. restreet.com), I have been trying to have a community conversation about the future of our streets and to do so using technology (Riggs, 2018).

We have become a mobile phone-based and networked society (Hampton et al., 2011) for personal and business mobility purposes (Evans-Cowley and Kubinski, 2012; Riggs and Gordon, 2015). Since one of the fastest-growing and most invested-in industries in recent years have been networked and data-driven personal travel, why not harness that for good? Many of the ride-sharing companies we have already discussed connect riders with drivers through mobile smartphone apps and facilitate first- and last-mile connections and complement transit—why not harness that (Rassman, 2014; Rayle et al., 2016)? Perhaps mobile technology offers not only an illustration of what the autonomous future might look like but a technological medium to envision safe, slow and sustainable streets.

So, how can we rethink streets using technology? In the case of our work, we created a mobile application designed to help users illustrate a picture of what a future street should look like. We demonstrated this with a participatory street design project in San Luis Obispo, CA. While the idea of using technology platforms to help drive community participation was not new, the infusion of things such as autonomy was (Evans-Cowley and Kubinski, 2012; Riggs and Gordon, 2015). Our goal was to capture data from citizens about what their future vision for that street, space or urban area was. Participants sat at computer terminals and added (or subtracted) whatever they wanted to a set street they saw on the screen—whether it was more bike lanes or less parking. As data were gathered at a public event where our team was available to assist with any issues, the team set up a bank of computers with wifi-enabled hotspots for the public to congregate and submit their "street plans." One it was submitted, we combined this information for all participants and articulated what the public-at-large preferred and how they wanted to allocate transportation resources. We could show what the community preferences were, inform street-section planning, design traffic modeling and simulation and then use the results to help policy makers take action.

While we anticipated that the tool could be used to collect data in a virtual environment, we could not believe how powerful it was in an on-site, community event. The process of having citizens work through design options alongside others was amazing. People talked earnestly with each other about the trade-offs they faced. For example, if you want to have more space dedicated to bicycles then that leaves less space not only for cars but also for pedestrians. They also made decisions based on those discussions and worked through issues with others—considering opinions and alternatives that they may not have thought of otherwise. This idea of breaking down the barriers of self-reinforcement was important to us because we felt that it addressed many of the problems with digital discussions we have in our society. It helped break down the echo-chamber that digital mediums sometimes create.

I have also used ReStreet to study streets for the autonomous future, and I believe that harnessing the benefits of automation could be one of the ways we kill the idea of the street. Streets could see the right-of-way needs for automobiles eroding based on the efficiency of space use and reduced need for wide travel lanes. Related policy decisions could support allocating that physical space to other forms of transportation. The streets we illustrated showed right-of-way needs for cars decreasing because of these trends—an opportunity for traffic calming and lane reductions that support the humanized transportation. If we took this devolution of the roadway further, we could be asking radical questions like: what if we eliminated all the streets in front of homes and converted them to parks or areas for play? What might that mean to the physical, social and spiritual wellness of people who live there? What if we made the lines between the green space and transportation space disappear?

Beyond idealism to logistics and drones

At the same time, this vision of place can't work without a picture of increasingly segmented travel that requires a logistics backbone. Yet planners and engineers rarely consider these factors. While we have tried

Figure 10.1: Street section redesigned for the autonomous future ending with a modest but radical proposal for the future of a street that looks like a garden

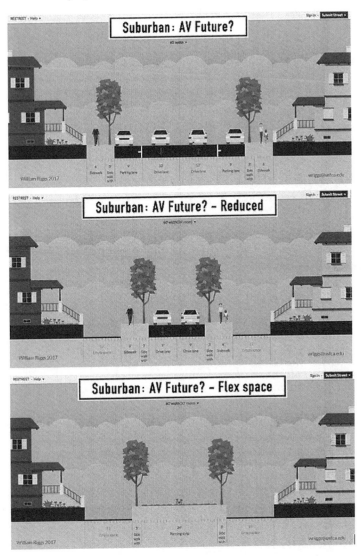

to solve the final link in personal transportation, or what we call the "last mile," with many sharing-economy technologies (Shaheen and Chan, 2016), we don't often think about the less sexy topic of logistics and how a street needs to evolve to accommodate deliveries, whether it is boxes or people. Most logistics companies (for example UPS, FedEx, OnTrac) have found the last mile the least profitable component of their business (Lee and Whang, 2001; Cleophas and Ehmke, 2014; Faccio and Gamberi,

2015). In addition to high personnel costs, contributions to congestion (7 percent of urban traffic) and air pollution, UPS, for example, paid almost $19 million in parking fines to New York City in 2006 (Schrank et al., 2015; Zaleski, 2017).

There have been few attempts to innovate in this area. While UPS has explored cargo bike delivery in select urban markets (Nickelsburg, 2018), most experts speculate that the future of urban deliveries will be a combination of same-day delivery drones and robots and autonomous vehicles (Joerss et al., 2016; Kunze, 2016). While some academics hypothesize that "parcel drop" or "box" facilities may play a role in future local logistics (Punakivi et al., 2001; Dell'Amico and Hadjidimitriou, 2012), requiring customers to come to the drop facility that could be maintained, at least in-part, by crowdsourced delivery services, research by McKinsey & Company finds that there is a strong consumer preference for direct home delivery (Joerss et al., 2016).

Drones may be part of the solution. They are becoming more common and I believe we have to think about them and streets at the same time. Sometimes called Unmanned Aerial Vehicles (UAVs), most drones use a similar kind of technology to automated cars: combination sensors and lidar and mapping that work to assist in obstacle detection and collision avoidance. While there's been little talk about the potential noise implications of these platforms, Amazon intends to launch UAVs to safely get packages to customers in 30 minutes or less, having devised a series of hive-like towers to launch throughout the cities (Atherton, 2017).

Other applications of drones and autonomous robots include public safety and firefighting. In places such as Santa Rosa and Paradise, California drones were used to provide thermal imaging to fight fires in 2019. There are also numerous companies exploring drones that spray water on and in buildings while in flight—essentially becoming the flying firefighters of the future (Margaritoff, 2017; Johnson, 2019). In Greensboro, North Carolina, a drone technology firm is looking for a $5.7 million investment into emergency-response drones (Arcieri, 2015). The company aims to get drones to designated destinations in under 90 seconds while transmitting live video to first responders to give them information about the situation before they arrive and help them better respond. Nelson County, North Dakota, intends to use drones for the protection of US customs and border and would operate eight predator drones to assist local, state and federal law (Bennett, 2011). In Ann Arbor, Michigan, researchers at Michigan Tech want to utilize UAVs for mapping roads as well as providing roadside features, for example identifying potholes and understanding traffic (Wood, 2014). They would use UAVs for a project that assesses and predicts repairs needed on unpaved roads. In Poland, drones are being used to monitor and optimize crop production (Mazur, 2016). In Delhi, India, the local government is considering employing drones to monitor forest areas (Janwalkar, 2015).

These concepts are a lot to digest and extend far beyond what we can cover in a book focused on streets, but they are important things that cities need to consider as we move into the future. Since federal agencies govern the air in most countries, we are in for some controversial discussions about privacy and how air and land connect. But these developments also relate to streets. They may mean that planners and engineers can think even more radically about the future of curbs, pivoting away from the requirements of emergency services. I have been to many public meetings where fire and emergency services access becomes a key limitation to road diets. They become linchpin issues that impede projects that reduce vehicular service in favor of increased bicycle and pedestrian service. Could it be that firefighting drones are an antidote? Perhaps planners and engineers need to think more about appropriate landing areas for vehicles in the future. Likewise, maybe we need to start considering zoning landing pads on the tops of buildings for parcel and goods deliveries or having designated drop-spaces every block for logistics. This is interesting because it would free up traditional loading zones (usually yellow and white) on the street for increased passenger delivery or other uses.

Best practices for future design: becoming the antifragile city

The idea of freeing up street space for alternative uses is an important precursor to how we can rethink streets in the future. Whether or not we are talking about automation, drones, scooters or whatever the next big thing may be, cities can use these disruptions to reconsider how the built environment works for travel. In some cases, it could be that a more sophisticated economic nudge incentive system might encourage people to walk or bike to pick up packages. It might cost more to get a parcel delivered by drone to your doorstep than to a central zone where you could walk to pick it up. Likewise, it could be that smart technology installed within roadways could capture real-time data such as weather conditions or more precise traffic volume. This could lead to better data being delivered to travelers that a walk, bike ride or train trip will take them less time or be safer than getting in a car.

Put simply, as the future unfolds, we have an opportunity to design streets differently. And to achieve this, I believe there should be two guiding principles. First, that future streets are *safe, slow and sustainable*, and second that we can reach this outcome through three simple actions that you may have noticed echoed throughout this book: *thinning lanes, removing parking* and *thinking "shared"*. I have been working with these simple principles for my entire career, and they have recently become crystalized in work that I've done with colleagues at the University of Oregon. Technology offers the opportunity to thin lanes and reduce roadway width. In addition to the reduction of on-street parking, automation will remove the human error in driving and reduce the number of collisions and accidents. With reduced human error, vehicle travel lanes can be reduced and thereby ensure that lane widths can be decreased. Reduced lane widths can provide additional space that could be reused or repurposed for various uses that can be safe, slow, sustainable and shared.

Likewise, technology and mobility shifts can reduce parking demand and city planners and engineers should reduce on-street parking as a result. As automated vehicles become more widely used and available, private vehicle ownership will decrease in favor of shared services—mobility-as-a-service (MaaS) or transportation-as-a-service (TaaS) options—where you can easily and affordably get a reliable and convenient ride from your mobile device. This means that, instead of owning a vehicle, individuals will pay for rides as they are needed. With these services, vehicles could operate 24/7, so instead of sitting parked 95 percent of the time, as most vehicles are, cars can be more efficient and continually serve consumers. As a result, the need for on-street parking will decrease.

Finally, I emphasize again that cities need to think "shared." Automated technology is being designed to know the environment around the vehicle visually—which means that cities can consider integrated and mixed-flow opportunities. They can repurpose the streets with pedestrian facilities, bike lanes, sidewalks and other features that can support sustainable travel behaviors.

These actions and ideas are rooted in idealism, but they are also realistic as we saw during the move to make streets safe for walking and cycling during the COVID-19 pandemic. They are small actions that can be taken incrementally and phased to match the way technology is changing transportation in our cities. I recognize that all cities are different and that these changes may not be all without pain. But I also think that the shocks to cities that urban technology provides can make them better and stronger.

In his book, *Antifragile*, Nassim Nicholas Taleb introduces the idea that,

> Some things benefit from shocks; they thrive and grow when exposed to volatility, randomness, disorder, and stressors and love adventure, risk, and uncertainty. Yet in spite of the ubiquity of the phenomenon, there is no exact word for the exact opposite of fragile. Let us call it antifragile. (Taleb, 2014, p 3)

Applying this concept to transportation, it could be that these changes and stressors to our urban systems will make us stronger and more resilient (Isted, 2014). Maybe we should be encouraging shocks and disruptions to our transportation systems to make them antifragile. And perhaps if we manage our streets with this concept in mind we won't, in the words of Eisenhower, "lay down on the tracks of history."

A Call to Action: Streets as the Heart of the City

When we speak of the "environment", what we really mean is a relationship existing between nature and the society which lives in it. Nature cannot be regarded as something separate from ourselves or as a mere setting in which we live. [...] We are faced not with two separate crises, one environmental and the other social, but rather with one complex crisis which is both social and environmental. (Pope Francis, Laudato Si' On Care for Our Common Home, 2015)

If part of what cities need to do is become antifragile and embrace streets not roads, then how do we do this? We've spent time talking about the history, methods and rationale for a new way to think about roads. In sum, I've argued that we can kill the concept of the road and potentially reinvigorate cities through a new vision for streets. But, particularly in an era where we face an unprecedented need to restore the environmental sanctity and social justice of our cities, I think it is important to consider how we take action. It is import that we do as Pope Francis suggests in his recent encyclical and not separate environment and social challenges.

So how do we do this? In my experience, while plans and visions are important, they are simply words until we (citizens, policy makers, engineers and planners) take unabashed actions, exercise leadership and use management inertia to make change. And there is so much work to do to change that we need to make a start on our streets and in our cities. There are so many streets that are not friendly to walking and biking. There are so many roadways that are hostile to public discourse and transactional exchanges. There are many streets where we need to take action on both environmental and social challenges.

I have spent a large portion of my career focused on trying to reinvigorate a dialogue about how streets can be a catalyst for change. I observed forms of social segregation and environmental marginalization as central cities gentrified and have long argued that walkable places need to become more available to poor and minority populations. In this light, I have always been careful to say that economic development and gentrification are not necessarily the problem, but when uncontrolled they can be a symptom and have negative consequences. Just like how the uneven distribution of vaccines can contribute to the spread of a contagious disease in a pandemic, unbalanced economic growth can lead to urban inequity. And as we have discussed in this book, structural inequities have become a problem in our society. A dialogue about transportation equity could fill an entire book in itself, but the topic relates closely to the dialogue about reinvigorating the street in this book and it serves as a cautionary reminder.

Efforts to reinvent the street must involve diverse communities—communities that have been unheard for a long time—be they the Black, urban poor, or the White, working class. Each should have a voice in reshaping the street in places that have been historically neglected. To borrow words from Pope Francis, these are places that have experienced

> disproportionate and unruly growth ... become unhealthy to live in, not only because of pollution caused by toxic emissions but also as a result of urban chaos, poor transportation, and visual pollution and noise. (Pope Francis, 2015)

Transportation planners and engineers invoke terms such as "complete streets" or "multimodal levels of service" that imply every street should be available to every mode—but, as we've discussed in this book, these terms are insufficient for what we need to do as a society. And words alone do not represent all that we need to do to help our communities reinvent themselves—to solve environmental and social problems and encourage people to "live wisely, to think deeply and to love generously." We need to end the old idea of the road and reimagine what a street can be. And maybe, in doing so, we can save the planet. Maybe we can help cure many of the social ills that exist in Western cities and many of the disparities that plague America.

I know this idea sounds bold, but it is not a stretch to say that democracy lives and dies on our streets. From the marches in the Arab Spring to the calls of the civil rights movement and protest after the 2020 murder of George Floyd, our streets give us voice. In cities around the globe, citizens have taken voice to change the way streets worked for them and taken to streets to reshape cities and countries.

We have talk about places such as San Francisco where, for many years, planners and engineers tried to frame Market Street as a road where cars, bikes, pedestrian, buses and taxis could coexist. This never worked. It was unsafe and did not reflect what citizens actually wanted—a street that was dedicated to bikes and pedestrians. But citizens spoke up and changed this. Now, for certain segments, private auto traffic is not allowed and there are expanded bike lanes and sidewalks. While there is still work to do on recreating the streets of San Francisco, in simplest terms, citizens took action and set in motion a new way of thinking about the street.

Similarly, on the Berkeley campus, when I was the lead transportation planner, students wanted to prioritize green travel so we made the choice that the campus would be for pedestrians. This meant that, while we would not prohibit bikes from going through the campus, we not encourage them to. Pedestrians would be our priority. We tried to prioritize safe, slow and sustainable streets.

These prioritization and implementation discussions are modest gestures but they show that action can be the start. Drawing on examples from urban thinkers ranging from Jane Jacobs to Jan Gehl, cities can use simple actions to invoke change on their streets. For example, in Copenhagen, car-free Sundays have grown to large portions of the city being inaccessible to cars all the time, and in Stockholm many roads in the central city are being reduced and deconstructed to prioritize pedestrians, with only a minor amount of space given to cars (Goodyear, 2015; O'Sullivan, 2017).

In this context, it is not a stretch to argue that our cities can move to new "antifragile" ways of looking at landscape urbanism—to move to a new praxis of streets.

A praxis of streets

Much of this book has been spent developing a history of how we have thought about streets and then arguing for a more radical view of making streets disappear into green space—to make streets safe, slow and sustainable by supporting measures such as lane thinning, removing parking and thinking shared. I have also argued that cities need to become antifragile. This is all quite a mouthful, yet to argue it simply I might just say that we need "a praxis of streets."

The idea of praxis is that of managed or planned action. In framing our street planning activity this way, I believe that our cities can create a series of planned actions that change streets. Cities can engage in actions that kill the street. This is the definition of praxis. And these actions, this praxis, would not only support the notion of livable and sustainable streets, but of places that can support human relationships, community and social equity.

I do not take this notion of action lightly. One of the strongest adult memories I have was when my first son was born. I remember the first night in the hospital. He was laying next to my wife and I and we were so excited. Neither of us could sleep. We just wanted to look at him and listen to him breathe—this little life that we had created. We were also extremely scared and I particularly had a deep sense of urgency that I had to make change—that I had to make the world a better place for him.

This pit in my stomach to make change never really subsided. When my second son was born, I proceeded to call my father and tell him that I had to run political office and, like Ghandi, "be the change." In retrospect, I realize that, not only was I being dramatic, I was forgetting the power that was right in front of me. We can all make change—we can engage in praxis—both in ourselves and in the world around us.

One of the first places we can start with making change is on the streets of our own neighborhoods. We can take ownership of the streets in front of our own houses and businesses. We can make sure that we have the infrastructure to support walking and biking on our own blocks, and that our kids can safely get to school or their friends' houses without getting in a car. We can put planter boxes or bike racks in parking spaces. We can do what my friends in England did when they converted an old telephone booth at the end of their block into a community book share.

We can make changes such as converting directions and reducing drive lanes. Like what happened in Louisville, Kentucky, we can experiment with street conversions and placemaking. When Louisville converted one-way streets in their downtown core to two-way, they were not sure what would happen but they were intentional. The result was safer streets and economic growth but the bigger lesson was the impact of thoughtful action. They took planned actions that experimented with the street.

I believe we can achieve similar successes through a spirit of experimentation that uses three practices (or praxes): harness funding; thinking beyond the street; and embracing tactical concepts and experimenting. Each of these practices embodies a deliberate management strategy, which is an idea we will talk about more later. But for now, let us focus on the specific practices.

Harnessing funding

One of the first questions that I get asked when I talk about changing the design of streets is "how do I pay for all of this?" While the question is important and I do not take this lightly, I usually chuckle because I think the answer is straightforward. It is about priorities.

If you look at some of the top bicycle and pedestrian cities in the country, you find that simple tools such as general fund allocations and sales tax measures are used by most cities to fund bicycle and pedestrian improvements. This means that cities are targeting normal, everyday funds for non-automotive transportation. Sales tax measures are equally as important since they fill in gaps in funding and can be very flexibly spent. They also allow for cities to capture the impacts of non-residents on their city—people who do not live in a town but use the streets.

These traditional methods provide a core, but there are also cities using more futuristic methods that harness emerging technology. For example, the cities of Memphis, Denver and Christchurch (New Zealand) are using private crowdsourcing to fund and implement certain components of their bicycle infrastructure (Anderson, 2013; Andersen, 2014). Other locations are using the concept of the local-business-financed infrastructure (such as parklets) to create appealing and creative streetscape features adjacent to businesses who pay for those features (Loukaitou-Sideris et al., 2012; City of San Francisco, 2013).

London, Singapore, Stockholm and Milan have successfully used cordon pricing systems to reduce vehicle congestion related delay in their financial and urban centers (May et al., 2002; Broaddus, 2014; Liu et al., 2014; Broaddus et al., 2015). For example, the city of London began charging private vehicles this type of fee to enter Central London on weekdays as of 2003 (Litman, 2006).

In London, this pricing strategy has been combined with improvements to transit and safety and access for bicyclists and pedestrians. The result has been reduced congestion, fewer delays in central city roadways during peak hours and a safer roadway environment for non-motorized travelers (Komanoff, 2013). Furthermore, using fees collected from London's pricing system, the city has paid for vastly enhanced bicycle and pedestrian infrastructures. As of 2007, approximately three percent of total net revenues ($4 million of $137 million in revenues) were spent on support for new pedestrian crossings and cycling initiatives (Transport for London, 2008).

These kind of prioritization decisions are also echoed elsewhere. Cities such as Bogotá and Seoul have looked at capturing the value of increased property taxes after the installation of bicycle and pedestrian infrastructures. Capturing this "value" has been shown to be very significant with transit but there has been very little work that showed the same for bike and pedestrian infrastructure (Kang and Cervero, 2009; Munoz-Raskin, 2010). Yet research does allude to a potential price premium for bicycle and pedestrian infrastructure project investments, so this kind of "tax-increment financing" (TIF) may be another method of paying for new visions of streets (Pivo and Fisher, 2011; Pivo, 2013; Gilderbloom et al., 2015).

Furthermore, in the future I think there will be opportunities to think about the value of roadway real estate gained from the efficiency that autonomous vehicles have on streets. If they can operate in an 8-foot lane or shared lane, that could yield a minimum 4 linear feet on every standard 12-foot roadway. In a recent paper on autonomous vehicles and livability with my friend Bruce Appleyard, we thought about the value of that space and suggest that,

Cities could conduct "right-of-way recapture" and then choose to repurpose that for bicycle or pedestrian infrastructure, or for things like gardens and play areas. They could also consider deeding this real estate back to private owners for them to do what they please—an action that would not only increase property value for owners but municipal property tax revenue on an annual basis. (Appleyard and Riggs, 2017, p 14).

This kind of innovation could hold value in providing new, creative and flexible financing solutions for street design in our funding-constrained urban environments. We also may see blockchain technology allow for more localized finance, and I believe there is potential for citizens to do what I have started to call IIOs, or initial infrastructure offerings, on a block-by-block basis to invest in their own streets, let alone local roads.

This could be a radical new way to empower local cities to invest in their own streets, and we could spend more time dreaming up other ideas of how to pay for bicycle and pedestrian infrastructure. But let's stop on that for now because this is not the only practice that needs focus. We also need to think beyond the street.

Thinking beyond the street

In addition to thinking about the nuts and bolts of project funding, it is also important to focus on things that are outside of the traditional arena of transportation—things such as density and how we use land and build housing. For example, one transportation professional I interviewed a while back felt that the most important factor at reshaping streets for all was density. I can still remember his passion when he described that,

> "The single biggest difference (around the world) that you see everywhere is density. Even in small towns out in green fields the housing is all five stories high and all in apartment blocks with mixed-use below ... (Even in) the absolute cookie cutter standard of good housing ... is this basic density assumption—which means there's almost always some transit and always something to walk to. You get the bars on the street with the cafes ... grocery stores and smaller retail." (Interview)

This idea of encouraging density and destination forms a catalyst for two suggested policy interventions that would break down barriers for minorities and allow for access to more walkable and bikeable places. Specifically, capitalizing on vacant land or space and providing more options to live in a walkable environment could allow for greater access and sorting into walkable locations for every person, regardless of race.

Former industrial properties, vacant parcels, large surface parking lots or driveways are all the kind of opportunity sites that could increase the supply of walkable housing and creating new (and more equitable) places. As one person I talked to described,

> "(In Europe) they are creating a lot of new spaces (by developing on vacant parcels and former parking in urban areas). I think the biggest opportunities are that they're undergrounding all sorts of things (including) parking. In Madrid, Barcelona and Torino, they're taking rail yard space and putting train tracks underground, or capping the top of what had been a train canyon right through the middle of the city and creating a new boulevard on top of it with a pedestrian mall. That's where they're getting all of these beautiful new pieces of the city." (Interview)

While the idea of undergrounding infrastructure (as the interviewee alluded) might counteract the goal of affordability, the principle of creative identification of vacant or underutilized land holds promise. Cities can and should increase the supply of land for housing so that minorities, low- and middle-income individuals can have the opportunity to stay in and choose to move to dense, urban, walkable and bikeable neighborhoods.

Policy makers could also encourage more interactive uses (shops, restaurants, experiential retail, amenities and so on) in neighborhoods and more places to go to. In my discussions with people about what makes them walk or bike, by-and-large people talk about where they are going. They talk about local places such as barbershops, salons, manicurists, dry-cleaners, drug stores, grocery stores and churches. If policy could be implemented to reinfuse or reinject these types of places into cities, then they could be transformational.

One way I like to think about this is to encourage pop-up businesses by loosening planning and zoning codes (some of which have helped shape a segregated environment, especially in more suburban environments). As one interviewee put it:

> "I think that's the problem with a lot of the cul-de-sacs. They're great for walking if you want to walk for long stretches for leisure, but if you're walking for utilitarian purposes, for example kids are walking to school, they are not necessarily the best. If they had set aside pedestrian routes directly to the school, had safe street crossings and had (routes) that maybe cut across lots, that would have made sense. But the way that neighborhood was laid out, you don't have space between houses to do that." (Interview)

This creates dissonance in life, work and play connections, and in the transportation, housing and school connections. Loosening planning and zoning restrictions would diversify these locations and reduce this kind of dissonance. The concept has parallels around the world. Loose, pop-up or informal businesses make many streets lively and there are great examples in Central and South America. As one individual I talked to remembered about a neighborhood in Nicaragua:

"You had these things that the called pulporillas, or octopus stores (from the world pulpo for octopus). That was the joke because the person would just stand in a little window of their house and reach for everything 'like an octopus.' They would sell a couple of light bulbs, some matches, some cokes, and cheese and bread; kind of like a 7–11, just out of their closet. They would have one window that opened to the street, and a sales person manned the window just for the block." (Interview)

But how could this be achieved in less walkable or bikeable areas? The same person had additional thoughts about how more local businesses (such as beauty shops and convenience stores) might create more destinations and places to walk to:

"If you could afford to design a walkable life for yourself, map out wherever the nail salon should go, where does the grocery store go, where would your neighbors and your friends be … it might not be too different from the suburbs—you just wouldn't be so far from people. You would need to walk; need to go pick up milk and beer on the corner; and this stuff would really need to be two hundred yards away or five hundred yards away. It can't be any more than that or it's just not somewhere to dash down to get your milk. It can't be like walking a mile to the grocery store.

So, the distances in the suburbs just mean that some of those houses have to become stores. (Geometrically) it's a very interesting question because in some suburbs, that is what's happening. People are cooking tacos out of their garage and selling them for a buck, and doing nails in the basement—all unregulated business activity in the suburbs.

But it again gets to land use policy, because those aren't permitted uses and there are underground businesses. And the question is—what would it take to permit those businesses? All of the inspectors are going to freak out—you're going to have nail polish solvent in somebody's garage and no ventilation, so there's no way you're going to get that approved. But you could take the opposite approach that it's lost business revenue for the city. So the building inspectors might freak out, but your economic development people might be saying 'yeah, go for it, we love small businesses here.'" (Interview)

New flexible zoning codes would complement street size and connectivity and enable places such as the corner grocery store—possibly a new spin on the idea of *pulporillas*. More flexible zoning could enable these small businesses to prosper by doing things such as providing for one commercial conversion of a single-family home per block in a residential area. This might be very effective in retrofitting the suburbs—allowing for corner stores in places that planners might never fathom. It could support small, walkable businesses serving minority communities—businesses that might be run out of a garage in a suburban cul-de-sac.

Perhaps the idea of "land banking" could also be used to enable this concept. Land banking involves establishing a quasi-governmental organization which controls a "land bank." This organization then has responsibility for vacant lots or foreclosed on homes. These lots can be used for varied public-serving land uses, parks and community facilities that might enable more inclusive, walkable and bikeable environments.

These ideas and proposed frameworks might open the door for more facilities, such as parks and greenways, focused in areas of clustered minority populations. They might incentivize individuals to tear down backyard fences and create playing fields and footpaths similar to what has been done in many cohousing developments, not only increasing the accessibility of walkable resources but the probably of walking behavior to those that need it most (Whyte, 1988; Corti et al., 1996; Giles-Corti et al., 2005).

Yet they also reflect a new way of thinking about housing, and in the US particularly we have had limited ways of doing so. We have been very bound by the idea of what a single-family home is and the identity that it shapes. But what if we were to change this? Could we encourage more walking and cycling while at the same time creating stronger communities? Research indicates that we could and creating more affordable, small unit housing with flexible zoning would be a start in getting there. Yet, to certain degree, design needs to evolve.

By saying that design needs to evolve, I mean that it can change to capture the imagination and desire of the public. This might be in the form of changing the idea of multi-family, high-rise "housing" to that of "homes" along a walkable streetscape (Davis, 1997). It might mean embracing some of the ideas of Japanese designer Maki and thinking about the beauty and individuality of how single elements could aggregate into a larger pattern of "group form" like many towns, villages, or pueblos across the globe.

Good design standards can help to influence alternative preferences toward smaller housing and one-small-car (or even car-free) lifestyles. For example, recent projects in the US have taken advantage of efficiency and single room zoning limitations to create independent living units.

Because they are very small (350 square feet or roughly 32 meters at the largest), these units require new design thinking—using ambient light from wrap around windows, high ceilings and individual balconies to add to the perceived spaciousness of small units. This kind of design provides housing options that evoke the styles of Italian hill towns, making design better match preferences in organic groups of buildings, designed as a unit but with individual components (Maki, 1970). Other factors that can be employed include:

- Providing units with individual architectural identities and independence while being a part of the whole community / neighborhood, with independent addresses, front doors, balconies and so on, relating to the traditional American value of independence espoused in the single-family home.
- Balancing repetition with architectural variation, including repeated elements such as structural frames, bathrooms, kitchens, cabinets and so on, but making statements with things such as entries and windows where they are most visible, and matching preferences toward individualism.
- Offering private space immediately adjacent to the public areas, with transitional space in between, and a semi-public space such as a central courtyard that is controllable and viewable by the resident. This can also facilitate preferences toward multi-family, multi-generational and multi-cultural lifestyles.
- Providing large spaces (such as combined kitchen-living areas), high ceilings, light colored interiors that bleed indoor to outdoor, and lots of light to make smaller units feel larger, matching preferences for larger spaces.
- Providing reduced parking that can be unbundling from unit costs, offering the ability for those who want to own a car that capability, but tempering that desire by reducing the number of spaces available and offering financial incentives for non-vehicle owners.

I know that some of these spaces were espoused in where I used to live, UC Berkeley's University Village, Albany (UVA), designed for families by my friend and mentor Sam Davis. The development works both to establish individual housing unit identity and to make a distinction between the private, semi-private and public spaces appealing to American residential desires toward single-family living. One of the things I liked most about the design is that the development used mailboxes and different colors of paint on the doorways to create individuation between units.

Embracing tactical opportunities and experiment

At the same time as engaging in these intentional design features that soften the environment, citizens and cities should also do what they can do now—and embrace tactical opportunities as a key practice. We can all engage in what Pope Francis (2015) describes as "ecological citizenship." We can recycle, reduce water, turn of the lights, take the bus and walk or bike whenever it is possible. Each of these things can be an act of love for our planet, our god and each other.

We can also push for small and simple transformational opportunities. I call these "tactical" projects, meaning those that are short-term tests with no definitive, long-range plan. I recently discussed this tactical, action-oriented approach with my colleague Ryan McClain at the transportation engineering firm Fehr and Peers.

Ryan was looking at putting in a roundabout in a community but there was resistance not only from the city but also the local fire department. The fire department was specifically concerned about running their engines around the circle. They did not think they could make the turn around the circle without hitting the curb.

In response, the Fehr and Peers team went out and threw hay bales into the road. No, literally, they took a weekend and put hay bales out in the roadway to mimic the curb. Then they tested the fire engines. Guess what happened? It turned out that turning was not an issue. The city got the roundabout. They radically experimented and transformed a road to a street.

The same thing has happened with many communities that have participated in park(ing) days (Schneider, 2017). These are days when citizens create installations in parking spaces to illustrate alternative uses for that space. It turns out that people like places to sit along the street and many of these temporary demonstration projects have been implemented on a permanent basis. I suspect many of the slow streets that were implemented during the COVID-19 pandemic will become more permanent. They allowed for a reimaging of the street for things such as playing and dining and showed that cities can take tactical steps to change with small experiments.

All of these little experiments remind me of a quote from former US President Franklin Delano Roosevelt. He has been quoted as saying "… the country demands bold, persistent experimentation" (Roosevelt, 1932). I agree. Simply spending time, effort and a small amount of funding on piloting and testing can be invaluable. And if we can spend this money in advance of investing millions, or even billions, in infrastructure funding, then there can be substantial savings as we reshape our streets. Moreover, experimentation can help us avoid mistakes as we move forward.

From experimentation to management

But experimentation is not everything. Seeing our roads change and killing ideas that have been with us for over a century also takes focused management—especially in the realm of public process and policy making.

Making good rules and reviewing projects can be thankless and frustrating. Having been a local planning commissioner, I understand this. I have sat through many meetings where there were strong and unclear opinions on just about everything. I have heard vocally passionate citizens who all have different desires and then seen all these ideas be incorporated into terrible plans—with vague and confused visions.

In these situations, I have sometimes felt frustrated. While I think inclusivity, dialogue and debate is important, it does not always make for the best policy. This is why I think Janet Sadik-Kahn described her efforts in New York as a "street fight" as opposed to a plan or compromise (Sadik-Kahn and Solomonow, 2017). Yet I think that the term "fight" is too harsh. And while I do not disagree with the action-oriented sentiments of Sadik-Kahn, I believe our work to change roads into streets is more of a collective and collaborative journey rather than a fight.

For example, in a recent meeting, I was asked to review a project providing walkable downtown housing. The project met all the city policy with regard to street design and more, but we (the civic leaders and policy makers) wanted more. We dialogued, proposed and agreed to many livability improvements. Yet when it came to the vote to approve the project, there was additional debate and the desire to increase the expectations and demands of the project.

While I thought this dialogue were interesting, it was also clear that the discussion was not pertinent to the project. Moreover, the suggestions were burdensome to the project, and as a group we were at risk of threatening something that was good because it was not perfect. We needed to embrace not only a spirit of empathy but also one of managed expectations and balance.

Designing cities is about dialogue and I believe that balanced and empathetic management can provide one of the best paths for creating both policy and action. I believe we can work together to shape change in our cities, including some small changes in our own neighborhoods, but we need to listen; we need to empathize and then manage action. This can start with being individual, ecological citizens, making better decisions about our own behavior and how it impacts the planet. After that, it can translate to collective and managed action—and perhaps through this process we can save the planet.

Ending roads to save the planet

Save the planet? That sounds somewhat "out there." Yet when you think about much of what is wrong with society—from climate change, social injustice, economic development, traffic and obesity to a more open political dialogue—there are issues at the street level. In America particularly, we saw frustration with many of these things manifest itself on streets of our nation's capital in the tragic political uprising in January of 2021. However, there are solutions that start with the street—many of which we have discussed in this book. The street can become a place for commerce, a place to slow down traffic and encourage exercise, interaction, protest and political discourse. So, is it really too much of a stretch to say that, if we reimagine what road can be, if we truly kill and then resurrect the idea, that we can save society? In my opinion, probably not.

For a long while, we have seen an eroding civic environment in the US at the same time that we have seen dramatic innovation and entrepreneurship in our business sectors. A 2016 Harvard Business School study illustrated this deterioration in the public sector (Porter et al., 2016). The study showed that confidence has gone down in many areas that make up our civic lives, such as our legal framework, health care, tax code, schools, logistics and politics.

While the reasons for this deterioration are complicated, the results can be seen all around our cities, whether through acute housing shortages, failing infrastructure or lack of transit. In my mind they are local problems, problems of streets and neighborhoods, and these problems underscore much of what we have discussed in this book.

I have argued that we need to invest in simple things such as signs, lines and pavements as we reshape our roadways but also that there are basic strategies that we can employ—for example harnessing funding, thinking tactically and then experimenting. Ultimately, however, the problems with our roads have neither policy nor political basis—they are systems problems.

I recently attended a talk by economists Michael Porter and Katherine Gehl that was largely focused on applying strategy and strategic planning to government. One of the things they talked about was how many of our problems are not problems with the private sector but with public "industry." They argue that unhealthy political competition is working against strategic solutions and sophisticated management—that we need more ideas, competition in the public sector and disruption to regenerate our cities.

I agree and believe that if policy makers and planners are honest with themselves they might see this. We, the students, policy makers, planners, engineers and civic leaders of the future, cannot let the brokenness of politics thwart strategic business decisions to run government, cities and transportation systems. We cannot stifle new things, be they rideshares or shuttles, scooters or skateboards, fearing the unknown. We cannot operate on assumptions or hypotheticals about what "the next big thing" might do to our urban environs. On the contrary, maybe competition makes us better and perhaps we should be encouraging more competitive innovation to improve transportation. Maybe we should embrace and accelerate disruption since it facilitates our evolution (or even devolution).

While there may be incentives to avoid problems and improve competition at the state and national level, I think we can still save our cities and our streets. While forces at the national scale may work against this change, there is hope—audacious hope—that our cities can still compete and drive innovative ideas that disrupt the status quo.

We can start with our roads. We can instigate change and lead from the local. We can reshape our roads to change our cities, increase competition, build housing and save the planet. We can end the road and embrace the street. We can reinvigorate our local and national communities in the US and around the world by taking simple actions. We can be the best versions of ourselves in order to bring out the best in other people—to be like the character from my grandmother's favorite poem "a friend to man." We can engage in an ecological conversation where our "goodness of spirit" that can become evident in our relationship with the street and with one another.

I began this book talking about the moment when I ruptured my Achilles tendon. In the drama of my youth, I felt my life was over, that I would never run again. I felt that I would never experience the street in the same way again. In truth, what happened was quite the opposite and quite remarkable.

I embraced the disruption and an audacious hope that propelled me to rethink roads. I recovered my health and ran again with a new perspective on the street—that it could be so much more than a space for travel. Rather than thinking about the brash idea that I had borrowed from Corbusier that we should "kill the street," I realized that roads could evolve. That they could become places respected and accommodated by many different kinds of travelers and experiences. I learned a street could be a place that could change the world—a place for commerce, culture and community.

My hope is that you can capture the same vision—that streets can be so much more than a places for travel. That they can be green and beautiful. That streets can tear down the barriers to racial, gender and social inequality. That they can be non-binary, both formal and informal at the same time. That they can be places for love, life and spiritual awakening. That they can be the heart of our cities.

So, onward. Let's end the road.

APPENDIX

Natural (Green) Streets – Data Collection Template

Site: _____ Investigator: _____
Date: _____ Start Time: _____ Finish Time: _____

Site Data

Number of blocks: _____ Length: _____ Lanes (cars): _____
Street width: _____ Weather (sunny, cloudy, etc.): _____
Posted speed limit: ____ ☐ none posted Observed speed (if possible):____
Land use:_____

Upkeep and Maintenance
("Physical condition" is cracks in sidewalks or pavements and other things
that require construction solutions; "Upkeep" is things that are non-structural
such as trash, health of plants, etc.):
Physical condition: *Needs repair* ←1——2——3——4——5→ *Well-maintained*
Upkeep of site: *Needs attention* ←1——2——3——4——5→ *Well-maintained*
NOTES: _____

Complete Street

Sidewalks: ☐ yes ☐ no *Notes*: _____
Road diet (reduced lanes or width): ☐ yes ☐ no *Notes*: _____
Bike lanes: ☐ yes ☐ no *Type*: ☐ class 1 ☐ class 2 ☐ sharrow
Notes (locations): _____
Shelter: ☐ yes ☐ no *Notes*: _____
Bus stops: ☐ yes ☐ no *Notes (nearest if not on street)*: _____

Crosswalks: ☐ yes ☐ no # of intersections with (#/total): _____
Bulb outs? Signals?:_____
Seating: ☐ yes ☐ no #/block: _____ *Notes*: _____
Stop signs: (#)_____ Other traffic controls: _____

Connectivity: Bike ☐ yes ☐ no Bus ☐ yes ☐ no Sidewalk ☐ yes ☐ no
Other Observations (e.g. barriers and other elements good or bad): _____

Green Stormwater Infrastructure

Curb cuts (street runoff): ☐ yes ☐ no *Notes:* _____

Bioretention cells or bioswales: ☐ yes ☐ no __Cells/distance or block: __

Flow-through planters: ☐ yes ☐ no *Notes:* _____
Pervious paving (pavement, blocks, etc.): ☐ yes ☐ no
Location: _____
Drop structures (conventional sewer inlets): ☐ yes ☐ no
Notes (include location): _____
Perched intake (intentional ponding): ☐ yes ☐ no
Retention basins (conventional SW): ☐ yes ☐ no
Notes: _____
Velocity disturbance (e.g. at entry to bioretention cells or through swale): ☐
yes ☐ no
Notes: _____
LID upkeep
("Needs work" refers to sediment accumulation that the limits functionality
of a system. Keep in mind that all systems will have sediment (they're
supposed to), but too much can cause huge problems such as blocked inlets
or no ponding)
Upkeep: *Needs work* ←1——2——3——4——5→ *Well-maintained*
Adjacent GSWI implementation (Private Property): ☐ yes ☐ no *(note on
site sketch)*
Educational signage: ☐ yes ☐ no *Notes:* _____

Co-benefits

Tree: ☐ yes ☐ no Tree Density (#/block): _____ Tree size (Diameter at
4.5'): _____
Shade Provision: *Zero shade* ←1—2—3——4—5→ *Ample availability*
Health of tress: __High_____ Medium_____Low
Street users (use hash marks): Bike – _____ Peds – _____
Social Lingering (solo 20+ sec. in place): sitting – _____ standing – _____
Social behavior (2+ pp): greeting – _____ eating – _____ discussion – _____
Non-tree greenery: ☐ yes ☐ no__Level of maintenance: High_____
Medium__ Low

Quality of travel corridors (broken pavement, cracks, discontinuity of sidewalk or bike lane):

_____

_____

Lighting: ☐ yes ☐ no *Notes:* _____

_____

Photo Log

Photo #	Description of street element photo documents

Site Sketch (Indicate major elements, non–vehicular street users, stores and other LU, major landscape features.)

_____

Pedestrian and Bicycle Volume Data Collection Tool

This document describes the procedure that one can use to count pedestrians, bicyclists and autos at intersections. The directions and sheets have evolved and been adapted from some of my work with Bob Schneider and others at the UC Berkeley Traffic Safety Center in the early 2010s. I have used these resources to successfully gather field data by hand with my students and employees for many years. Many times, this observational data can yield richer information about travel behavior than what can be gathered from traffic signal cameras or automated counters. The sheets that follow can be adapted for many locations and I'd encourage you to review this document and make it a template for your own data collection efforts—efforts that can facilitate better design of streets and the end of roads in your own neighborhood.

BRING COUNT MATERIALS:

- Data Collection Sheets
- Pencil or Pen
- Clipboard (or something to write on)
- Watch (or other timing device that can identify 15-minute periods)
- Approval letter from

FILL IN GENERAL INFORMATION:

- Record your name as the observer
- Record the date and time period of the count
- Estimate the current temperature (°F) and weather (sunny, cloudy, rainy, etc.)
- Describe the intersection, including surrounding buildings (e.g., restaurants, single-family houses, offices, etc.) and roadway characteristics (traffic signals, median islands, fast traffic, etc.)

FOLLOW BICYCLIST COUNTING PROCEDURE:

- Tally each time a bicyclist enters the campus at the designated intersection from each of the three approaches. Do not count bicyclists exiting campus or traveling parallel to without entering campus.
- Record whether the bicyclist is riding in the travel lane ("T"), the bike lane if applicable ("B") or on the sidewalk ("SW"). If a bicyclist changes their position during observation, mark the position they took the majority of the time.
- Record whether the bicyclist is wearing a helmet by circling "Y" or "N."
- Record the gender of the bicyclist by circling "M" or "F." If unsure, make your best guess.
- Record the approximate age of the bicyclist by circling the appropriate age group.
- Count bicyclists who may be riding on the wrong side of the street (against traffic).
- Observe each bicyclist as they pass through the next intersection. Note how the bicyclist behaves at the intersection ("GY" = bicyclist passes through light on green/yellow, "RS" = bicyclist stops at red light and waits until green to enter the intersection, "RX" = bicyclist enters intersection when light is red, "SS" = bicyclist stops or slows significantly at stop sign before entering intersection, "SX" = bicyclist enters intersection without slowing significantly at a stop sign). A quick reference key is provided on the data collection sheets.
- Mark a "W" next to the row if a bicyclist dismounts his or her bicycle to cross the intersection. Do not count bicyclists who only walk and do not ride their bike throughout the observation.
- Mark a line below the latest completed observation every 15 minutes, and label that line with the current time.
- Count for three hours. Enter tally marks in a new row after each 15-minute period.

Intersection Pedestrian Count Sheet

Date/Time: _____

Mainline Roadway: _____

Intersecting Roadway: _____

Observer Name (s): _____

Observation Time: (Start) _____ (End) _____

Temp. (°F): _____ Sunny, cloudy, rainy, etc.: _____

Description of Specific Observation Location: _____

Write the compass direction next to each intersection leg (A, B, C, D) and each corner (1, 2, 3, 4) on the diagram. Also label road names.

Leg A   Leg B

Leg D   Leg C

Tally each time a pedestrian crosses each leg of the intersection(count all crossings within 50 ft. of the crosswalk). If the pedestrian is female, mark an "O"; if male, mark an "X"; unknown, mark a "+".

Pedestrian Counts

Time Period #	Crossing Leg A		Crossing Leg B		Crossing Leg C		Crossing Leg D	
	From 4 to 1	OR From 1 to 4	From 1 to 2	OR From 2 to 1	From 2 to 3	OR From 3 to 2	From 3 to 4	OR From 4 to 3

Intersection Bicycle Count Sheet

Mainline Roadway: _____
Intersecting Roadway: _____
Observer Name(s): _____
Date: _____
Observation Time: (Start) _____ (End) _____
Temp. (°F): _____ Sunny, cloudy, rainy, etc.: _____
Description of Specific Observation Location: _____

Write the compass direction next to each intersection leg (A, B, C, D) and each corner (1, 2, 3, 4) on the diagram. Also label road names.

Tally each time a bicyclist leaves each leg of the intersection (include bicyclists on sidewalks). If the pedestrian is female, mark an "O"; if male, mark an "X"; unknown, mark a "+".

Bicycle Counts

Time Period #	Crossing Leg A			Crossing Leg B			Crossing Leg C			Crossing Leg D		
	(Turning Left) T to W	(Going Straight) T to S	(Turning Right) T to E	(Turning Left) W to S	(Going Straight) W to E	(Turning Right) W to T	(Turning Left) S to E	(Going Straight) S to T	(Turning Right) S to W	(Turning Left) E to S	(Going Straight) E to W	(Turning Right) E to T

Intersection Auto Count Sheet

Mainline Roadway: _____
Intersecting Roadway: _____
Observer Name(s): _____
Date: _____
Observation Time: (Start) _____ (End) _____
Temp. (°F): _____ Sunny, cloudy, rainy,etc.: _____
Description of Specific Observation Location: _____

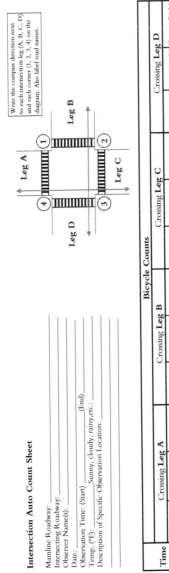

Write the compass direction next to each intersection leg (A, B, C, D) and each corner (1, 2, 3, 4) on the diagram. Also label road names.

Bicycle Counts

Time Period #	Crossing Leg A			Crossing Leg B			Crossing Leg C			Crossing Leg D		
	(Turning Left) T to W	(Going Straight) T to S	(Turning Right) T to E	(Turning Left) W to S	(Going Straight) W to E	(Turning Right) W to T	(Turning Left) S to E	(Going Straight) S to T	(Turning Right) S to W	(Turning Left) E to S	(Going Straight) E to W	(Turning Right) E to T

Notes

Chapter 1

[1] Sir Roger Bannister was the first runner known to have broken the 4-minute mile. He was notorious for doing his training to and from his medical classes at the University of Oxford.

[2] I ran and completed the California International Marathon in 2 hours and 46 minutes, automatically qualifying for the 2005 Boston Marathon. This was a lifelong dream and I completed it in 2 hours and 52 minutes!

Chapter 3

[1] More reading can be found at:

ITE Technical Committee. "Trip Generation." *Traffic Engineering*, 1976. http://nacto.org/docs/usdg/trip_generation_ite.pdf.

Metropolitan Washington Council of Governments. "Four-Step Travel Model," 2016. http://www.mwcog.org/transportation/activities/models/4step/step1.asp.

Schneider, Robert James, Kevan Shafizadeh and Susan L. Handy. "Method to Adjust Institute of Transportation Engineers Vehicle Trip-Generation Estimates in Smart-Growth Areas." *Journal of Transport and Land Use*, 0, no. 0 (January 11, 2015): 1–15. https://doi.org/10.5198/jtlu.v0i0.416.

[2] More reading can be found at:

Litman, Todd. "Introduction to Multi-Modal Transportation Planning." *Victoria Transport Policy Institute*, 15 (2011). http://www.vtpi.org/multimodal_planning.pdf

Milam, Ronald T., Marc Birnbaum, Chris Ganson, Susan Handy and Jerry Walters. "Closing the Induced Vehicle Travel Gap between Research and Practice." *Transportation Research Record: Journal of the Transportation Research Board*, no. 2653 (2017): 10–16. http://www.opr.ca.gov/docs/Closing_the_Induced_Vehicle_Travel_Gap-TRB_Paper-Milam_et_al.pdf

[3] More reading:

Victoria Transport Policy Institute. "Multi-Modal Level-of-Service Indicators Tools For Evaluating. The Quality of Transport Services and Facilities." Apr. 2015. http://www.vtpi.org/tdm/tdm129.htm

[4] More reading:

McNichol, T. Roads gone wild. *Wired Magazine*, 2004, 12(12), 108–112. http://urbanarchives.org/documents/articles/McNichol-Roads_Gone_Wild.doc

[5] More reading:

Frank et al. "The development of a walkability index: application to the Neighborhood Quality of Life Study." *British Journal of Sports Medicine*, Feb. 9 2009. http://bjsm.bmj.com/content/44/13/924.full

Riggs, William. "Inclusively Walkable: Exploring the Equity of Walkable Housing in the San Francisco Bay Area." *Local Environment*, 21, no. 5 (May 3, 2016): 527–54. https://doi.org/10.1080/13549839.2014.982080.

[6]   More reading:

Federal Highway Administration Livability Initiative: https://www.fhwa.dot.gov/livability/

[7]   More reading:

Bliss, Laura. "How Urban Designers Can Get Smaller Cities Walking." *City Lab*. Jul 29, 2015. http://www.citylab.com/design/2015/07/how-urban-designers-can-get-smaller-cities-walking/3995

Federal Highway Administration. "Bicycle and Pedestrian Program." Aug. 20, 2013. http://www.fhwa.dot.gov/environment/bicycle_pedestrian/guidance/design_flexibility.cfm

NACTO Green Book: http://nacto.org/publication/urban-bikeway-design-guide/bicycle-boulevards/green-infrastructure/

[8]   More reading:

Jaffe, Eric. "6 Places Where Cars, Bikes, and Pedestrians All Share the Road As Equals." *City Lab*. March 23, 2015. https://www.citylab.com/solutions/2015/03/6-places-where-cars-bikes-and-pedestrians-all-share-the-road-as-equals/388351/

Hockenos, Paul. "Where 'Share the Road' Is Taken Literally." *New York Times*. April 26, 2013. http://www.nytimes.com/2013/04/28/automobiles/where-share-the-road-is-taken-literally.html

Brandt, Steve. "Downtown Minneapolis gets its first 'woonerf'." *Minneapolis Star Tribune*. http://www.startribune.com/downtown-minneapolis-gets-its-first-woonerf/393491981/

Chapter 4

[1]   For example, to the north, cities such as Milwaukee and Minneapolis or St. Paul have made dramatic efforts to encourage active living and activity-based commutes. Minneapolis is focused on building the Nicolette Mall as a pedestrian area and has made a massive investment in a walking and biking infrastructure, including one of the nation's most expansive bike networks. Further, its investment in light rail has encouraged and allowed for more car-free living. Cities such as Indianapolis focused on creating greenways that extend along rivers running through the city, something that is being studied by Greg Lindsey who has shown not only that bike lanes and infrastructure increase activity level but they increase housing values and business transactions. The neighborhood of Broadripple has seen direct economic growth and become a thriving arts and entertainment district as a result of this kind of investment.

Chapter 5

[1]   The streets of Boston's North End are jokingly rumored to have been laid out by wandering cows.

Chapter 8

[1]   Looking at the San Francisco area in a present-day context, the two extremes of housing development are the ornate Victorian homes of the late 19th century and early 20th century, and the post-WWII tract-housing that inspired the photography of Ansel Adams and the music of Malvina Reynolds ("Little boxes made of ticky tacky"). Westwood

Highlands and most of the West of Twin Peaks area developments would fall in the middle between the Victorian and tract-housing extremes.

2   As one planner interviewed described, those in inner- and lower-income suburbs may experience "dissonant utopias" that are contradictory to the historically romanticized view of the American suburban experience or American dream.

3   Racial discrimination still exists within the housing industry. The Fair Housing Council of Washington found that Black people are discriminated against approximately 40 percent of the time when they attempt to buy or rent a home or apply for a mortgage loan (Squires and Friedman, 2001). An analysis from George Washington University's Survey Research Center shows that fewer than 20 percent of White people compared with 33 percent of Black people were denied their first choice when they moved into their current home. Moreover, more than 25 percent of Black people reported that they or someone they knew experienced discrimination in their efforts to find housing or a mortgage during the past three years. In San Francisco, the absence of middle-class Black people has left the impression to some that they "are not stakeholders in the community."

Chapter 10

1   I use the term automated as opposed to autonomous or self-driving. Among academics, this has become the most commonly used term since it recognizes the many things that might impede a car from being 100 percent self-driving, 100 percent of the time, in 100 percent of roadway conditions.

2   You can learn more about these ideas and others in my book *Disruptive Transport* as well as in the American Planning Association, PAS Report, *Planning for Autonomous Mobility*.

References

Abolghasem, S., Gómez-Sarmiento, J., Medaglia, A.L., Sarmiento, O.L., González, A.D., del Castillo, A.D., Rozo-Casas, J.F. and Jacoby, E. (2018) "A DEA-centric decision support system for evaluating Ciclovía-Recreativa programs in the Americas," *Socioeconomic Planning Sciences*, 61, 90–101.

Agyeman, J., Bullard, R.D. and Evans, B. (2012) *Just Sustainabilities: Development in an Unequal World*, London: Earthscan.

Akar, G., Clifton, K. (2009) "Influence of Individual Perceptions and Bicycle Infrastructure on Decision to Bike," *Transportation Research Record: Journal of the Transportation Research Board*, 2140, 165–172. https://doi.org/10.3141/2140-18

Alexander, C. (1979) *The Timeless Way of Building*, Oxford: Oxford University Press.

Alexander, C., Ishikawa, S. and Silverstein, M. (1977) *A Pattern Language: Towns, Buildings, Construction*, New York: Oxford University Press.

Alfonzo, M.A. (2005) "To Walk or Not to Walk? The Hierarchy of Walking Needs," *Environment and Behavior*, 37(6): 808–836, doi:10.1177/0013916504274016.

Alpert (2016) "Copenhagen uses this one trick to make room for bikeways on nearly every street," Greater Greater Washington, Available at: https://ggwash.org/view/43010/copenhagen-uses-this-one-trick-to-make-room-for-bikeways-on-nearly-every-street [Accessed October 4, 2021].

Amir, O., Ariely, D., Cooke, A., Dunning, D., Epley, N., Gneezy, U., Koszegi, B., Lichtenstein, D., Mazar, N., Mullainathan, S., Prelec, D., Shafir, D and Silva, J. (2005) "Psychology, behavioral economics, and public policy," *Marketing Letters*, 16, 443–454.

Andersen, M. (2014) "How Denver got an oil company to help crowdfund a protected bike lane," People Bikes, Available at: http://www.peopleforbikes.org/blog/entry/how-denver-got-an-oil-company-to-help-crowdfund-a-protected-bike-lane?utm_source=twitterfeed&utm_medium=twitter [Accessed December 16, 2014].

Anderson, J.M., Nidhi, K., Stanley, K.D., Sorensen, P., Samaras, C. and Oluwatola, O.A. (2014) Autonomous vehicle technology: A guide for policymakers. Santa Monica, CA: Rand Corporation.

Anderson, M. (2013) "What caused Portland's biking boom?," BikePortland. org, Available at: http://bikeportland.org/2013/07/02/what-caused-portla nds-biking-boom-89491 [Accessed December 16, 2014].

APHA (1948) Planning the neighborhood: standards for healthful housing, Chicago: Public Administration Service: American Public Health Association.

Appleyard, B. and Riggs, W. (2017) Measuring and Doing the Right Things: A Livability, Sustainability and Equity Framework for Autonomous Vehicles (SSRN Scholarly Paper No. ID 3040783), Rochester, NY: Social Science Research Network, Available at: https://papers.ssrn.com/sol3/pap ers.cfm?abstract_id=3040783 [Accessed December 12, 2021].

Appleyard, D. (1980) 'Livable streets: protected neighborhoods?', *The ANNALS of the American Academy of Political and Social Science*, 451(1): 106–117.

Appleyard, D., Gerson, M.S. and Lintell, M. (1981) *Livable Streets*, Berkeley: University of California Press.

Archer, J. (2009) "Suburbia and the American Dream House," in D. Rubey (ed.) *Redefining Suburban Studies: Searching for New Paradigms*, Hofstra University: National Center for Suburban Studies.

Arcieri (2015) "Greensboro will consider a $5.7 million citywide unmanned aircraft system that performs robotic 911 emergency response in 90 seconds or less," *Triad Business Journal*, Available at: https://www.bizjournals.com/ triad/news/2015/07/20/greensboro-to-consider-5-7m-drone-deal.html [Accessed June 24, 2019].

Ariely, D. (2008) *Predictably Irrational: The Hidden Forces That Shape Our Decisions*, New York: Harper.

ASLA (2021) "Interview with Jan Gehl," *American Society of Landscape Architects*, Available at: https://www.asla.org/contentdetail.aspx?id=31346 [Accessed November 29, 2021].

Atherton (2017) "Amazon's delivery drone hive patent is an urban planning nightmare," *Popular Science*, Available at: https://www.popsci.com/amazons- patented-drone-towers-dont-make-any-sense/ [Accessed June 24, 2019].

Badland, H. and Schofield, G. (2005) "Transport, urban design, and physical activity: an evidence-based update," *Transportation Research Part D: Transport and Environment*, 10, 177–196.

Bartholomew, K. and Ewing, R. (2011) "Hedonic price effects of pedestrian- and transit-oriented development," *Journal of Planning Literature*, 26, 18–34. https://doi.org/10.1177/0885412210386540

Batty, M. (2007) *Cities and Complexity: Understanding Cities With Cellular Automata, Agent-Based Models, and Fractals*, Cambridge, MA: MIT Press.

Batty, M. and Torrens, P.M. (2001) "Modeling complexity: the limits to prediction," *Cybergeo: European Journal of Geography*, Available at: http:// cybergeo.revues.org/1035?file=1 [Accessed February 17, 2015].

Ben-Elia, E., Erev, I. and Shiftan, Y. (2008) "The combined effect of information and experience on drivers' route-choice behavior," *Transportation*, 35, 165–177.

Bennett (2011) "Police employ Predator drone spy planes on home front," *Los Angeles Times*, Available at: https://www.latimes.com/archives/la-xpm-2011-dec-10-la-na-drone-arrest-20111211-story.html [Accessed June 24, 2019].

Bergen, M. (2013) "Mumbai's walkability problem: plenty of pedestrians, not enough sidewalks," CityLab, Available at: http://www.theatlanticcities.com/commute/2013/01/mumbais-walkability-problem-plenty-pedestrians-not-enough-sidewalks/4297/ [Accessed December 27, 2014].

Berman, M. (1983) *All That Is Solid Melts Into Air: The Experience of Modernity*, New York: Verso.

Berrigan, D. and Troiano, R.P. (2002) "The association between urban form and physical activity in U.S. adults," *American Journal of Preventative Medicine*, 23, 74–79. https://doi.org/10.1016/S0749-3797(02)00476-2

Beyard, M., Pawlukiewicz, M. and Bond, A. (2003) Ten Principles for Rebuilding Neighborhood Retail, Washington DC: Urban Land Institute, Available at: http://www.uli.org/wp-content/uploads/2012/07/TP_NeighborhoodRetail.ashx_1.pdf [Accessed October 20, 2014.]

Bhan, G. (2009) "'This is no longer the city i once knew'. Evictions, the urban poor and the right to the city in millennial Delhi," *Environment and Urbanization*, 21, 127–142. https://doi.org/10.1177/0956247809103009

Bianco, M.J. (2000) "Effective transportation demand management: combining parking pricing, transit incentives, and transportation management in a commercial district of Portland, Oregon," *Transportation Research Record: Journal of the Transportation Research Board*, 1711, 46–54.

Blincoe, L., Miller T.R., Zaloshnja, E., and Lawrence, B.A. (2015) The economic and societal impact of motor vehicle crashes, 2010 (Revised), Report No. DOT HS 812 013, Washington, DC: National Highway Traffic Safety Administration, Available at: http://www-nrd.nhtsa.dot.gov/Pubs/812013.pdf [Accessed 12 December 2021].

Bowles, H.R., Rissel, C. and Bauman, A. (2006) "Mass community cycling events: Who participates and is their behaviour influenced by participation?" *International Journal of Behavioral Nutrition and Physical Activity*, 3, 39. https://doi.org/10.1186/1479-5868-3-39

Boyer, M.C. (1986) *Dreaming the Rational City: The myth of American City Planning*, Cambridge, MA: MIT Press.

Broaddus, A. (2014) "Sustainable transportation: lessons from London," *Focus*, 11, 10–14.

Broaddus, A. (2010) "Tale of two ecosuburbs in Freiburg, Germany: encouraging transit and bicycle use by restricting parking provision," *Transportation Research Record: Journal of the Transportation Research Board*, 2187, 114–122.

Broaddus, A., Browne, M. and Allen, J. (2015) "Sustainable freight: impacts of the london congestion charge and low emissions zone," *Transportation Research Record: Journal of the Transportation Research Board*, 2478, 1–11.

Brock, W. and Durlauf, S. (2003) A multinomial choice model with social interactions, Technical Working Paper 288, Cambridge: National Bureau of Economic Research, Available at: http://www.nber.org/papers/t0288 [Accessed November 11, 2015].

Brodsky, H. (1970) "Residential land and improvement values in a central city," *Land Economics*, 46, 229–247.

Brown, A., Gonder, J. and Repac, B. (2014) "An analysis of possible energy impacts of automated vehicle," in G. Meyer and S. Beiker (eds) *Road Vehicle Automation,* Cham: Springer International Publishing (Lecture Notes in Mobility), pp 137–153.

Brown, H. (1973) "The Impact of War Worker Migration on the Public School System of Richmond, California, 1940–1945," Ed.D. Dissertation, Stanford University.

Brownson, R.C., Hoehner, C.M., Day, K., Forsyth, A. and Sallis, J.F. (2009) "Measuring the built environment for physical activity: state of the science," *American Journal of Preventative Medicine*, 36, S99–S123.

Brulle, R.J. and Pellow, D.N. (2006) "Environmental justice: human health and environmental inequalities," *Annual Review of Public Health*, 27, 103–124. https://doi.org/10.1146/annurev.publhealth.27.021405.102124

Cabanek, A., Zingoni de Baro, M.E. and Newman, P. (2020) "Biophilic streets: a design framework for creating multiple urban benefits," *Sustainable Earth*, 3, 7. https://doi.org/10.1186/s42055-020-00027-0

CAI-Asia (2011) Walkability in Indian Cities. Available at: https://cleanai rinitiative.org/portal/node/155 [Accessed October 27, 2014].

Carr, L.J., Dunsiger, S.I. and Marcus, B.H. (2010) "Walk Score™ as a global estimate of neighborhood walkability," *American Journal of Preventative Medicine*, 39, 460–463.

Carr, L.J., Dunsiger, S.I. and Marcus, B.H. (2011) "Validation of Walk Score for estimating access to walkable amenities," *British Journal of Sports Medicine*, 45, 1144–1148.

CDC (2021) "Obesity is a common, serious, and costly disease," *Center for Disease Control and Prevention*, Available at: https://www.cdc.gov/obesity/data/adult.html [Accessed 22 September 2021].

Cervero, R. (2012) "Integrating Transit and Urban Development: Lessons and Challenges for Developing Countries," Faculty Research Series, University of California, Berkeley, 13 September.

Cervero, R. and Duncan, M. (2003) "Walking, bicycling, and urban landscapes: evidence from the San Francisco Bay Area," *American Journal of Public Health*, 93, 1478.

Cervero, R. and Kockelman, K. (1997) "Travel demand and the 3Ds: density, diversity, and design," *Transportation Research Record: Journal of the Transportation Research Board*, 2, 199–219.

Cervero, R. and Murakami, J. (2010) "Effects of built environments on vehicle miles traveled: evidence from 370 US urbanized areas," *Environment and Planning A: Economy and Space*, 42, 400–418.

Chatman, D. (2007) "Will transportation credit mortgages work in practice?" *Intransition Mag*, 5–6. Available at: http://ced.berkeley.edu/downloads/pubs/faculty/chatman_2007_will-trans-credit-mort.pdf [Accessed December 12, 2012].

Chetty, R., Friedman, J.N., Saez, E., Turner, N. and Yagan, D. (2020) "Income segregation and intergenerational mobility across colleges in the United States," *The Quarterly Journal of Economics*, 135, 1567–1633.

Chetty, R. and Hendren, N. (2018) "The impacts of neighborhoods on intergenerational mobility i: childhood exposure effects," *The Quarterly Journal of Economics*, 133, 1107–1162. https://doi.org/10.1093/qje/qjy007

Chin, G.K.W., Van Niel, K.P., Giles-Corti, B. and Knuiman, M. (2008) "Accessibility and connectivity in physical activity studies: the impact of missing pedestrian data," *Preventative Medicine*, 46, 41–45.

Chisholm, H. (1911) 'Haussmann, Georges Eugène, Baron', *Encyclopedia Britannica* 11th edition, Cambridge: Cambridge University Press.

Chiu, Y., Zhou, X. and Hernandez, J. (2007) "Evaluating urban downtown one-way to two-way street conversion using multiple resolution simulation and assignment approach," *Journal of Urban Planning and Development*, 133, 222–232. https://doi.org/10.1061/(ASCE)0733-9488(2007)133:4(222)

City of Chicago (2010) Green Alley Handbook, Chicago: City of Chicago.

City of Chicago (2012) Chicago Streets for Cycling Plan 2020, Chicago: Chicago Department of Transportation.

City of Chicago (2013) Complete Streets Guide, Chicago: City of Chicago.

City of Los Angeles (n.d.) "CicLAvia," CicLAvia, Available from: http://www.ciclavia.org/ [Accessed May 11, 2018].

City of Melbourne (2021) "Greening laneways," City Melb, Available at: https://www.melbourne.vic.gov.au/community/greening-the-city/green-infrastructure/pages/greening-laneways.aspx [Accessed October 1, 2021].

City of Portland (2021) "Green streets," City of Portland, Oregon, Available at: https://www.portlandoregon.gov/bes/45386 [Accessed October 1, 2021].

City of San Francisco (2013) "San Francisco parklet manual," Available at: http://pavementtoparks.sfplanning.org/docs/SF_P2P_Parklet_Manual_1.0_FULL.pdf [Accessed November 3, 2014].

City of San Francisco (n.d.) "Sunday Streets SF," Available at: http://www.sundaystreetssf.com/ [Accessed May 11, 2018].

City of Seattle (2021) "Bell Street Park," Available at: http://www.seattle. gov/parks/find/parks/bell-street-park [Accessed: December 13, 2021].

Clarke, P. and George, L.K. (2005) "The Role of the Built Environment in the Disablement Process," *Am J Public Health*, 95, 1933–1939. https://doi.org/10.2105/AJPH.2004.054494

Clay, R.A. (2001) "Green is good for you," *Monit. Psychol*, 32, 40–42.

Cleophas, C. and Ehmke, J.F. (2014) "When are deliveries profitable?" *Business & Information Systems Engineering*, 6, 153–163.

Clewlow, R.R. and Mishra, G.S. (2017) Disruptive transportation: the adoption, utilization, and impacts of ride-hailing in the United States (Research Report No. UCD-ITS-RR-17-07), Davis: University of California, Institute of Transportation Studies.

Cohen, D., Han, B., Derose, K.P., Williamson, S., Paley, A. and Batteate, C. (2016) "CicLAvia: evaluation of participation, physical activity and cost of an open streets event in Los Angeles," *Prev. Med*, 90, 26–33.

Cohen, D., Sehgal, A., Williamson, S., Sturm, R., McKenzie, T., Lara, R. and Lurie, N. (2006) Park use and physical activity in a sample of public parks in the city of Los Angeles. Available at: https://www.rand.org/pubs/technical_reports/TR357.html [Accessed December 11, 2021].

Colhouer, B. (2015) "Locally grown: the beginnings of downtown SLO Farmers' Market," *SLO City News*, Available at: http://www.tolosapressn ews.com/locally-grown-the-beginnings-of-downtown-slo-farmers-mar ket/ [Accessed May 11, 2018].

Collins, C.M. and Chambers, S.M. (2005) "Psychological and situational influences on commuter-transport-mode choice," *Environment and Behavior*, 37, 640–661. https://doi.org/10.1177/0013916504265440

Corburn, J. (2007) "Reconnecting with our roots: American urban planning and public health in the twenty-first century," *Urban Affairs Review*, 42, 688.

Corburn, J. (2005) *Street Science: Community Knowledge and Environmental Health Justice*, Cambridge, MA: MIT Press.

Corti, B., Donovan, R.J. and Holman, C.D.J. (1996) "Factors influencing the use of physical activity facilities: results from qualitative research," *Health Promotion Journal of Australia*, 6, 16–21.

Cortright, J. (2009) *Walking the Walk: How Walkability Raises Home Values in U.S. Cities*, Portland, OR: CEOs Cities.

Cromley, E.K. and McLafferty, S. (2002) GIS and Public Health, The Guilford Press.

Curbed (2013) "Belltown's Bell Street Park now open to pedestrians," *Curbed Seattle*, Available at: https://seattle.curbed.com/2013/7/25/10216320/bell-street-park [Accessed October 1, 2021].

Cutler, D.M., Glaeser, E.L. and Vigdor, J.L. (1999) "The rise and decline of the American ghetto," *Journal of Political Economy*, 107, 455–506.

Cutts, B.B., Darby, K.J., Boone, C.G. and Brewis, A. (2009) "City structure, obesity, and environmental justice: an integrated analysis of physical and social barriers to walkable streets and park access," *Social Science and Medicine*, 69, 1314–1322. https://doi.org/10.1016/j.socscimed.2009.08.020

Davis, B., Dutzik, T. and Baxandall, P. (2012) *Transportation and the new generation: why young people are driving less and what it means for transportation policy*, Santa Barbara: Frontier Group, Available at: https://trid.trb.org/view/1141470 [Accessed January 19, 2022].

Davis, S. (1997) *The Architecture of Affordable Housing*, Berkeley: University of California Press.

Deakin, E. (2001) *Sustainable development and sustainable transportation: strategies for economic prosperity, environmental quality, and equity*, Berkeley: Institute of Urban & Regional Development, Available at: https://escholarship.org/uc/item/0m1047xc.pdf [Accessed August 30, 2016].

Dekay, M. and O'Brien, M. (2001) "Gray city, green city," *Forum for Applied Research and Public Policy*, 16(2), 19–27.

Dell'Amico, M. and Hadjidimitriou, S. (2012) "Innovative logistics model and containers solution for efficient last mile delivery," *Procedia-Social and Behavioral Sciences*, 48, 1505–1514.

Diao, M. and Ferreira, J. (2010) "Residential property values and the built environment," *Transportation Research Record: Journal of the Transportation Research Board*, 2174, 138–147. https://doi.org/10.3141/2174-18

Diaz, J. (2011) "On the Oakland Experience / Jerry Brown's audacity," *San Francisco Chronicle*, Available at: https://www.sfgate.com/opinion/diaz/article/Jerry-Brown-s-audacity-3243435.php [Accessed December 12, 2021].

DiClemente, C.C. and Prochaska, J.O. (1998) "Toward a comprehensive, transtheoretical model of change: stages of change and addictive behaviors," in W.R. Miller and N. Heather (eds) *Treating Addictive Behaviors (2nd Ed.)*, Applied Clinical Psychology, New York: Plenum Press, pp 3–24.

Diez Roux, A.V. (2001) "Investigating neighborhood and area effects on health," *American Journal of Public Health*, 91, 1783.

Dong, H. (2015) "Were home prices in new urbanist neighborhoods more resilient in the recent housing downturn?" *Journal of Planning Education and Research*, 35, 5–18. https://doi.org/10.1177/0739456X14560769

Douglas, J.D. (1970) *Freedom & Tyranny: Social Problems in a Technological Society*, New York: Knopf.

Duany, A.E., Plater-Zyberk, E. and Speck, J. (2001) *Suburban Nation: The Rise of Sprawl And the Decline of the American Dream*, New York: North Point Press.

Dugundji, E. and Walker, J. (2005) "Discrete choice with social and spatial network interdependencies: an empirical example using mixed GEV models with field and panel effects," *Transportation Research Record: Journal of the Transportation Research Board*, 1921(1), 70–78.

Dumbaugh, E. and Rae, R. (2009) "Safe urban form: revisiting the relationship between community design and traffic safety," *Journal of the American Planning Association*, 75, 309–329.

Dunphy, R., Myerson, D. and Pawlukiewicz, M. (2003) "Ten principles for successful development around transit." Washington DC: Urban Land Institute. Available at: http://www.reconnectingamerica.org/assets/Uplo ads/bestpractice086.pdf [Accessed December 12, 2021].

Eberlein, S. (2011a) "City of the future. Part I: keeping what works (a photo diary)," *Dly. Kos*, Available at: https://www.dailykos.com/stories/2011/ 8/12/1000830/- [Accessed January 26, 2016].

Eberlein, S. (2011b) "Universal principles for creating a sustainable," Planetizen – Urban Plan. News Jobs Educ, Available at: https://www.pla netizen.com/node/50883 [Accessed March 14, 2018].

Eisenhower, D.D. (1952) "Quote from Time Magazine," Wikipedia, Available at: https://en.wikiquote.org/wiki/Dwight_D._Eisenhower [Accessed March 14, 2018].

Engelberg, J.K., Carlson, J.A., Black, M.L., Ryan, S. and Sallis, J.F. (2014) "Ciclovía participation and impacts in San Diego, CA: the first CicloSDias," *Preventative Medicine*, 69, S66–S73.

Essoka, J.D. (2010) "The gentrifying effects of brownfields redevelopment," *Western Journal of Black Studies*, 34, 299.

Evans-Cowley, J. and Kubinski, B. (2012) "A brave new world: how apps are changing planning," *Planetizen*, Available at: http://www.planetizen. com/node/58314 [Accessed December 15, 2014].

Ewing, R. (2005) "Can the physical environment determine physical activity levels?" *Exercise and Sport Science Reviews*, 33, 69–75.

Ewing, R. and Cervero, R. (2001) Travel and the built environment: a synthesis," *Transportation Research Record: Journal of the Transportation Research Board*, 1780, 87–114. https://doi.org/10.3141/1780-10

Ewing, R. and Cervero, R. (2010) "Travel and the built environment – a meta-analysis," *Journal of the American Planning Association*, 76(3), 265–294. https://doi.org/10.1080/01944361003766766

Ewing, R., Handy, S., Brownson, R.C., Clemente, O. and Winston, E. (2006) "Identifying and measuring urban design qualities related to walkability," *Journal of Physical Activity & Health*, 3, 223–240.

Ezzati, M., Martin, H., Skjold, S., Hoorn, S.V. and Murray, C.J.L. (2006) "Trends in national and state-level obesity in the USA after correction for self-report bias: analysis of health surveys," *JRSM*, 99, 250–257.

Faccio, M. and Gamberi, M. (2015) "New city logistics paradigm: From the 'last mile' to the 'last 50 miles' sustainable distribution," *Sustainability*, 7, 14873–14894.

Fagnant, D.J. and Kockelman, K.M. (2014) "The travel and environmental implications of shared autonomous vehicles, using agent-based model scenarios," *Transportation Research Part C: Emerging Technologies*, 40, 1–13. https://doi.org/10.1016/j.trc.2013.12.001

Farrell, M. (2009) "Blacks abandon San Francisco," *Christian Science Monitor*, Available at: https://www.csmonitor.com/USA/2009/0615/p02s04-usgn. html [Accessed December 12, 2021.]

Ferguson, E. (2000) *Travel demand management and public policy.* New York: Routledge.

Fiske, A.P. (1992) "The four elementary forms of sociality: framework for a unified theory of social relations," *Psychological Review*, 99(4), 689–723. https://doi.org/10.1037/0033-295X.99.4.689

Florida, R.L. (2002) *The Rise of the Creative Class: And How It's Transforming Work, Leisure, Community and Everyday Life*, New York: Basic Books.

Florida, R.L. (2003) "Cities and the creative class," *City & Community*, 2(1), 3–19. https://doi.org/10.1111/1540-6040.00034

Flyvbjerg, B. (2001) "Beyond the limits of planning theory: response to my critics," *International Planning Studies*, 6(3), 285–292. http://dx.doi.org/10.1080/13563470120069706

Forchey, A.I. (1890) "Sans moteur, sans ailes et... aussi vite avec; la bicyclette "Presto"," *Gallica*, Available at: https://gallica.bnf.fr/ark:/12148/btv1b9 012951m [Accessed October 1, 2021].

Forsyth, A., Hearst, M., Oakes, J.M. and Schmitz, K.H. (2008) "Design and destinations: factors influencing walking and total physical activity," *Urban Studies*, 45, 1973–1996. https://doi.org/10.1177/0042098008093386

Forsyth, A., Oakes, J.M., Schmitz, K.H. and Hearst, M. (2007) "Does residential density increase walking and other physical activity?" *Urban Studies*, 44, 679–697.

Foss, S.W. (1897) *Dreams in Homespun*, Boston, MA: Lothrop, Lee & Shepard Company.

Foster, S. and Giles-Corti, B. (2008) "The built environment, neighborhood crime and constrained physical activity: an exploration of inconsistent findings," *Preventative Medicine*, 47, 241–251. https://doi.org/10.1016/j.ypmed.2008.03.017

Frank, L., Kerr, J., Chapman, J. and Sallis, J. (2007) "Urban form relationships with walk trip frequency and distance among youth," *American Journal of Health Promotion*, 21, 1–8.

Frank, L.D., Andresen, M.A. and Schmid, T.L. (2004) "Obesity relationships with community design, physical activity, and time spent in cars," *American Journal of Preventative Medicine*, 27, 87–96.

Frank, L.D., Sallis, J.F., Saelens, B.E., Leary, L., Cain, K., Conway, T.L. and Hess, P.M. (2009) "The development of a walkability index: application to the Neighborhood Quality of Life Study," *British Journal of Sports Medicine*, 44(13), 924–933. http://dx.doi.org/10.1136/bjsm.2009.058701

Frank, L.D., Schmid, T.L., Sallis, J.F., Chapman, J. and Saelens, B.E. (2005) "Linking objectively measured physical activity with objectively measured urban form: findings from SMARTRAQ," *American Journal of Preventative Medicine*, 28, 117–125.

Frumkin, H., Frank, L.D. and Jackson, R. (2004) *Urban Sprawl and Public Health: Designing, Planning, and Building For Healthy Communities*, Washington DC: Island Press.

Fulton, L., Mason, J. and Meroux, D. (2017) Three revolutions in urban transportation, Davis, CA: Institute for Transportation & Development Policy.

Galea, S., Freudenberg, N. and Vlahov, D. (2005) "Cities and population health," Soc. Sci. Med, 60, 1017–1033.

Gaspard, F. (1995) *A Small City in France*, Cambridge: Harvard University Press.

Gayah, V.V. and Daganzo, C.F. (2012) "Analytical capacity comparison of one-way and two-way signalized street networks," *Transportation Research Record: Journal of the Transportation Research Board*, 2301, 76–85.

Gaydos, T. (2014) "How useful is Bell Street Park, actually?" *Crosscut*, Available at: https://crosscut.com/2014/07/bell-street-park-belltown-tim-gaydos [Accessed October 1, 2021].

Gehrke, S.R., Felix, A. and Reardon, T.G. (2019) "Substitution of ride-hailing services for more sustainable travel options in the Greater Boston region," *Transportation Research Record: Journal of the Transportation Research Board*, 2673(1), 438–446. https://doi.org/10.1177/0361198118821903

GeoLytics (2010) *Census Neighborhood Change Database*, Available at: https://geolytics.com/products/normalized-data/neighborhood-change-database [Accessed December 14, 2021].

Gilderbloom, J. (2016) "Ten Commandments of urban regeneration: creating healthy, safe, affordable, sustainable, and just neighbourhoods," *Local Environment*, 21(5), 653–660. https://doi.org/10.1080/13549839.2015.1005467

Gilderbloom, J.I., Riggs, W.W., Meares, W.L. (2015) "Does walkability matter? An examination of walkability's impact on housing values, foreclosures and crime," *Cities*, 42, 13–24. https://doi.org/10.1016/j.cities.2014.08.001

Giles-Corti, B., Broomhall, M.H., Knuiman, M., Collins, C., Douglas, K., Ng, K., Lange, A. and Donovan, R.J. (2005) "Increasing walking how important is distance to, attractiveness, and size of public open space?" *American Journal of Preventative Medicine*, 28, 169–176.

Ginwright, S. and Akom, A. (2007) *African American Out-Migration Trends Initial Scan of National and Local Trends in Migration and Research on African Americans*, San Francisco State University: Public Research Institute. Available at: https://sfmohcd.org/sites/default/files/FileCenter/Documents/2127-Product%20I%2007-18-07.pdf [Accessed December 12, 2021].

Glaeser, E. (2011) *Triumph of the City: How Our Greatest Invention Makes Us Richer, Smarter, Greener, Healthier, and Happier*, New York: Penguin.

Glazier, R.H., Creatore, M.I., Weyman, J.T., Fazli, G., Matheson, F.I., Gozdyra, P., Moineddin, R., Shriqui, V.K. and Booth, G.L. (2014) "Density, destinations or both? A comparison of measures of walkability in relation to transportation behaviors, obesity and diabetes in Toronto, Canada," *PLoS ONE*, 9, e85295. https://doi.org/10.1371/journal.pone.0085295

Gómez, L.F., Mosquera, J., Gómez, O.L., Moreno, J., Pinzon, J.D., Jacoby, E., Cepeda, M. and Parra, D.C. (2015) "Social conditions and urban environment associated with participation in the Ciclovia program among adults from Cali, Colombia," *Cad. Saude Publica*, 31, 257–266.

Goodyear, S. (2015) "Why the streets of Copenhagen and Amsterdam look so different from ours," *CityLab*, Available at: http://www.theatlanticcities.com/commute/2012/04/why-streets-copenhagen-and-amsterdam-look-so-different-ours/1849/ [Accessed June 26, 2018].

Greater London Authority (2015) Mayors Vision for Cycling in London, London: London Councils, Available at: https://www.london.gov.uk/sites/default/files/cycling_vision_gla_template_final.pdf [Accessed February 26, 2018].

Guo, Z. (2013) "Does residential parking supply affect household car ownership? The case of New York City," *Journal of Transportion. Geography*, 26, 18–28. https://doi.org/10.1016/j.jtrangeo.2012.08.006

Hall, J.D., Palsson, C. and Price, J. (2018) "Is Uber a substitute or complement for public transit?" *Journal of Urban Economics*, 108, 36–50. https://doi.org/10.1016/j.jue.2018.09.003

Hall, P. (1996) *Cities of Tomorrow: An Intellectual History of Planning and Design in the Twentieth Century* (rev. ed), Cambridge: Blackwell.

Hamilton, B. (2008) "The transportation demand management experience at Stanford University," *TDM Review*, 16(2), 16–21.

Hampton, K.N., Sessions, L.F. and Her, E.J. (2011) "Core networks, social isolation, and new media: how Internet and mobile phone use is related to network size and diversity," *Information, Communication & Society*, 14, 130–155.

Handy, S., Cao, X. and Mokhtarian, P. (2005) "Correlation or causality between the built environment and travel behavior? Evidence from Northern California," *Transportation Research Part D: Transport and Environment*, 10, 427–444.

Handy, S., Cao, X. and Mokhtarian, P.L. (2006) "Self-selection in the relationship between the built environment and walking: empirical evidence from Northern California," *Journal of the American Planning Association*, 72, 55–74.

Handy, S., Sallis, J.F., Weber, D., Maibach, E. and Hollander, M. (2008) "Is support for traditionally designed communities growing? Evidence from two national surveys," *Journal of the American Planning Association*, 74, 209–221.

Handy, S.L., Boarnet, M.G., Ewing, R. and Killingsworth, R.E. (2002) "How the built environment affects physical activity," *American Journal of Preventative Medicine*, 23, 64–73.

Heath, G.W., Brownson, R.C., Kruger, J., Miles, R., Powell, K.E. and Ramsey, L.T. (2006) "The effectiveness of urban design and land use and transport policies and practices to increase physical activity: a systematic review," *Journal of Physical Activity & Health*, 3(1), 55–76. https://doi.org/10.1123/jpah.3.s1.s55

Heyman, J. and Ariely, D. (2004) "Effort for payment a tale of two markets," *Psychological Science*, 15, 787–793. https://doi.org/10.1111/j.0956-7976.2004.00757.x

Hipp, J.R. and Lakon, C.M. (2010) "Social disparities in health: disproportionate toxicity proximity in minority communities over a decade," Health & Place, 16, 674–683. https://doi.org/10.1016/j.healthplace.2010.02.005

Hirt, S. (2015) *Zoned in the USA: The Origins and Implications of American Land-Use Regulation*, Ithaca, NY: Cornell University Press.

Howard, E. (1902) *Garden Cities of To-morrow*, London: S. Sonnenschein & Co., Ltd.

Howard, R. (2006) "Ballet company's comeback is short-lived / Low ticket sales, donor 'fatigue' feed demise." *San Francisco Chronicle*, Available at: http://www.sfgate.com/cgi-bin/article.cgi?f=/c/a/2006/02/01/OAKBALLET.TMP [Accessed June 14, 2011].

Hurst, R. (2006) *Art of Cycling: A Guide to Bicycling in 21st-Century America*, Guilford, CT: Falcon.

Igarta, D. (2017a) Signs posted: Portland Community College Southeast campus, 2305 SE 82nd and Division. Personal email. March 1.

Igarta, D. (2017b) Street Design and Right of Way in Portland. Interview by William Riggs, 24 April.

Isaacson, W. (2011) *Steve Jobs*, New York: Simon & Schuster.

Isted, R. (2014) "The use of antifragility heuristics in transport planning," Australian Institute of Traffic Planning and Management (AITPM) National Conference, Adelaide, Australia.

ITE Technical Committee (1976) "Trip Generation," *Traffic Engineering*, 42–47, Available at: https://nacto.org/docs/usdg/trip_generation_ite.pdf [Accessed December 12, 2021].

Jackson, K.T. (1987) *Crabgrass Frontier: The Suburbanization of the United States*, Oxford: Oxford University Press.

Jacobs, A. and Appleyard, D. (1987) "Toward an urban design manifesto," *Journal of the American Planning Association*, 53, 112–120.

Jacobs, J. (1958) "Downtown is for People," *Fortune Magazine*, Available at: http://innovationecosystem.pbworks.com/w/file/fetch/63349251/DowntownisforPeople.pdf [Accessed December 12, 2021].

Jacobs, J. (1961) *The Death and Life of Great American Cities*, London: Peregrine Book.

James, H. (1917) *The Portrait of a Lady*, New York: P.F. Collier & Son.

Jankowski, M.S. (1991) *Islands in the Street: Gangs and American Urban Society*, Berkeley: University of California Press.

Janwalkar (2015) "Delhi govt to get drones to keep an eye on its forests," *Indian Express*, Available at: https://indianexpress.com/article/cities/delhi/delhi-govt-to-get-drones-to-keep-an-eye-on-its-forests/ [Accessed December 12, 2021].

Jariyasunant, J., Carrel, A., Ekambaram, V., Gaker, D., Sengupta, R., and Walker, J. L. (2012) 'The quantified traveler: changing transport behavior with personalized travel data feedback', UC Berkeley: University of California Transportation Center. Available at: https://escholarship.org/uc/item/3047k0dw [Accessed December 15, 2021].

Jariyasunant, J., Carrel, A., Ekambaram, V., Gaker, D., Sengupta, R., and Walker, J. L. (2015) 'Quantified traveler: travel feedback meets the cloud to change behavior', *Journal of Intelligent Transportation Systems*, 19(2), 109–124. doi:10.1080/15472450.2013.856714.

Joerss, M., Schröder, J., Neuhaus, F., Klink, C. and Mann, F. (2016) *Parcel Delivery: The Future of Last Mile, Travel, Transport and Logistics*, Mckinsey & Company, Available at: https://www.mckinsey.com/~/media/mckinsey/industries/travel%20transport%20and%20logistics/our%20insights/how%20customer%20demands%20are%20reshaping%20last%20mile%20delivery/parcel_delivery_the_future_of_last_mile.ashx [Accessed December 12, 2021].

Johnson (2019) "DJI R&D head dreams of drones fighting fires by the thousands in 'aerial aqueduct'," *VentureBeat*, Available at: https://venturebeat.com/2019/04/20/dji-rd-head-dreams-of-drones-fighting-fires-by-the-thousands-in-aerial-aqueduct/ [Accessed June 24, 2019].

Johnson, M.S. (1991) "Urban arsenals: war housing and social change in Richmond and Oakland, California, 1941–1945," *Pacific Historical Review*, 60, 283–308.

Kahneman, D., Knetsch, J.L. and Thaler, R.H. (1991) "Anomalies: the endowment effect, loss aversion, and status quo bias," *Journal of Economic Perspectives*, 5, 193–206.

Kain, J. and Quigley, J. (1972) "Housing market discrimination, home-ownership, and savings behavior," *The American Economic Review*, 62, 263–277.

Kang, C.D. and Cervero, R. (2009) "From elevated freeway to urban greenway: land value impacts of the CGC Project in Seoul, Korea," *Urban Studies*, 46, 2771–2794. https://doi.org/10.1177/0042098009345166

Kaplan, S. (1989) *The Experience of Nature: A Psychological Perspective*, Cambridge: Cambridge University Press.

Keating, W.D. and Krumholz, N. (2000) "Neighborhood planning," *Journal of Planning Education and Research*, 20, 111–114.

Komanoff, C. (2013) "Lessons from London after 10 years of the congestion charge," *Streetsblog*, Available at: http://www.streetsblog.org/2013/02/15/lessons-from-london-after-10-years-of-the-congestion-charge/ [Accessed December 16, 2014].

Konecny, K.D. (2011) "Urban form and home value: a hedonic analysis in Sacramento, California," dissertation, Sacramento: California State University.

Krafcic, J. (2019) A Decade of Disruption. Automotive News: Shift Discussions, Waymo Headquarters, Mountain View, CA, 11 June.

Kuchar, S. (2013) "Turning Hayes Valley's Alleys into pretty pedestrian-friendly public spaces," *Curbed SF*, Available at: https://sf.curbed.com/2013/7/12/10221092/turning-hayes-valleys-alleys-into-pretty-pedestrian-friendly-public [Accessed March 14, 2018].

Kunze, O. (2016) "Replicators, ground drones and crowd logistics a vision of urban logistics in the year 2030," *Transportation Research Procedia*, 19, 286–299.

Lacitis, E. (2013) "Belltown streets fill as the bars are closing," *The Seattle Times*, Available at: https://www.seattletimes.com/seattle-news/belltown-streets-fill-as-the-bars-are-closing/ [Accessed October 1, 2021].

Lang, R. (2003) *Edgeless Cities: Exploring the Elusive Metropolis*, Washington DC: Brookings Institution Press.

Larco, N. (2017) "When are AVs coming? (10 car companies say within the next 5 years…)," Urbanism Next, Available at: https://urbanismnext.uoregon.edu/2017/08/28/when-are-avs-coming-10-car-companies-say-within-the-next-5-years/ [Accessed September 29, 2017].

Larice, M. and Macdonald, E. (2013) *The Urban Design Reader*, New York: Routledge.

Lawton, M. P. (1999). "Environmental taxonomy: generalizations from research with older adults," in S.L. Friedman and T.D. Wachs (eds) *Measuring Environment Across the Life Span: Emerging Methods and Concepts*, American Psychological Association, pp 91–124. https://doi.org/10.1037/10317-004

Le Corbusier (1930) *Précisions: Sur Un État présent de L'architecture et de L'Urbanism*, Paris: Collection de l'Esprit Nouveau.

Leavitt, J.W. (1996) *The Healthiest City: Milwaukee and the Politics Of Health Reform*, Madison: University of Wisconsin Press.

Leber (2014) "On a new shared street in Chicago, there are no sidewalks, no lights," Fast Co., Available at: https://www.fastcompany.com/3037 471/on-a-new-shared-street-in-chicago-there-are-no-sidewalks-no-lig hts-and-no-signs [Accessed September 26, 2021].

Lee, H.L. and Whang, S. (2001) "Winning the last mile of e-commerce," *MIT Sloan Management Review*, 42, 54–62.

Lennard, S.H.C. and Lennard, H.L. (1995) *Livable Cities Observed: A Source Book of Images and Ideas For City Officials, Community Leaders, Architects, Planners and All Other Committed to Making Their Cities Livable*, Carmel, CA: Gondolier Press.

Leslie, E., Saelens, B., Frank, L., Owen, N., Bauman, A., Coffee, N. and Hugo, G. (2005) "Residents' perceptions of walkability attributes in objectively different neighbourhoods: a pilot study," *Health & Place*, 11, 227–236. https://doi.org/10.1016/j.healthplace.2004.05.005

Li, F., Fisher, K.J., Brownson, R.C. and Bosworth, M. (2005) "Multilevel modelling of built environment characteristics related to neighbourhood walking activity in older adults," *Journal of Epidemiology and Community Health*, 59, 558–564. https://doi.org/10.1136/jech.2004.028399

Li, W. (1998) "Anatomy of a new ethnic settlement: the Chinese ethnoburb in Los Angeles," *Urban Studies*, 35, 479–501. https://doi.org/10.1080/ 0042098984871

Li, W. (2009) *Ethnoburb: The New Ethnic Community in Urban America*, Hawaii: University of Hawaii Press.

Lieberman, J.K. (1970) *The Tyranny of the Experts*, New York: Basic Books.

Lipson, H. and Kurman, M. (2016) *Driverless: Intelligent Cars and the Road Ahead*, Cambridge: MIT Press.

Litman, T. (2006) "London congestion pricing. Implications for other cities," Victoria BC: Victoria Transport Policy Institute, Available at: https://www. vtpi.org/london.pdf [Accessed July 2, 2015].

Litman, T. (2011) "Introduction to multi-modal transportation planning," Victoria BC: Victoria Transport Policy Institute, Available at: https:// www.vtpi.org/london.pdf [Accessed July 2, 2015].

Litman, T.A. (2003) "Economic value of walkability," *Transportation Research Record: Journal of the Transportation Research Board*, 1828, 3–11.

Liu, Z., Wang, S., Qu, X. and Shiwakoti, N. (2014) "Congestion pricing with distance tolls: a review and new developments," CICTP 2014: Safe, Smart and Sustainable Multimodal Transportation Systems. American Society of Civil Engineers, 3459–3469.

Lo, R.H. (2009a) "The city as a mirror: transport, land use and social change in Jakarta," *Urban Studies*, 47(3) 529–555. https://doi.org/10.1177/ 0042098009348557

Lo, R.H. (2009b) "Walkability: what is it?" *Journal of Urbanism: International Research on Placemaking and Urban Sustainability*, 2, 145–166. https://doi.org/10.1080/17549170903092867

Lo, R.H. (2011) "Walkability planning in Jakarta," doctoral dissertation, Berkeley: University of California. Available at: http://escholarship.org/uc/item/05p5r596 [Accessed December 14, 2021].

Loeb, C.S. (2001) *Entrepreneurial Vernacular: Developers' Subdivisions in the 1920s*, Baltimore: Johns Hopkins University Press.

Loukaitou-Sideris, A., Brozen, M., Callahan, C.K., Brookover, I., LaMontagne, N. and Snehansh, V. (2012) Reclaiming the right-of-way: a toolkit for creating and implementing parklets. Los Angeles, CA: Luskin School of Public Affairs. Available at: https://nacto.org/docs/usdg/reclaiming_the_right_of_way_brozen.pdf [Accessed July 7, 2015].

Lövdén, M., Schaefer, S., Pohlmeyer, A.E. and Lindenberger, U. (2008) "Walking variability and working-memory load in aging: a dual-process account relating cognitive control to motor control performance," *The Journals of Gerontology Series B: Psychological Sciences and Social Sciences*, 63(3), P121–P128.

Lynch, K. (1960) *The Image of the City*, Cambridge, MA: MIT Press.

Macintyre, S., Ellaway, A. and Cummins, S. (2002) "Place effects on health: how can we conceptualise, operationalise and measure them?" *Social Science and Medicine*, 55, 125–139.

Maki, F. (1970) "The theory of Group Form," *The Japan Architect*, February, 39–42.

Maller, C., Townsend, M., Pryor, A., Brown, P. and St Leger, L. (2006) "Healthy nature healthy people: 'contact with nature' as an upstream health promotion intervention for populations," *Health Promotion International*, 21, 45–54.

Marchal, F. and Nagel, K. (2005) "Modelling location choice of secondary activities with a social network of cooperative agents," *Transportation Research Record: Journal of the Transportation Research Board*, 1935, 141–146. Available at: http://trrjournalonline.trb.org/doi/abs/10.3141/1935-16 [Accessed December 14, 2021].

Margaritoff, M. (2017) "Drones in firefighting: how, where and when they're used," *The Drive*, Available at: https://www.thedrive.com/aerial/16770/drones-in-firefighting-how-where-and-when-theyre-used [Accessed June 24, 2019].

Massey, D.S. (2008) "Origins of economic disparities: the historical role of housing segregation," in J.H. Carr and N.K. Kutty (eds) *Segregation: The Rising Costs in America*, pp 39–80.

Massey, D.S. and Denton, N.A. (1993) *American Apartheid: Segregation and the Making of the Underclass*, Cambridge, MA: Harvard University Press.

Matthews, J.W. and Turnbull, G.K. (2007) "Neighborhood street layout and property value: the interaction of accessibility and land use mix," *The Journal of Real Estate Finance and Economics*, 35, 111–141. https://doi.org/10.1007/s11146-007-9035-9

May, A.D., Liu, R., Shepherd, S.P. and Sumalee, A. (2002) "The impact of cordon design on the performance of road pricing schemes," *Transport Policy*, 9, 209–220. https://doi.org/10.1016/S0967-070X(02)00031-8

Maynard, M. (2017) "The Starbucks unicorn tastes like a naughty child's birthday party," *Forbes*, Available at: https://www.forbes.com/sites/michelinemaynard/2017/04/19/review-the-starbucks-unicorn-tastes-like-a-naughty-childs-birthday-party/ [Accessed September 26, 2021].

Mazur, M. (2016) "Six ways drones are revolutionizing agriculture," *MIT Technology Review*, Available at: https://www.technologyreview.com/2016/07/20/158748/six-ways-drones-are-revolutionizing-agriculture/ [Accessed September 26, 2021].

McNichol, T. (2004) "Roads gone wild," *Wired Magazine*, 12, 108–112.

Mehta, V. (2007) "Lively streets determining environmental characteristics to support social behavior," *Journal of Planning Education and Research*, 27, 165–187.

Melkonian, M.J. and Whitman, P.A. (1968) "The Oakland Leased Housing Program," *Stanford Law Review*, 20, 538–570. https://doi.org/10.2307/1227514

Melosi, M.V. (2000) *The Sanitary City*, Baltimore, MD: Johns Hopkins University Press.

Metropolitan Washington Council of Governments (2016) Four-step travel model. Available at: http://www.mwcog.org/transportation/activities/models/4step/step1.asp [Accessed December 8, 2017].

Middlecamp, D. (2010) Cruisin' San Luis Obispo ends, the birth of Farmer's Market. Photos from the Vault. San Luis Obispo Telegram Tribune. Available at: https://mustangnews.net/the-birth-of-farmers-market-was-the-death-of-cruising/ [Accessed December 8, 2017].

Mims, C. (2016) "Driverless cars to fuel suburban sprawl – WSJ," Available at: https://www.wsj.com/articles/driverless-cars-to-fuel-suburban-sprawl-1466395201 [Accessed July 8, 2018].

Mohai, P. and Saha, R. (2006) "Reassessing racial and socioeconomic disparities in environmental justice research," *Demography*, 43, 383–399.

Muir, J. (1894) *The Mountains of California*, New York: Dorset Press.

Munnell, A.H., Tootell, G.M.B., Browne, L.E. and McEneaney, J. (1996) "Mortgage lending in Boston: interpreting HMDA data," *American Economic Review*, 86, 25–53.

Munoz-Raskin, R. (2010) "Walking accessibility to bus rapid transit: does it affect property values? The case of Bogotá, Colombia," *Transport Policy*, 17, 72–84.

Myers, D. (2016) "Peak millennials: three reinforcing cycles that amplify the rise and fall of urban concentration by millennials," *Housing Policy Debate*, 26, 928–947. https://doi.org/10.1080/10511482.2016.1165722

NACTO (2021) "Case study: laneways of Melbourne," *Global Designing Cities Initiative*, Available at: https://globaldesigningcities.org/publicat ion/global-street-design-guide/streets/pedestrian-priority-spaces/lanew ays-and-alleys/case-study-laneways-of-melbourne-australia/ [Accessed December 2, 2021].

New York City Department of Transportation (2020) *Street Design Manual*. New York: New York City Department of Transportation, Available at: https://www.nycstreetdesign.info/ [Accessed December, 12 2021].

Nickelsburg, M. (2018) "UPS launches cargo e-bike delivery in Seattle, returning to bicycle courier origins a century later," *GeekWire*, Available at: https://www.geekwire.com/2018/ups-launches-cargo-e-bike-deliv ery-seattle-returning-bicycle-courier-origins-century-later/ [Accessed June 21, 2019].

Nussbaum, M. (1986) "The discernment of perception: an Aristotelian conception of private and public rationality," Proceedings of the Boston Area Colloquium in Ancient Philosophy, p. 151. Available at: http://chi cagounbound.uchicago.edu/journal_articles/3156/ [Accessed December 14, 2021].

Nussbaum, M.C. (2011) *Creating Capabilities*, Cambridge, MA: Harvard University Press.

Oakes, J.M. (2004) "The (mis) estimation of neighborhood effects: causal inference for a practicable social epidemiology," *Social Science and Medicine*, 58, 1929–1952.

Obama, B. (2015) "Remarks by the President at the 50th Anniversary of the Selma to Montgomery Marches," *Whitehouse.Gov*, March 7. Available at: https://obamawhitehouse.archives.gov/the-press-office/2015/03/ 07/remarks-president-50th-anniversary-selma-montgomery-marches [Accessed December 14, 2021].

Olmsted Jr, F.L. (1911) "The City Beautiful," *The Builder*, 101, 15–17.

O'Sullivan, F. (2017) "Stockholm starts a friendly rivalry over car-free planning," *CityLab*, Available at: https://www.citylab.com/design/2017/ 05/stockholm-pedestrian-downtown-plans-oslo/526464/ [Accessed June 27, 2018].

Palermo, P.C. and Ponzini, D. (2010) *Spatial Planning and Urban Development*, Amsterdam: Springer.

Perry, C.A. (1929) "City planning for neighborhood life," *Social Forces*, 8(1), 98–100.

Peterson, J. (1979) "The impact of sanitary reform upon American urban planning," *Journal of Social History*, 13, 84–89.

Pi-Sunyer, F.X. (1993) "Medical hazards of obesity," *Annals of Internal Medicine*, 119, 655.

Pivo, G. (2013) "The effect of transportation, location, and affordability related sustainability features on mortgage default prediction and risk in multifamily rental housing," *Journal of Sustainable Real Estate*, 5(1), 149–170

Pivo, G. and Fisher, J.D. (2011) "The walkability premium in commercial real estate investments," *Real Estate Economics*, 39, 185–219. https://doi.org/10.1111/j.1540-6229.2010.00296.x

Pomfret, J. (2006) "Where did all the children go?" *The Washington Post*, 19 March. Available at: http://www.washingtonpost.com/wp-dyn/cont ent/article/2006/03/18/AR2006031801034.html [Accessed November 10, 2014].

Pope Francis (2015) "Laudato si'," Available at: http://w2.vatican.va/cont ent/francesco/en/encyclicals/documents/papa-francesco_20150524_en ciclica-laudato-si.html [Accessed May 1, 2018].

Porter, M., Rivkin, J.W., Desai, M.A. and Raman, M. (2016) Problems unsolved and a nation divided, Cambridge: Harvard Business School. https://adminlb.imodules.com/s/1738/images/gid8/editor_documents/2017/problems_unsolved_and_a_nation_divided.pdf?sessionid=a192c2a4-e1ac-4368-9453-2273425ad40b&cc=1

Prohaska, T.R., Eisenstein, A.R., Satariano, W.A., Hunter, R., Bayles, C.M., Kurtovich, E., Kealey, M. and Ivey, S.L. (2009) "Walking and the preservation of cognitive function in older populations," *The Gerontologist*, 49, S86.

Punakivi, M., Yrjölä, H. and Holmström, J. (2001) "Solving the last mile issue: reception box or delivery box?" *International Journal of Physical Distribution & Logistics Management*, 31, 427–439.

Putnam, R.D. (2001) *Bowling Alone: The Collapse and Revival of American Community*, New York: Simon & Schuster.

Quastel, N. (2009) "Political ecologies of gentrification," *Urban Geography*, 30, 694–725.

Rassman, C.L. (2014) "Regulating rideshare without stifling innovation: examining the drivers, the insurance gap, and why Pennsylvania should get on board," *Pittsburgh Journal of Technology Law & Policy*, 15(1), 81–100.

Rauterkus, S.Y. and Miller, N.G. (2011) "Residential land values and walkability," *Journal of Sustainable Real Estate*, 3, 23–43.

Rawls, J. (1988) "The priority of right and ideas of the good," *Philosophy and Public Affairs*, 17, 251–276.

Rayle, L., Dai, D., Chan, N., Cervero, R. and Shaheen, S. (2016) "Just a better taxi? A survey-based comparison of taxis, transit, and ridesourcing services in San Francisco," *Transport Policy*, 45, 168–178. https://doi.org/10.1016/j.tranpol.2015.10.004

Riggs, W. (2011) "Walkability and Housing: A Comparative Study of Income, Neighborhood Change and Socio-Cultural Dynamics in the San Francisco Bay Area," doctoral dissertation, Berkeley: University of California.

Riggs, W. (2014a) "Steps toward validity in active living research: research design that limits accusations of physical determinism," *Health & Place*, 26, 7–13. https://doi.org/10.1016/j.healthplace.2013.11.003

Riggs, W. (2014b) "inclusively walkable: exploring the equity of walkable neighborhoods in the san francisco bay area," *Local Environment*, https://doi.org/10.1080/13549839.2014.982080

Riggs, W. (2015) "Walkability: to quantify or not to quantify," *Journal of Urbanism*, 0, 1–3. https://doi.org/10.1080/17549175.2015.1111926

Riggs, W. (2016) "Inclusively walkable: exploring the equity of walkable housing in the San Francisco Bay Area," *Local Environment*, 21, 527–554. https://doi.org/10.1080/13549839.2014.982080

Riggs, W. (2017a) "Revisiting location efficiency: strategies to graduate thinking on mortgage policy", *Housing & Society*, 43(3), 195–216. https://doi.org/10.1080/08882746.2017.1340056

Riggs, W. (2017b) Reduced perception of safety for cyclists on multi-lane, one-way and two-way streets: opportunities for behavioral economics and design (SSRN Scholarly Paper No. ID 3011680). Rochester, NY: Social Science Research Network.

Riggs, W. (2017c) "Painting the fence: social norms as economic incentives to non-automotive travel behavior," *Travel Behaviour & Society*, 7, 26–33. https://doi.org/10.1016/j.tbs.2016.11.004

Riggs, W. (2018) "Technology, Civic Engagement and Street Science: Hacking the Future of Participatory Street Design in the Era of Self-driving Cars," Proceedings of the 19th Annual International Conference on Digital Government Research: Governance in the Data Age, Dgo '18. ACM, New York, pp 4:1–4:6. https://doi.org/10.1145/3209281.3209383

Riggs, W. (2019) *Disruptive Transport: Driverless Cars, Transport Innovation and the Sustainable City of Tomorrow, Routledge Equity, Justice and the Sustainable City Series*, London: Routledge.

Riggs, W. and Gilderbloom, J. (2015) "Two-way street conversion evidence of increased livability in Louisville," *Journal of Planning Education and Research*, 0739456X15593147. https://doi.org/10.1177/0739456X15593147

Riggs, W. and Gordon, K. (2015) "How is mobile technology changing city planning? Developing a taxonomy for the future," *Environment and Planing. B Planning and Design*, 0265813515610337. https://doi.org/10.1177/0265813515610337

Riggs, W. and Gross, S. (2017) Pedestrian use of urban alleys: analyzing plans and surveying route choice (SSRN Scholarly Paper No. ID 3057848). Rochester, NY: Social Science Research Network.

Riggs, W. and Kuo, J. (2015) "The impact of targeted outreach for parking mitigation on the UC Berkeley campus," *Case Studies in Transport Policy*, 3, 151–158. https://doi.org/10.1016/j.cstp.2015.01.004

Riggs, W. and McDade, E. (2016) "Moving from planning to action: exploring best practice policy in the finance of local bicycling and pedestrian improvements," *Case Studies in Transport Policy*, 4, 248–257. https://doi.org/10.1016/j.cstp.2016.06.004

Riggs, W. and Yudowitz, L. (2021) "Snap judgements and availability bias in travel decisions," *Transportation Research Record: Journal of the Transportation Research Board*, 2675(11) 89–96. https://doi.org/10.1177/03611981211015992

Riis, J. (1890) *How the Other Half Lives*, New York: Simon & Schuster.

Rittel, H.W.J. and Webber, M.M. (1973) "Dilemmas in a general theory of planning," *Policy Sciences*, 4(2), 155–169. https://doi.org/10.1007/BF01405730

Rocha, A. (2007) "Chinatown alley plan: $2M down, 24 alleys to go," San Francisco Examiner, Available at: https://www.sfexaminer.com/news/chinatown-alley-plan-2m-down-24-alleys-to-go/ [Accessed December 14, 2021].

Roosevelt, F. (1932) Franklin D. Roosevelt Speeches, Oglethorpe University Address, Available at: https://publicpolicy.pepperdine.edu/academics/research/faculty-research/new-deal/roosevelt-speeches/fr052232.htm [Accessed December 14, 2021].

Roosevelt, T. (1910) "Presidential addresses and state papers," The Review of Reviews Company.

Roth, M. (2010) "Streetsblog San Francisco. BART board member urges agency to consider unlimited monthly pass," Available at: http://sf.streetsblog.org/2010/09/21/bart-board-member-urges-agency-to-consider-unlimited-monthly-pass/ [Accessed January 13, 2011].

Rothstein, R. (2017) *The Color of Law: A Forgotten History of How Our Government Segregated America*, New York: Liveright Publishing.

Roxburgh (2017) "China's 'sponge cities' are turning streets green to combat flooding," *The Guardian*, Available at: https://www.theguardian.com/world/2017/dec/28/chinas-sponge-cities-are-turning-streets-green-to-combat-flooding [Accessed October 1, 2021].

Ruiz-Apilanez, B., Arnaiz, M. and De Urena, J. (2015) "Beyond lively streets," in L. Vaughan (ed.) *Suburban Urbanities*, London: University College London Press, pp 130–150.

Rutheiser, C. (2008) "Beyond the radiant garden city beautiful: notes on the new urbanism," *City & Society*, 9, 117–133.

Sadik-Khan, J. and Solomonow, S. (2017) *Streetfight: Handbook for an Urban Revolution*, New York: Penguin.

Saelens, B, Sallis, J. and Frank, L. (2003) "Environmental correlates of walking and cycling: findings from the transportation, urban design, and planning literatures," *Annuals of Behavioral Medicine*, 25, 80–91. https://doi.org/10.1207/S15324796ABM2502_03

Saito, M. (2011) " 'Land bank' knocks out some foreclosure problems," *NPR*. Available at: https://www.npr.org/2011/08/29/139971310/land-bank-knocks-out-some-foreclosure-problems [Accessed March 14, 2018].

Sallis, J.F., Frank, L.D., Saelens, B.E. and Kraft, M.K. (2004) "Active transportation and physical activity: opportunities for collaboration on transportation and public health research," *Transportation Research-Part A Policy and Practice*, 38, 249–268.

Sallis, J.F. and Glanz, K. (2006) "The role of built environments in physical activity, eating, and obesity in childhood," *Future Child*, 16, 89–108.

San Francisco Planning Department (2015a) "Market octavia living alleys program," Available at: http://sf-planning.org/market-octavia-living-all eys-program [Accessed March 14, 2018].

San Francisco Planning Department (2015b) "Better market street environmental review process," Available at: http://sf-planning.org/bet ter-market-street-environmental-review-process#bms [Accessed March 14, 2018].

Schafran, A. (2009) "Outside Endopolis: Notes from Contra Costa County," *Critical Planning*, 16, 10–33.

Schafran, A. (2013) "Discourse and dystopia, American style." *City*, 17(2), 130–148. https://doi.org/10.1080/13604813.2013.765125

Schaller, B. (2017) "Unsustainable? The growth of app-based ride services and traffic, travel and the future of New York City," Brooklyn: Schaller Consulting.

Schneider, B. (2017) "How park(ing) day sparked a global parklet movement," *CityLab*, Available at: https://www.citylab.com/life/2017/09/from-park ing-to-parklet/539952/ [Accessed June 27, 2018].

Schrank, D., Eisele, B., Lomax, T. and Bak, J. (2015) 2015 Urban Mobility Scorecard, College Station: Texas A&M Transportation Institute. Available at: https://static.tti.tamu.edu/tti.tamu.edu/documents/umr/archive/mobil ity-scorecard-2015-wappx.pdf [Accessed December 14, 2021].

Scott, M.M., Cohen, D.A., Evenson, K.R., Elder, J., Catellier, D., Ashwood, J.S. and Overton, A. (2007) "Weekend schoolyard accessibility, physical activity, and obesity: The Trial of Activity in Adolescent Girls (TAAG) study," *Preventative Medicine*, 44, 398–403.

Sen, A. (1999) *Commodities and Capabilities*, Oxford: Oxford University Press.

Sen, A. (2004) *Rationality and Freedom*, Cambridge: Harvard University Press.

Shaheen, S. and Chan, N. (2016) "Mobility and the sharing economy: potential to facilitate the first-and last-mile public transit connections," *Built Environment*, 42, 573–588.

Shirgaokar, M., (2012) "The rapid rise of middle-class vehicle ownership in Mumbai," doctoral dissertation, Berkeley: University of California.

Shoup, D.C. (1997) "The high cost of free parking," *Journal of Planning Education and Research*, 17, 3–20. https://doi.org/10.1177/0739456X9701700102

Shoup, D.C. (2005) "The high cost of free parking," Washington DC: Planners Press, American Planning Association.

Silver, C. (1985) "Neighborhood planning in historical perspective," *Journal of the American Planning Association*, 51, 161–174.

Slowik, P. and Kamakaté, F. (2017) New mobility: today's technology and policy landscape, Washington DC: International Council on Clean Transportation.

Smith, A. (1776) *An Inquiry Into the Nature and Causes of the Wealth of Nations*, London: Whitestone.

Smith, E. (2017) "A brief history of Santiago's street art scene with local graffiti artist," *Upscape*, Available at: https://upscapetravel.com/blog/street-art-santiago/ [Accessed December 3, 2021].

Smith, E. (2021) *Hate Crime Recorded by Law Enforcement, 2010-2019*. Statistical Brief NCJ 301554, Washington DC: US Department of Justice, Available at: https://bjs.ojp.gov/library/publications/hate-crime-recorded-law-enforcement-2010-2019 [Accessed January 17, 2022].

Sole-Smith, V. (2006) "Nature on the threshold," *New York Times*, Available at: https://www.nytimes.com/2006/09/07/garden/07bio.html [Accessed December 12, 2021].

Solnit, R. (2016) "We don't need self-driving cars – we need to ditch our vehicles entirely," *The Guardian*, Available at: https://www.theguardian.com/commentisfree/2016/apr/06/self-driving-cars-public-transportation [Accessed July 8, 2018].

Solnit, R. (2001) *Wanderlust: A History of Walking*, New York: Penguin Group USA.

Southworth, M. (2005) "Designing the walkable city," *Journal of Urban Planning and Development*, 131, 246–257. https://doi.org/10.1061/(ASCE)0733-9488(2005)131:4(246)

Southworth, M. and Ben-Joseph, E. (1995) "Street standards and the shaping of suburbia," *Journal of the American Planning Association*, 61, 65–81.

Spencer, R.C. (2005) Inside the Panther Revolution: The Black Freedom Movement and the Black Panther Party in Oakland, California. Groundwork: Local Black Freedom Movements in America. New York: New York University Press.

Sperling, D. (2018) *Three Revolutions: Steering Automated, Shared, and Electric Vehicles to a Better Future*, Washington DC: Island Press.

Spielman (2021) "Raised bike lanes to be installed in Chicago to better protect cyclists," *Chicago Sun-Times*, Available at: https://chicago.suntimes.com/2021/5/11/22431094/raised-bike-lanes-copenhagen-chicago-bicycle-commuting [Accessed December 4, 2021].

Squires, G. and Friedman, S. (2001) "Coloring the American Dream," *Washington Post*. Available at: https://www.washingtonpost.com/archive/opinions/2001/09/09/coloring-the-american-dream/7398106d-2a8a-4731-84fa-7a560e325669/ [Accessed: 21 March 2017].

Sturm, R. and Cohen, D.A. (2004) "Suburban sprawl and physical and mental health," *Public Health*, 118, 488–496.

Sunstein, C. and Thaler, R. (2016) "The two friends who changed how we think about how we think," *New Yorker*, Available at: http://www.newyorker.com/books/page-turner/the-two-friends-who-changed-how-we-think-about-how-we-think [Accessed: 21 March 2017].

Taggart (2018) "Busy city street in Santiago is turned into a colorful pedestrian promenade," *My Modern Met*, Available at: https://mymodernmet.com/paseo-bandera-urban-art/ [Accessed December 3, 2021].

Takano, T., Nakamura, K. and Watanabe, M. (2002) "Urban residential environments and senior citizens' longevity in megacity areas: the importance of walkable green spaces", *Journal of Epidemiology and Community Health*, 56, 913–918.

Taleb, N.N. (2014) *Antifragile: Things that Gain from Disorder*, New York: Random House Trade Paperbacks.

Tan, T.H. (2011) "Measuring the willingness to pay for houses in a sustainable neighborhood," Available at: https://mpra.ub.uni-muenchen.de/30446/ [Accessed June 25, 2015].

Thompson, S.R., Watson, M.C. and Tilford, S. (2018) "The Ottawa Charter 30 years on: still an important standard for health promotion," *International Journal of Health Promotion and Education*, 56, 73–84.

Transport for London (2004) *Making London a walkable city*, London: Transport for London.

Transport for London (2008) "London Low Emission Zone: impacts monitoring," London: Transport for London. Available at: https://content.tfl.gov.uk/lez-impacts-monitoring-baseline-report-2008-07.pdf [Accessed December 12, 2021].

Tranter, R.T., Slater, R. and Vaughan, N. (1991) "Barriers to mobility: physically-disabled and frail elderly people in their local outdoor environment," *International Journal of Rehabilitation Research*, 14, 303–312.

Troy, A. and Grove, J.M. (2008) "Property values, parks, and crime: a hedonic analysis in Baltimore," *Landscape and Urban Planning*, 87, 233–245.

Tversky, A. and Kahneman, D. (1973) "Availability: a heuristic for judging frequency and probability," *Cognitive Psychology*, 5, 207–232.

Tversky, A. and Kahneman, D. (1992) "Advances in prospect theory: cumulative representation of uncertainty," *Journal of Risk and Uncertainty*, 5, 297–323.

Twain, M. (1899) *Pudd'nhead Wilson and Those Extraordinary Twins*, New York: Harper.

UBS (2019) "How China is radically reinventing urban architecture to go green," *Mashable*, Available at: https://mashable.com/article/green-cities-china [Accessed October 1, 2021].

Ulrich, R.S. (1984) "View through a window may influence recovery from surgery," *Science*, 224, 420.

Ulrich, R.S., Simons, R.F., Losito, B.D., Fiorito, E., Miles, M.A. and Zelson, M. (1991) "Stress recovery during exposure to natural and urban environments," *Journal Environmental Psychology*, 11, 201–230.

US PIRG (2014) Millennials in motion, Washington DC: United States Public Interest Research Group. Available at: https://uspirg.org/reports/usp/millennials-motion [Accessed December 14, 2021].

Waldheim, C. (2012) *The Landscape Urbanism Reader*, New York: Chronicle Books.

Weinberger, R., Seaman, M. and Johnson, C. (2008) "Suburbanizing the city: how New York City parking requirements lead to more driving," Available at: https://trid.trb.org/view/1153742 [Accessed December 14, 2021].

Westneat, D. (2015) "Belltown ticket trap turns drivers into 'sitting ducks'," *The Seattle Times*, Available at: https://www.seattletimes.com/seattle-news/belltown-ticket-trap-turns-drivers-into-sitting-ducks/ [Accessed October 1, 2021].

White, E. (2001) *The Flâneur: A Stroll Through the Paradoxes of Paris*, New York: Bloomsbury.

WHO (2018) *Global status report on road safety 2018*, Geneva: World Health Organization, Available at: https://www.who.int/publications/i/item/9789241565684 [Accessed: 14 December 2021].

Whyte, W.H. (1988) *City: Rediscovering the Center*, New York: Doubleday.

Williams, D. and Jackson, P. (2005) "Social sources of racial disparities in health," *Health Affairs*, 24, 325-334.

Willson, R.W. and Shoup, D.C. (1990) "Parking subsidies and travel choices: assessing the evidence," *Transportation*, 17, 141–157.

Wilson, J.D., Tierney, P., Kim, M.-S. and Zieff, S. (2012) "Temporary parks? Sunday Streets, serving the need for urban outdoor recreation," *Journal of Park and Recreation Administration*, 30(4), 38–52.

Wolch, J., Wilson, J.P. and Fehrenbach, J. (2005) "Parks and park funding in Los Angeles: an equity-mapping analysis," *Urban Geography*, 26, 4–35.

Wood (2014) Michigan Studies Unpaved Roads from the Sky – Government. Available at: https://www.govtech.com/transportation/Michigan-Studies-Unpaved-Roads-from-the-Sky.html [Accessed June 24, 2019].

Yiftachel, O. (1998) "Planning and social control: exploring the dark side," *CPL Bibliography*, 12, 395–406.

Yiftachel, O. (2001) "Can theory be liberated from professional constraints? on rationality and explanatory power in Flyvbjerg's Rationality and Power," *International Planning Studies*, 6, 251–255. https://doi.org/10.1080/713672902

Zaleski, A. (2017) "How cities are coping with the delivery truck boom," *CityLab*, Available at: https://www.citylab.com/transportation/2017/04/cities-seek-deliverance-from-the-e-commerce-boom/523671/ [Accessed June 21, 2019].

Zavestoski, S. and Agyeman, J. (2014) *Incomplete Streets: Processes, Practices, and Possibilities*, New York: Routledge.

Zhang, Y., Zhang, L. and Benton, F. (2021) "Hate crimes against Asian Americans", *American Journal of Criminal Justice*, 1–21. doi:10.1007/s12103-020-09602-9

Zieff, S.G., Hipp, J.A., Eyler, A.A. and Kim, M.-S. (2013) "Ciclovía initiatives: engaging communities, partners, and policy makers along the route to success," *Journal of Public Health Management and Practice*, 19, S74–S82. https://doi.org/10.1097/PHH.0b013e3182841982

Index

Page numbers in **bold** refer to tables; page numbers in *italics* refer to figures and photographs; 'n' after a page number indicates the endnote number.